# The Religious Foundations of Francis Bacon's Thought

# Eric Voegelin Institute Series in Political Philosophy: Studies in Religion and Politics

Other Books in the Eric Voegelin Institute Series in Political Philosophy

*The American Way of Peace: An Interpretation,* by Jan Prybyla

*Art and Intellect in the Philosophy of Étienne Gilson,* by Francesca Aran Murphy

*Augustine and Politics as Longing in the World,* by John von Heyking

*Eros, Wisdom, and Silence: Plato's Erotic Dialogues,* by James M. Rhodes

*Faith and Political Philosophy: The Correspondence between Leo Strauss and Eric Voegelin, 1934–1964,* edited by Peter Emberley and Barry Cooper

*A Government of Laws: Political Theory, Religion, and the American Founding,* by Ellis Sandoz

*Hans Jonas: The Integrity of Thinking,* by David J. Levy

*Lonergan and the Philosophy of Historical Existence,* by Thomas J. McPartland

*The Narrow Path of Freedom and Other Essays,* by Eugene Davidson

*New Political Religions, or an Analysis of Modern Terrorism,* by Barry Cooper

*Robert B. Heilman and Eric Voegelin: A Friendship in Letters, 1944–1984,* edited by Charles R. Embry

*Transcendence and History: The Search for Ultimacy from Ancient Societies to Postmodernity,* by Glenn Hughes

*Voegelin, Schelling, and the Philosophy of Historical Existence,* by Jerry Day

# The Religious Foundations of Francis Bacon's Thought

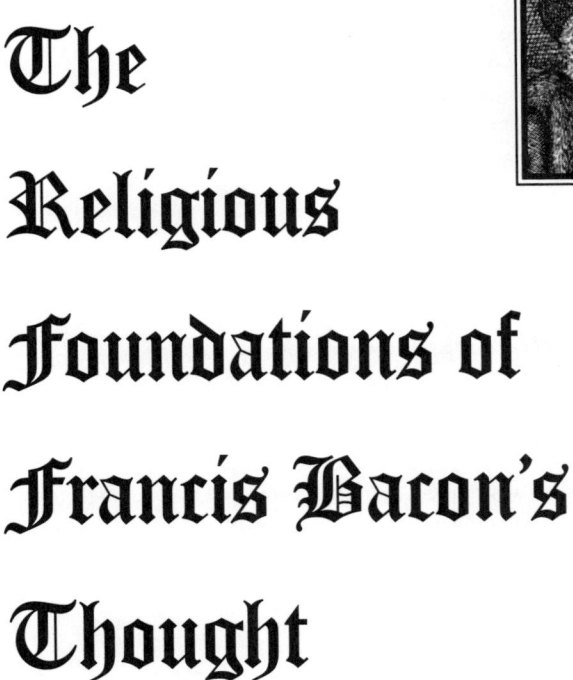

Stephen A. McKnight

University of Missouri Press   Columbia and London

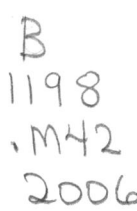

© Copyright 20006 by
The Curators of the University of Missouri
University of Missouri Press, Columbia, Missouri 65201
Printed and bound in the United States of America
All rights reserved

5  4  3  2  1    10  09  08  07  06

Library of Congress Cataloging-in-Publication Data

McKnight, Stephen A., 1944–
   The religious foundations of Francis Bacon's thought / Stephen A. McKnight.
      p. cm. — (Eric Voegelin Institute series in political philosophy)
   Summary: "Presents close analysis of eight of Francis Bacon's texts in order to investigate the relation of his religious views to his instauration. Attempts to correct the persistent misconception of Bacon as a secular modern who dismissed religion in order to promote the human advancement of knowledge"—Provided by publisher.
   Includes bibliographical references and index.
   ISBN-13: 978-0-8262-1609-0 (alk. paper)
   ISBN-10: 0-8262-1609-9 (alk. paper)
   1. Bacon, Francis, 1561–1626.  2. Bacon, Francis, 1561–1626.—Religion.  I. Title.  II. Series.
   B1198.M42  2006
   192—dc22                                          2005022339

♾™ This paper meets the requirements of the American National Standard for Permanence of Paper for Printed Library Materials, Z39.48, 1984.

Designer: Kristie Lee
Typesetter: Phoenix Type, Inc.
Printer and binder: The Maple-Vail Book Manufacturing Group
Typeface: Adobe Garamond and Old English

Publication of this book has been assisted by a generous contribution from the Eric Voegelin Institute.

**For**

*Alen, Kim,
Emma, Jeffrey,
and, most of all,
for Becky*

# Contents

**Acknowledgments** ix
**References and Abbreviations** xi

**Introduction.** Bacon's Religion Obscured:
The Problem of Reading in the "Future Indicative"   1

**Chapter 1.**   The *New Atlantis*   10

**Chapter 2.**   *The Great Instauration*   45

**Chapter 3.**   *The New Organon*   72

**Chapter 4.**   Themes and Images in Bacon's Early Writings   103

**Conclusion.**   Four Key Baconian Themes:
Instauration, Providence, Vocation, and Charity   151

**Notes**   161
**Bibliography**   175
**Index**   189

# Acknowledgments

I would like to acknowledge two sources of funding that assisted with the preparation of this book. The Earhart Foundation generously provided a summer research grant, which allowed me to complete the research and prepare the initial full draft of the book. I should also like to acknowledge support from the Volkswagen Foundation. I am one of four principal investigators of a project on "Mysticism and Modernity," which was funded under the foundation's program "Key Themes in the Humanities." The grant permits collaborative research by an international team of senior scholars and postdoctoral fellows, who have an opportunity to meet annually to report on their work in progress. I was, therefore, able to present my work to this international team as I was preparing this book. The grant also provided for some research assistance as I was preparing the manuscript for publication.

I also want to express my gratitude to three colleagues from the fields of religion and the history of science who read the manuscript and made helpful suggestions for improvement. They are Jay Malone, Eugene Webb, and Steven Matthews.

Finally, I want to thank my wife, Becky, who has patiently and expertly prepared each of the manuscripts from the first working draft to the final published version.

# References and Abbreviations

Quotations of Francis Bacon's writings are taken from two sources. The majority are from *The Works of Francis Bacon,* ed. James Spedding, Robert L. Ellis, and Douglas D. Heath, 14 vols. (London: Longman, 1857–1874). References to this edition will be abbreviated in the text as *WFB,* followed by the volume number and page cited. The other source for quoted material is Benjamin Farrington, *The Philosophy of Francis Bacon: An Essay on Its Development from 1603 to 1609 with New Translations of Fundamental Texts* (Chicago: University of Chicago Press, 1964). This work contains English translations of six of Bacon's early Latin writings, which the editors of the *WFB* did not translate. Citations of this text will be abbreviated as *PFB,* followed by appropriate page numbers.

# The Religious Foundations of Francis Bacon's Thought

# Introduction

## Bacon's Religion Obscured
### The Problem of Reading in the "Future Indicative"

Marina Leslie recently observed that Francis Bacon's writings are frequently read in the "future indicative."[1] She means by this that many scholars treat Bacon as a visionary advocate of the social and political benefits to be derived from science and technology, and that they judge the merits of his work in terms of his influence on eighteenth-, nineteenth-, and twentieth-century developments. While Professor Leslie's reference is to recent scholarship, her observation is apposite to earlier interpretations as well. The Enlightenment, for example, valorized Bacon as the heroic promoter of human rational action over passive faith in divine Providence and portrayed him as a secular humanitarian, who realized that "relief of man's estate" depended on human action and not on God's saving acts in history.[2] Early interpreters, who shaped this point of view, and those who have subsequently followed it, associate Bacon with empiricism, rationality, and secularization.[3] Because of this focus, many scholars give little attention to Bacon's use of religious themes, images, and motifs or they contend that Bacon uses them in a manipulative, cynical fashion in order to establish rapport and influence with intellectual and political elites, whose support was vital to his enterprise but who were less enlightened than he.[4]

Interpretations from the perspective of the "future indicative" have been and continue to be the predominant approach to Bacon's work.[5] A survey of the period from 1990 to 2000 shows that 35 books and 105 articles or book chapters were devoted to Bacon.[6] Of these, 20 books and 61 articles trace key elements of modern thought to Bacon, and many of these dismiss Bacon's religious references as disingenuous.[7] While this continues to be the prevailing approach to Bacon, it has not been the exclusive one. In recent years, early modern historians and historians of science have undertaken significant reassessments of the interrelation of science and religion in the early modern period; and this work is opening new perspectives on Bacon's writings.[8] Perez Zagorin and John C. Briggs, for example, make convincing arguments that Bacon's use of religious terms and images is a genuine reflection of his belief, not a cynical manipulation of prevailing religious sentiment.[9] This eleven-year period has also seen the beginning of the new critical edition of Bacon's collected works.[10] These volumes provide detailed textual analyses of Bacon's writings in relation to contemporary politics, philosophy, and religion. Still, there is much left to be done with regard to the investigation of Bacon's religious views and the influence of religion on his program of instauration.[11] For the most part, studies of Bacon's religion have attempted to situate his views within a particular belief system, e.g., Puritanism or in relation to an influential doctrine or belief, such as millenarianism. Less attention has been given to the ways in which Bacon draws from competing forms of Protestantism or how he shapes apocalyptic or millenarian views into his own unique doctrines.[12] There is still no book-length analysis of Bacon's use of religious images and themes in his major works, and there is no systematic development of Bacon's religious outlook.

This study investigates the relation of Bacon's religious views to his program of instauration through an advancement of learning and explores the range of religious motifs appearing in Bacon's writings. The method used involves close textual analysis to establish the themes and issues that consistently recur in Bacon's work from 1603 to 1626. Such close textual analysis is necessary because there are so many contradictory interpretations of the same key texts and because prevailing scholarship often ignores Bacon's religious ideas or dismisses them as part of the cultural iconography that Bacon manipulates to conceal or disguise his modern, secular, materialistic, rationalist views. This textual analysis will begin with the *New Atlantis* (1626) because it offers the fullest articulation of Bacon's vision of instauration and because the principal religious themes in Bacon's writings are all contained within it. Then the analysis will turn to the *Instauratio Magna* (*The Great Instauration*) and the *Novum Organum* (*The New Organon*), which were published in 1620, to show the centrality of religious concepts in two of his major philosophical works. The study will then examine five of Bacon's early published and unpublished works, including *The Advancement of Learning* (1605) and *De sapientia veterum* (*Wisdom of the Ancients*) (1609), to demonstrate that religious imagery and biblical themes permeate Bacon's program of reform from the outset.[13]

Analysis of these texts will demonstrate that Bacon's vision of reform or instauration is drawn from the Judaeo-Christian scriptures, particularly the Genesis account of the Creation and the Fall; from apocalyptic expectation of renewal in the Old Testament; and from soteriological themes of the New Testament. Careful examination will also demonstrate that Bacon's Christian ideas are augmented and transmuted by related themes and imagery found in the *prisca theologia*, a highly elastic collection of Neoplatonism, Hermeticism, alchemy, magic, and Jewish esoteric traditions. Bacon, like many Christian thinkers of his day, was convinced that Scholastic error and ecclesiastical dogma obscured religious truth and required a search for a truer, deeper level of understanding of the scriptures and of God's saving acts in history. Moreover, Bacon, like many philosophers and theologians, saw in the religious, esoteric, and pseudoscientific traditions of the *prisca theologia* elements of truth that could be refined and employed in the recovery and the advancement of Christian natural philosophy and theology.

The analysis of the *New Atlantis* will have three aims. First, it will highlight the pervasive religious imagery in the text. These images center around themes of salvation and deliverance and include references to the Exodus-Sinai events, the Davidic-Solomonic kingdom, the wisdom of Solomon, the motif of special election as God's *am segullah,* or chosen people, and the theme of messianic and millenarian restoration of humanity and nature. The second aim is to demonstrate the influence of the *prisca theologia,* or ancient wisdom tradition. Part of this analysis will require a careful examination of Bacon's use of the myth of Atlantis and its account of a primordial golden age of order, harmony, and prosperity. The third aim of this analysis of the *New Atlantis* is to provide a close examination of the activities of

Solomon's House. Particular attention will be given to the descriptions of the role and function of the members of Solomon's House in comparison with descriptions in the Old Testament of priests as the guardians and preservers of the Ark and of the Temple. In developing this priestly function, it will also be necessary to relate the functions of the members of Solomon's House to the noncanonical traditions of priests as recipients and preservers of Mosaic esoteric knowledge. A key element of this analysis will be to highlight the esoteric tradition of the secret wisdom given to Moses, preserved in the Ark, and then transferred to the Temple of Jerusalem. This tradition, in turn, will be related to the esoteric traditions of Solomonic wisdom and to the legends of the Temple as an omphalos or microcosm, through which nature could be commanded to obey. The argument will be that these Jewish esoteric traditions complement and reinforce the reference to the pagan ancient wisdom that was lost in the calamities that destroyed Atlantis. These themes, in turn, will be shown to be essential to understanding Bacon's use of the term *instauration*. The analysis will show that Bacon gives this term several connotations, including the rebuilding or re-edification of learning and the restoration of humanity to its prelapsarian state.

The analysis of the *New Atlantis* prepares the context for examination of Bacon's other writings in four important ways. First, it shows that Bacon presents his vision of an ideal or reformed utopian society in predominantly biblical language of special election, salvation, and deliverance. These themes are augmented by specific allusions to apocalyptic and millenarian fulfillment—for example, the key use of references to Jerusalem, to the Ark, and to Solomon. Second, Bacon adds to these traditional biblical themes, images, and patterns from pagan and Jewish esoteric traditions. Third, the *New Atlantis* demonstrates that Bacon's utopian reform depends on education or, more precisely, edification. As we shall see, Bacon's treatment of the term *edification* stresses that knowledge is essential to understanding God, to fulfilling human potential, and for drawing from nature all of the innate potential that God intends for humanity's use. Fourth, the theme of the divine vocation of the Brethren of Solomon's House will be related to Bacon's self-understanding of himself as a priest or prophet chosen by God to help restore order to a disordered world.

# Introduction

Part two of the study will focus on *The Great Instauration*. The published text is only a small portion of what Bacon had envisioned. His original plan called for a substantial work of six parts that would set out the philosophical principles for the study of nature and catalog all pertinent empirical findings. While the extant text is much briefer, Bacon devoted a great amount of time to a careful formulation of this work, and it does contain his principles for epistemological reform and presents a carefully conceived explanation of what can be achieved through his reform. The analysis in this section will demonstrate that "instauration" involves both tearing down and clearing away outmoded, deteriorated modes of knowledge and then rebuilding from the original foundations. In developing this key symbol, this study will follow Charles Whitney's excellent analyses of the root meaning of instauration as re-edification.[14] At the first level of meaning, Bacon is proposing a rehabilitation of learning. This philosophical enterprise, it is important to note, requires an edifice, that is, the institutionalization of learning. At the second level, this analysis of instauration will focus on the basic question of what exactly is to be restored and will show that there are two fundamental dimensions to Bacon's program. The first links Bacon's philosophical advance to a recovery of ancient wisdom. The second component is much broader in scope, and its goal is humanity's dominion over nature. This second element of instauration will be developed in relation to Bacon's several discussions of Original Sin and the restoration of humanity's proper relation to God and to nature. The method used in this section will be similar to that used in the analysis of the *New Atlantis:* it will move from the opening sections through the body of the text; and it will show how the "front matter" of the book, that is, the frontispiece, the "Proemium," and the "Dedicatory Letter," are permeated with biblical themes of providential restoration and redemption of humanity and nature.

The third part of the study will examine *The New Organon*, which was published simultaneously with *The Great Instauration*. As the title indicates, Bacon is proposing a new methodology or epistemology to replace Aristotle's organon. The structure of the work is not, however, comparable to Aristotle's propositional development of his method. *The New Organon* consists of two sets of aphorisms. The first describes the current state of epistemological disorder and then offers evidence or "signs of hope" that the current state can be overcome and that progress can be achieved. The second set comes closer to what might be expected as an epistemological statement, providing a detailed criticism of Aristotelian and Scholastic philosophy and introducing Bacon's inductive method. This study will focus primarily on the first set of aphorisms, paying close attention to the key themes and images, which present Bacon's view of his own time as a providential age in which God will intervene to provide "new mercies" by showing humanity the way to recover its dominion over nature. The procedure used here will be the same as with the *New Atlantis* and *The Great Instauration*. The analysis will develop from a close textual reading, which will seek to identify key terms, images, and themes that Bacon utilizes in this text. This procedure is particularly appropriate for this text's aphoristic style. This literary genre seeks to be suggestive and provocative, and Bacon chooses the wording and phrasing in each aphorism to prompt his reader to carefully consider the themes in each and the relation of each to the whole, and to freely associate his language and phrasing with other familiar settings in which they occur. Analysis will show that the overarching motif of this work is one of apocalyptic transformation. The ignorance and error that have characterized human history are giving way to advancements in learning that will bring relief to the human condition. Within this leitmotif, we will examine Bacon's repeated references to "reasons for hope" that the mind's proper relation to nature can be restored; evidence of providential action in Bacon's own time; the crucial need for humanity to respond to the opportunities provided by divine providence; and Bacon's understanding of his role in ushering in the new age of peace, harmony, and prosperity. In carrying out this analysis, the themes prominent in *The New Organon* will be related to key themes and symbols found in the *New Atlantis* and *The Great Instauration*.

The fourth part of the study will examine five of Bacon's published and unpublished texts prepared between 1603 and 1609. These early works include *The Advancement of Learning*, *De sapientia veterum* (*Wisdom of the Ancients*), *Temporis Partus Masculus* (*The Masculine Birth of Time*), *Redargutio Philosophiarum* (*The Refutation of Philosophies*), and *Cogitata et Visa* (*Thoughts and Conclusions*). Of these, the text that has received the most attention is *The Advancement of Learning*. A host of scholars have prepared commentaries and book-length studies that focus both on Bacon's critique of classical and medieval epistemology and on his presentation of his method for advancing knowledge and bringing "relief to man's estate." Often this text is used to demonstrate that Bacon is one of the "moderns," who replaces theology and metaphysics with inductive reasoning. Careful textual analysis will show, however, that biblical and religious themes and motifs permeate this work and will demonstrate that Bacon saw the reign of James I as the beginning of a providential age of peace, harmony, and prosperity. *The Advancement of Learning* was published shortly after the coronation of James I and contains two dedications in which Bacon compares the king to Solomon and portrays England as the New Zion. While this was familiar court imagery, Bacon concentrates on James's reputation for wisdom and argues that the king cannot install the "New Jerusalem" without Bacon's epistemological reforms to complement the spiritual reform already under way. Developing this aspect of Bacon's text will provide a fuller understanding of the two dimensions of Bacon's vision of the "great instauration" that will restore humanity's proper relation to God and to nature.

When *Wisdom of the Ancients* was published, it enjoyed enormous success; but it was largely ignored during the eighteenth and nineteenth centuries because it seemed marginal to Bacon's contribution to modern epistemological reform. More recently, however, Paolo Rossi, Howard White, and others have argued that *Wisdom of the Ancients* is a central text for understanding Bacon's views on the history of natural philosophy, its derailment by the Platonic and Aristotelean schools, and its reform through his advancement of knowledge.[15] The analysis offered here will demonstrate that *Wisdom of the Ancients* contains important elements essential to understanding Bacon's concept of instauration as rebuilding. Rather than attempting to discuss the work *in toto*, however, only four of the fifty-six fables will be examined. In the selected fables Bacon describes the methods and goals of the earliest, purest forms of natural philosophy, investigates the reasons for the decline of true knowledge, and explores the prospects for recovering and advancing true philosophy. The focus of the analysis of these representative fables will be on their relation to the primary theme of instauration and on the ways in which the fables and allegories augment the biblical motifs used in Bacon's other key texts.

The other three texts, *The Masculine Birth of Time, The Refutation of Philosophies,* and *Thoughts and Conclusions,* are not nearly as well-known as *The Advancement of Learning* and *Wisdom of the Ancients*. In fact, they were never prepared for publication; and if they were circulated in manuscript, it was among a close circle of theologians and philosophers, whose opinions Bacon valued. Even when these works were posthumously published as part of Bacon's collected works, they garnered little interest. For the most part, they were considered preliminary statements of themes developed more carefully and clearly in Bacon's later published work. To a great extent, this assessment remains valid. The main themes of these works do appear in *The Great Instauration, The New Organon,* and other later works. Still, these texts are useful to our analysis for two primary reasons. First, these early writings allow us to examine Bacon's attempts to find the proper literary mode for presenting his program of reform. Second, these early texts, which were read by Bacon's close acquaintances, often contain sharper, clearer statements of Bacon's primary themes than do the later, more public writings.

A fifth and concluding part of the study will draw together the principal motifs that emerged through the detailed examinations of these key texts and will show how a careful, objective study of Bacon's writings demonstrates that Baconianism and other approaches, which look at Bacon from the perspective of the "future indicative," distort Bacon's program of instauration by ignoring or minimizing its religious dimension. A careful reading of Bacon's writings shows that four religious motifs predominate. The central motif is that of instauration, an apocalyptic concept, which refers ultimately to the restoration of humanity to its prelapsarian condition. The second motif running through Bacon's writings is that of providential intervention. The third is that of "vocation" and reflects Bacon's conviction that he has been called by God to help usher in a new age of harmony and prosperity. The fourth element is Christian charity, which can eradicate human selfishness, pride, and materialism.

The demonstration of the centrality of these four major religious motifs in Bacon's writings will, it is hoped, add to the recent attention given to the role of religion in Bacon's program of scientific advancement by early modern historians and historians of science. In doing so, it will, perhaps, offer a corrective to the persistent view of Bacon as a secular modern, who dismisses religion in order to promote the human advance of knowledge. And while it does not propose to tackle the larger issue, this exploration of Bacon's religious convictions suggests that the origins of modernity are more complex than many current approaches allow. Given Bacon's extraordinary influence, it is evident that modernity is deeply steeped in apocalyptic yearning and that the goals and aims of science cannot be separated from the dream of a restoration of a prelapsarian relation of humanity, God, and nature.

# Chapter 1

## The *New Atlantis*

In 1968 Howard B. White published *Peace among the Willows,* the first book-length analysis of Bacon's *New Atlantis.* White, a political theorist who regards Bacon as a principal shaper of modern political ideas, maintains that it is this utopian work and not one of Bacon's philosophical treatises that provides the fullest statement of Bacon's political theory. White is especially interested in what he regards as Bacon's secularization of politics and in his glorification of the power of science to serve the interests of the secular state. In developing his argument, White maintains that the *New Atlantis* must be read with meticulous care in order to understand Bacon's complex interweaving and transformation of political iconography, ancient history and fables, religious symbols, scientific methodologies, and pseudoscientific concepts. White devotes considerable attention to Bacon's use of religious themes and argues that he manipulates them in order to subvert Christian ideas and transform them into a culturally acceptable justification for a preoccupation with luxury and materialism. According to White, Bacon's purpose is to transform the human quest from the search for the "heavenly city" to the creation of the well-governed country and to change the philosophical quest from an effort to understand God, God's Creation, and humanity's place in it to a pursuit to understand what humans can make of themselves.

White's work has been highly influential and has been augmented by that of another political philosopher, Jerry Weinberger. Weinberger also argues that Bacon's utopia provides a primary source for understanding the transitional phase from early modern political ideas to those of the modern age; and he maintains that Bacon manipulates religious language and concepts to conceal his secular agenda.[1] Recently, considerable attention to Bacon's *New Atlantis* has also come from the new historical criticism. Studies by Charles Whitney, Amy Boesky, and others have analyzed utopian literature as a primary source for understanding the "founding fictions" and political ideologies underpinning nationalism, imperialism, colonialism, and overseas expansion.[2] Like White and Weinberger, many cultural historians treat Bacon's manipulation of the religious ideas as a way of providing cultural authority for his political agenda. Marina Leslie, for example, asserts that Bacon inverts the spiritual and material worlds and claims that Bacon transforms spiritual salvation into material well-being accomplished by humans and not by God (*Renaissance Utopias and the Problem of History,* 91, 93). David Innes, a theologian influenced by White, contends that Bacon is responsible for transmuting Christian hope for spiritual salvation into a secular dream of material comfort and argues that the Christianity of Bensalem is actually a "fundamental assault upon, transformation of and ultimate displacement of Christianity" ("Bacon's New Atlantis: The Christian Hope and the Modern Hope," 4–5). Denise Albanese asserts that Bensalemite Christianity "first serves as yet another instance of reverse colonialism, with the natives' conversion already an accomplished fact" and as the "code for an intellectual imperialism" ("The *New Atlantis* and the Uses of Utopia," 510–11).

Because the *New Atlantis* has received so much attention from political philosophers and cultural historians, it offers an excellent point of departure to demonstrate how the analysis offered here differs from those that portray Bacon's use of religious language and concepts as disingenuous and manipulative. This study maintains that Bacon's program of utopian reform presented in the *New Atlantis* is grounded in genuinely and deeply felt religious convictions and contends that it serves as the foundation for his program of political and social prosperity to be achieved through the advancement of learning. The *New Atlantis* is also an appropriate beginning point for an analysis of Bacon's work because it offers a compact statement of the main themes that run through his philosophical writings from his earliest unpublished manuscripts through his most-often-cited philosophical texts, including *The Advancement of Learning*, *The Great Instauration*, and *The New Organon*.

Developing the evidence to support a position that stands in marked contrast to prevailing interpretations requires careful attention to the details of Bacon's utopian narrative. This investigation will, therefore, closely examine each episode, from the storm that brings European sailors to Bensalem, through the Europeans' interviews with the Governor of the Strangers' House and with Joabin, to the climactic audience with a Father of Solomon's House. Careful attention will also be given to the accounts of Bensalem's conversion to Christianity and to the early history of Bensalem, Atlantis, and other great seagoing civilizations. While only one of these accounts, the conversion to Christianity, appears to be explicitly religious, analysis of the other episodes will demonstrate Bacon's pervasive use of religious themes of providential deliverance and of special election. In discussing the primordial history of Bensalem and Atlantis, it will be important to compare Bacon's version of the myth of Atlantis to the one found in Plato's *Critias* and *Timaeus*. Analysis will show that Bacon uses this primordial history to portray a golden age that has been virtually lost from memory; and as a result, humanity has been left with a truncated account of its past achievements. This primordial history will then be related to Bacon's references to an ancient wisdom that has been lost and replaced by impotent, inferior philosophies. The purpose of the Platonic myth and Bacon's use of it, however, is to instill hope that this knowledge can be recovered and the state of civilizational excellence restored. The analysis will then turn to the complex themes surrounding the activities of Solomon's House. This episode is the one that most often receives extended discussion, but the focus is usually on Bacon's description of collaborative efforts of specialized sciences to collectively advance empirical knowledge and bring relief to the human condition. The analysis offered here will place Bacon's references to Solomon and Solomon's House in the context of the iconography of the court of James I, particularly portrayals of James I as the new Solomon who would restore Solomon's Temple and usher in a providential age of peace, harmony, and prosperity. This analysis will show that Bacon conceives of Solomon's House, that is, the recovery of natural philosophy, as the complement to the rebuilding of Solomon's Temple, that is, the restoration of true religion. Understanding this context is essential to understanding Bacon's program of instauration, and a proper understanding of the concept of instauration demonstrates that it has two dimensions. The first is a thoroughgoing reform of religion that restores humanity's relation to God, and the second is a thoroughgoing recovery of the principles of natural philosophy, which restores humanity's dominion over nature.

When the "scientific" work of Solomon's House is recontextualized within the religious themes of salvation and deliverance that permeate the *New Atlantis*, the full scope of Bacon's "great instauration" can be seen; and this project is not the one usually portrayed in scholarly treatments of the *New Atlantis*. Bacon's instauration is not a secular, scientific advance through which humanity gains dominion over nature and mastery of its own destiny. Bacon's instauration is a program for rehabilitating humanity and its relation to nature that is to be guided by divine Providence and achieved through pious human effort.

To develop Bacon's key themes and symbols, the analysis will follow the story as it unfolds.

## The Fortuitous Discovery of Bensalem

The story begins with a European expedition, sailing from Peru en route to China and Japan, being blown off course and becoming lost "in the greatest wilderness of the waters in the world" (*WFB*, 3:129). Helpless and disoriented, the sailors pray to God, begging for mercy and deliverance. Night closes in, leaving them to wonder at their fate. When dawn comes, they discover that their prayers have been answered and that they have been brought within sight of land. As they approach the island, people on shore warn the Europeans not to disembark. The Europeans beg for assistance, explaining that they have several sick sailors on board who might die without medical attention. In response to this urgent need, an official of the country sails out to their ship and offers provisions, medication, and repairs that will enable the Europeans to get under way. This offer is presented on a scroll written in four languages (Hebrew, Latin, Greek, and Spanish) and marked by a cross and a pair of cherubim's wings.[3] The apprehension of the Europeans is relieved by the obvious charity and learning of the inhabitants of this country and, most of all, by the familiar sign of the cross. Similarly, the Bensalemites modify their guarded reception of the foreigners when they declare themselves to be from a Christian land, and the Europeans are invited to the island to recuperate.

This opening segment is noteworthy for its introduction of the leitmotif of divine intervention and salvation. In describing the event, the Europeans compare their experience to that of Jonah and acknowledge that it was divine grace that brought them to Bensalem. This motif of rescue from treacherous waters will be repeated in several forms throughout the narrative. Were these the only references to deliverance or salvation and to Bensalem as an ideal Christian society (the Kingdom of God on earth), their significance could be discounted or be attributed to the language conventions of Bacon's day. This is not the case, however. The theme of salvation and deliverance is developed further as the Europeans experience the charity of the Bensalemites. The sailors are so struck by the people and by the society that they say that it "seemed to us that we have before us a picture of our salvation in heaven; for we . . . were awhile since in the jaws of death"; on another occasion they say that they had "come into a land of angels" or that they are presented with a "picture of salvation in heaven" (*WFB*, 3:136).

## The Conversion of Bensalem

When given an opportunity to learn about this remarkable island, the first question that the Europeans hope to have answered is how the island had been converted to Christianity. The Governor of the Strangers' House is pleased with this question because, he says, it indicates that these travelers are seeking the Kingdom of Heaven (*WFB*, 3:137). The Governor explains that the conversion occurred as the result of a miraculous event that happened about twenty years after the Resurrection and Ascension. One night a great column of light topped by a cross appeared about a mile out on the ocean. A few brave souls from Renfusa, the nearest city, boarded boats and sailed out toward the hierophany. When they had come within about sixty yards, they were mysteriously restrained from drawing closer. One of the boats, however, had a member of Solomon's House on board, and he said: "Lord God of heaven and earth, thou hast vouchsafed of thy grace to those of our order, to know thy works of creation, and the

# The *New Atlantis*

secrets of them; and to discern... between divine miracles, works of nature, works of art, and impostitures and illusions of all sorts" (*WFB*, 3:137). He then declared the column to be a genuine miracle and begged God to reveal its true meaning. The wise man was then allowed to move closer, and as he did, the Pillar of Cloud was transformed, leaving an ark (small chest) floating in the water. As the wise man moved toward it, the chest opened to reveal a book and a letter. The book found in the ark contained canonical books familiar to the Europeans and "some other books of the New Testament which were not at that time written" (*WFB*, 3:138). The letter was from the apostle Bartholomew, who stated that he had received a vision in which God instructed him "to commit the ark to the floods of the sea." When the ark reached its appointed destination, the people of that land would receive "salvation and peace and goodwill from the Father and from the Lord Jesus" (*WFB*, 3:138). Several aspects of this account deserve comment and development.

- Bensalem's conversion does not occur through ordinary missionary activity. It results from direct intervention by God, who has chosen the island for a special benediction. Also, Bensalem's conversion occurred shortly after Christ's Ascension—a period when Christ's teachings and deeds were vivid in the minds of the Apostles. The Christianity of Bensalem, therefore, is pure and unadulterated by human error and misinterpretation that occur with the passage of time; and this is a primary difference between Europe and Bensalem.

- The sacred texts available to the Bensalemites are more extensive than those available to European Christianity. So Bensalem not only has a purer form of gospel Christianity than does Europe, it also has a fuller scriptural base to guide it. Moreover, the Bensalemites have evidently been able to preserve the purity of the Christian kerygma and have founded a true Christian kingdom, one that the Europeans likened to Heaven and its inhabitants to angels. Again, the purity of religion in Bensalem stands in contrast to the degenerated Christianity of Europe, where doctrinal disputes and ecclesiastical corruption have contaminated the lifeblood of the faith.

- The ark that brings salvation to Bensalem calls to mind the ark that saved Noah and his family from the devastating flood that destroyed all other peoples. An ark is also an integral part of the history of God's selection of the Hebrews as His chosen people. The culminating event of the Exodus-Sinai experience is Moses' placement of the God-given law in the Ark of the Covenant, which served as the throne of God's presence among his chosen people. This ark is, therefore, the most sacred object in Hebrew history, playing a ritual role in the crossing of the Jordan River into the Promised Land, the establishment of the Davidic-Solomonic kingship, and in the consecration of Jerusalem as the seat of religious and political order. The ark functions similarly in the account of Bensalem's conversion, where it is a prime symbol of the special election of the Bensalemites as God's new chosen people. Perhaps this is why the country is named Bensalem: heir of peace or inheritor of Jerusalem's renown.[4]

- The choice of Bartholomew as the apostle who receives the vision and sends the ark on its way is also noteworthy. According to tradition, Bartholomew was the great missionary to the remote parts of the world: India, Persia, and Mesopotamia; and Bartholomew is also the apostle who had a special ability to receive and interpret dreams and revelations. Tradition also holds that Bartholomew was the author of two noncanonical works: the Gospel of Bartholomew and the Book of the Resurrection of Christ, both of which contain accounts of Christ's Resurrection, harrowing of Hell, and rescue of Adam. Bartholomew is, therefore, another important symbol of a pure religion capable of healing the ruptured union with God and recovering humanity's condition prior to the Fall.

- These symbols and episodes of providential rescue refer to an entire people or nation, not to a few select individuals. The Pillar of Cloud and the Ark are symbols of the selection of the Hebrews as God's chosen people. Adam, as his name indicates, represents humanity. Even Jonah's rescue is a prelude to the conversion of the people of Nineveh. Within the *New Atlantis,* salvation also comes to the entire nation. The European sailors, in the context of this utopia, are representative of European society as the whole.

- The function of the member of Solomon's House is important to note and to understand properly. Although this appearance is brief, it establishes Solomon's House as the interpreter of both natural and supernatural or divine events. So from the first, Solomon's House is presented in a religious context and is not depicted as a secular, scientific think-tank. The description of the activities of Solomon's House, which is provided in a later interview, makes it clear that the Brethren study the Creation in order to better understand God. Theirs is a pious search for the benefits in nature provided by the divine. Howard White is wrong when he says that the ability to interpret the miracle serves to grant "power over miracles to the wise men of Solomon's House" and means "control of natural philosophy over theology" (*Peace among the Willows,* 158–59). The wise man is not a secular scientist who is able to command the supernatural to obey. This first appearance of a member of Solomon's House makes it clear that their efforts are devoted to the search for truth in its natural and supernatural forms. The demeanor of the member of Solomon's House is reverent as he prays to God to reveal the meaning of a supernatural event that he is able to recognize as a miracle but cannot interpret without divine revelation. In this episode he is referred to as a "member" and as a "wise man." In other places in the *New Atlantis* the members are referred to as "Brethren," "Fellows," and "Fathers." The climactic meeting of the Europeans is with a "Father" of Solomon's House. "Father" and "Brethren" clearly carry religious connotations. Here the wise man serves as an agent for interpreting divine revelation.

- The role of the wise man in the episode is important to understand, not only to establish the scope of the efforts by Solomon's House to discover truth in all its forms, but also in order to understand why Bensalem was chosen for this special benediction. Christian revelation comes to the land because the Bensalemites already believed in an all-knowing, all-powerful God; they devoted efforts to studying both the natural and the divine and were able to distinguish the two. That the ark comes to Bensalem is, therefore, not a result of accident or caprice. God selects Bensalem because it is capable of receiving and perpetuating a pure form of gospel Christianity.

- The account of the island's conversion establishes parallels between the experience of the Bensalemites and those who first received the good news of Christ's birth. The community that first sees the hierophany is called Renfusa, or sheep people. The person on the ship who is able to interpret the miracle is a wise man. This is parallel with the miraculous announcement of the birth of the Messiah to the shepherds and to the Magi. White chooses to associate the name of the community with gullibility (*Peace among the Willows*, 143–62), and Laurence Lampert claims that Renfusa is evidence that "Christianity was introduced by a wise scientist as an instrument to lead the sheep" (*Nietzsche and Modern Times*, 31). These interpretations are difficult to maintain or support when the reference to Renfusa is read in relation to the other symbols and motifs associated with the conversion of Bensalem.

## The Prehistory of Civilization and Why Bensalem Remains Hidden

During the second interview with the Governor of the Strangers' House, the Europeans ask why such a great civilization has chosen to remain hidden from the rest of humanity, while it obviously knows about all other existing civilizations, including Europe. The Governor begins his answer with an account of ancient history virtually unknown to the Europeans. In the distant past worldwide navigation and commerce were commonplace, until disrupted by natural catastrophe. The only vestige of the golden age known to the Europeans is in Plato's account of the glorious civilization of Atlantis, which was destroyed by earthquake and flood as punishment for its avarice and will to power.[5] According to the Governor's account, early navigation was far more advanced than even the impressive recent accomplishments of the Europeans. In the ancient past many great civilizations sailed to the farthest regions of the world and carried on trade with Bensalem and its neighbor Atlantis. This period was brought to an end by earthquakes and floods that "Divine Revenge" used to punish Atlantis for its proud enterprises. These calamities devastated the country, the people, and the great civilization they had created. Human civilization was never able to recover fully following these catastrophes; the civilization of Atlantis left only the primitive culture of America and the New World. "So you see," the Governor explains, "by this main accident of time, we lost our traffic with the Americans.... As for the other parts of the world, it is most manifest that in the ages following (whether it were in respect of wars, or by a natural revolution of time) navigation did every where greatly decay; and specially far voyages" (*WFB*, 3:143).

This account explains how other civilizations had been cut off from Bensalem and knowledge of its greatness had been lost to the rest of the world. It does not explain, however, why Bensalem chose to keep its existence secret even though it was in contact with other nations. To give an adequate explanation requires the Governor to discuss the policies of the great king Solamona and his creation of Solomon's House. The Governor explains that about 1900 years earlier the Bensalemite king Solamona decided that his nation was far superior to any other in every way and could not benefit from direct intercourse with them. His country was wholly self-sufficient, morally upright, and could be "a thousand ways altered to the worse, but scarce any one way to the better" (*WFB*, 3:144) from traffic with other civilizations. Therefore, he took steps to prevent the influx of customs and ideas from inferior nations. One of his steps was to offer to allow all foreign travelers to take up residence in Bensalem rather than return to their own countries. The Governor reports that this policy had been followed ever since and that only thirteen individuals ever chose to leave during the 1900-year span. As a result, almost nothing has been reported back to other nations in two millennia; and the few reports that had been made were dismissed as fantasy because the quality of life in Bensalem seemed to be an improbable delusion. King Solamona also prohibited his subjects from leaving, to prevent them from revealing too much or from becoming corrupted by what they encountered abroad. Only members of Solomon's House are sent on secret reconnaissance missions. The purpose of these trips is to gather information about other nations, especially the "sciences, arts, manufacturers, and inventions of all the world; and withal to bring unto us books, instruments, and patterns in every kind" (*WFB*, 3:146). The Governor makes it clear that the purpose of these efforts is not to acquire "gold, silver, or jewels; nor for silks; nor for spices; nor any other commodity of matter; but only for God's first creature, which was Light" (*WFB*, 3:146–47). The Governor explains that King Solamona created Solomon's House to "find out the true nature of all things; (whereby God might have the more glory in the workmanship of them, and men the more fruit in the use of them)" (*WFB*, 3:145). This parenthetic statement links the pious study of the Creation and devotion to the Creator with the discovery of the benefits God placed in nature for humanity's use. Subsequent analysis will show that Bacon repeatedly warns that humanity cannot gain the benefits in nature without proper piety.

The Governor next explains that the name Solomon's House is inspired by the biblical Solomon's reputation for wisdom; but the Governor adds that Bensalem possessed Solomon's *Natural History,* a text that was lost to the Europeans. This text held special knowledge of the workings of nature, which Solomon's House used as the foundation of its remarkable work. Following his description of the founding of the House of Solomon, and of the reconnaissance missions of its members, the Governor offers to help the Europeans return to their country or to allow them to stay in Bensalem. The Europeans enthusiastically accept the offer to stay.

This account introduces or reinforces several critical themes:

- Atlantis is destroyed by the gods because of its drive to expand its empire through conquest and world domination. This *libido dominandi* stands in stark contrast to Bensalem, which is characterized as an embodiment of the cardinal Christian virtues of faith, charity, peace, and justice. Even after the series of natural disasters, which weakened or destroyed other civilizations, Bensalem does not seize the opportunity to invade lands and enslave their inhabitants. Instead, it chooses to withdraw in order to live in peace.

- While Atlantis used navigation and exploration for material gain, Bensalem seeks knowledge that it can use for the welfare of its people.

- The activities of Solomon's House have theological as well as scientific dimensions. The study of nature, which brings practical benefits, is also a study of the Creation in order to know the Creator. Also, the account of the conversion of Bensalem to Christianity makes it clear that the members of Solomon's House are able to discern the miraculous from the natural.

- This episode contains another reference to sacred texts unknown or lost to Europe, and these texts play an essential role in the well-being of the nation and its people.

- It is important to recognize that the age of Solomona and the founding of Solomon's House occur before the conversion to Christianity. The island, therefore, already is devoted to the spiritual and material well-being of its inhabitants. Perhaps this is why it is chosen by God for a "special benediction."

- In the discussion of the conversion to Christianity, reference was made to Bartholomew and the two writings attributed to him, which described Christ's harrowing of Hell and rescue of Adam. Before the Fall, humanity had dominion over nature and was able to draw from the Creation all of the benefits that God had placed in it. The work of Solomon's House reflects this prelapsarian condition in which humanity has mastery over nature and is able to create paradisiacal conditions.

- Finally, it is important to note that Bensalem is the only civilization that has been spared devastation. Neither natural catastrophes nor the ravages of war have interrupted its history. Therefore, it is able to preserve ancient truth and build upon it rather than being reduced to an infantile state of subsistence living and intellectual poverty.

These themes need further investigation in order to understand how they contribute to Bacon's concept of instauration, but three other episodes need to be examined first: the Feast of the Family ceremony, the meeting with Joabin, and the audience with a Father from Solomon's House.

## The Feast of the Family

As already noted, the Europeans readily accept the Governor's invitation to become citizens; and as they begin to move about the country in an attempt to learn more about Bensalem's customs and practices, they soon have the opportunity to observe the Feast of the Family ceremony. The account of the Feast of the Family serves primarily as a model to juxtapose to the pervasive disorder in European society, a theme taken up again during the Europeans' meeting with Joabin. Briefly, the stated purpose of the ceremony is to honor the patriarch of a family, who has supplied the king with many subjects. The celebration, then, is a ritual affirmation of the abundance and prosperity of the country.[6] More than fecundity is being celebrated, however. The ceremony stresses the patriarch's role as the source of order, justice, and moral instruction within the family and, by extension, within the nation as a whole.[7] The patriarch's first ceremonial duty, for example, is to resolve any conflict within the family before the actual celebration can begin (*WFB*, 3:148). Moreover, the honor accorded the patriarch is proportional to the success of his children as productive, responsible citizens of the state. That the moral dimension of family life is central to the ceremony and to the well-being of the country is made clear in the discussion with Joabin. This discussion begins when the European narrator asks Joabin if polygamy is practiced in Bensalem (since it is obvious that the country honors large families). "I desired to know of him what laws and customs they had concerning marriage; and whether they kept marriage well; and whether they were tied to one wife? For that where population is so much affected [desired] and such as with them it seemed to be, there is commonly permission of plurality of wives" (*WFB*, 3:152). Joabin replies that the marital bond is the nucleus of familial and social order in Bensalem and that the people are not given to passion or sexual excess: "there are no stews, no dissolute houses, no courtesans, nor any thing of that kind" (*WFB*, 3:152). He adds, however, that his familiarity with the deplorable condition of European society allows him to understand how such a question might be the paramount interest and logical assumption of the Europeans. "They [the Bensalemites] say ye have put marriage out of office: for marriage is ordained the remedy for unlawful concupiscence; and natural concupiscence seemeth as a spur to marriage. But when men have at hand a remedy more agreeable to their corrupt will, marriage is almost expulsed" (*WFB*, 3:152). This passage is followed by a scathing criticism of the libidinal immorality in Europe that has destroyed the family unit, the desire for children, and the orderly social life that emerges from a stable family. The disorder resulting from libidinal corruption in individuals is compounded by misguided social customs and laws. In order to prevent the greater evils of adultery, the deflowering of virgins, and unnatural lust, society permits "change and the delight in meretricious embracements." Such compromises and accommodations, however, are destined to fail. According to Joabin, lust is like a furnace: if you stop the flames altogether, it will go out, "but if you give it any vent, it will rage" (*WFB*, 3:153). He then asserts that vice and corrupt appetites reflect a profound disorder of the soul that obstructs religious and moral instruction; and without a firm moral and religious base, no society can endure.[8] The exchange between Joabin and the Europeans is interrupted by a messenger who has come to tell Joabin that a Father of Solomon's House is going to visit the city that and Joabin is needed to help make suitable arrangements.

## Joabin the Jew

Though Joabin appears only briefly, his role in Bacon's parable is crucial. The references to Solomon's House and Joabin's name provide the principal clue to his role in Bacon's parable. The stem of Joabin's name is Joab. The biblical Joab was one of King David's generals, whose most important role was in retrieving the Ark of the Covenant from the Philistines.[9] As we have already noted, the Ark of the Covenant is the prime symbol of the Hebrews' election as God's special people. The Ark's recovery and subsequent placement in the Temple were essential elements of the establishment of Jerusalem as a religious and political center for the Jewish people. So there is a direct connection between the biblical Joab, Jerusalem, and Solomon's Temple. Joabin also has a key function in Bensalem and has an important tie to the activities of Solomon's House. These equivalences of symbolization augment the earlier discussion of King Solamona and reinforce other symbols that associate Bensalem with God's chosen people and the New Jerusalem.

Joabin's connection with other key themes in the *New Atlantis* is found in his account of the ancestry of the Bensalemites. According to Joabin, the people of Bensalem are descended from Abraham and their laws were given by Moses. The descent from Abraham is supposed to come from his son Nachoran. Joabin's statement, therefore, further links the Bensalemites to a biblical benediction (Abraham is described elsewhere in the *New Atlantis* as "Father of the faithful"). The reference to Moses includes the statement that he "by a secret cabala ordained the laws of Bensalem which they now use" (*WFB,* 3:151). The political order of Bensalem, therefore, is founded on God's law. But the law available to Bensalem extends beyond the Old Testament. It includes the secret teachings revealed to Moses during the forty days on Mount Sinai. While Joabin speaks specifically of the Cabala in relation to political law, mention of the Cabala reinforces the discussion of Solomon's *Natural History.* From the Middle Ages into the Renaissance there was a widespread tradition that the secret teachings given to Moses were preserved in the Ark of the Covenant and transmitted to Solomon.

This complex of symbolic linkages between Bensalem and Jerusalem, Solomon's Temple, and Solomon's House is further augmented by the initial description of Joabin as a Jew unlike those in Europe. The chief difference between the Jews of Bensalem and the Jews of Europe is that the Bensalemite Jews expect that the coming of the Messiah will usher in a New Jerusalem or a Kingdom of God on earth, and they expect that the king of Bensalem, as a representative of a people who have received a special benediction, will sit on the right hand of the enthroned Messiah. Joabin's function, therefore, is to set the stage for the discussion of Solomon's House by introducing symbolic linkages between Solomon's House and Solomon's Temple. Joabin also serves as a representative of a pure form of Judaism, which complements Bensalem's pure form of Christianity. Joabin's pure form of Judaism follows the traditions of Abraham and Moses, respects Christianity, and waits for the Messiah, who will deliver his chosen people from spiritual and temporal disorder. Joabin's identification of Bensalem as a chosen people, whose king will sit on the right hand of God, reinforces the emphasis on piety, charity, faith, and good works as the traits of God's chosen people. God's "chosen" do not belong to a specific ethnic group. They are those who attempt to live under the Old and New Covenants.

### The Father of Solomon's House

Shortly after Joabin is called away to assist with the arrival of the Father from Solomon's House, the narrator gives a detailed description of the pomp and ceremony surrounding the Father's entry into the city. The people crowd the streets to catch a glimpse of this high-level state official, who is surrounded by religious paraphernalia. His attendants, for example, carry a crozier, a symbol of ecclesiastical authority, and a staff, a symbol of pastoral function. Moreover, his demeanor is clearly ecclesiastical, for he "held up his bare hand as he went, as blessing the people" (*WFB*, 3:155). Because the Europeans have heard about and have seen how highly the Brethren are valued, they are eager for an opportunity to gain an audience, and Joabin is able to make the arrangements. This interview is the climactic episode of the *New Atlantis.* When the Europeans enter, the Father greets them with a gesture of blessing, and they kneel to kiss the hem of his robe (as they have been instructed). The Father then provides an extended account of the purpose, the activities, and the contributions of Solomon's House. The purpose is first succinctly stated: "The End of our Foundation is the knowledge of Causes and secret motions of things; and the enlarging of the bounds of Human Empire, to the effecting of all things possible" (*WFB,* 3:156). A detailed description of the investigation of the natural world then follows: from caves to mountain observatories to marine investigations. These investigations produce a breadth and depth of knowledge beyond anything imagined in Europe, but they are only the preliminary stage. The intent is to use them to ameliorate the human condition through the improvement of existing orders and to create new phenomena. Experiments in the Lower Region, for example, produce new artificial metals, which are used for curing diseases. There is also a "great variety of composts, and of soils, for the making of the earth fruitful," as well as a number of artificial wells and fountains, including one called Water of Paradise, created by the Brethren "for health and the prolongation of life" (*WFB,* 3: 157–58). The Father further indicates that "we have also large and various orchards and gardens... [and] make them also by art greater much than their nature; and their fruit greater and sweeter.... And many of them we have so ordered as they become of medicinal use" (*WFB,* 3:155–58). The Father explains that Solomon's House has apothecaries, centers for the mechanical arts, furnaces, laboratories for light, acoustics, as well as houses for the study and exposure of deceit, impostitures, and illusions.

The Father next explains the duties or offices of the various members, which include advancing the practical aspects of research, developing new theoretical insights, and producing new products and inventions that benefit the nation. The Europeans are told that Solomon's House guards its work carefully and takes pains to prevent the government or the citizenry from obtaining information that might be misunderstood or misused. This last statement and the earlier statement that foreign travel was restricted to Solomon's House have prompted extensive comment by White, Weinberger, Boesky, and others, who see these practices as further evidence of totalitarian state control or of the creation of scientists as a new political-intellectual elite who are able to provide creature comforts to the citizens and produce political order and stability for political rulers. Such interpretations fail to take into account Bacon's concept of human nature, which is based upon the concept of Original Sin. Since the Fall, humans are prone to being self-centered and are inclined to become preoccupied with material concerns. Only the members of Solomon's House have attained the level of spiritual discipline to overcome this materialistic preoccupation and use the rich benefits to be derived from God's Creation for charitable purposes.

The Father ends by describing daily religious observances evidently intended to remind the Brethren of their religious and moral obligations to use their God-given wisdom prudently: "We have certain hymns and services, which we say daily, of laud, and thanks to God for his marvellous works: and forms of prayers, imploring his aid and blessing for the illumination of our labours, and the turning of them into good and holy uses" (*WFB*, 3:166).[10] Shortly after the statement that "we do also declare natural divinations of diseases, plagues, swarms of harmful creatures, scarcity, tempests, earthquakes, great inundations, comets and (etc.)," the text breaks off (*WFB*, 3:166).

This account of the collective efforts to advance the theoretical and practical applications of the study of nature is the reason Thomas Sprat and others describe Solomon's House as a model for the Royal Society, and it also justifies Bacon's place of honor in the frontispiece to Sprat's *History of the Royal Society*.[11] But the analysis offered here demonstrates that Bacon presents Solomon's House after establishing a context of religious imagery of salvation, deliverance, and rehabilitation. It is, therefore, important to consider in more detail the function of Solomon's House in relation to these motifs. More specifically, we need to examine the linkages Bacon establishes between Bensalem's Solamona and the biblical Solomon and between Solomon's House and Solomon's Temple. Investigating this latter connection will lead to a consideration of the meaning of Bacon's concept of instauration in relation to the religious motifs of rescue and renewal.

## Solamona and Solomon's House

We need to begin by recalling the Governor's account of King Solamona and his founding of Solomon's House.

> There reigned in this island, about nineteen hundred years ago, a King whose memory of all others we most adore; not superstitiously, but as a divine instrument, though a mortal man; his name was Solamona: and we esteem him as the lawgiver of our nation. This king had a *large heart,* inscrutable for good; and was wholly bent to make his kingdom and people happy.... amongst the excellent acts of that king, one above all hath the preeminence. It was the erection and institution of an Order or Society which we call *Salomon's House;* the noblest foundation (as we think) that ever was upon the earth; and the lanthorn of this kingdom. It is dedicated to the study of the Works and Creatures of God. Some think it beareth the founder's name a little corrupted, as if it should be Solamona's House. But the records write it as it is spoken. So as I take it to be denominate of the King of the Hebrews, which is famous with you, and no stranger to us. For we have some parts of his works which with you are lost; namely, that Natural History which he wrote, of all plants, from the *cedar of Libanus* to the *moss that groweth out of the wall,* and of all *things that have life and motion.* (*WFB,* 3:144–45)

The first notable feature of this account is the connection between Solamona's "large heart," that is, his piety and charity, and the establishment of Solomon's House. Bacon's reference to Solamona's "large heart" evokes the use of the phrase in 1 Kings 4:29 to describe Solomon. According to the text, Solomon found favor with God and God offered to grant him any wish. Solomon asked for wisdom in order to be able to rule his kingdom with intelligence and compassion. The request pleased God, and it was granted. God gave Solomon great material wealth as well. The biblical reference to a "large heart" is augmented in the Governor's account of Solamona's reign through descriptions of the king's devotion to making his kingdom and his people happy and to perpetuating peace and prosperity. This emphasis on the benevolence of the king also defines his kingship in terms of the primary Christian virtue: charity. The *New Atlantis* makes it clear that benevolence and charity are the motives for Solamona's establishing Solomon's House. It is referred to several times as "the lanthorn of the kingdom," providing enlightenment and prosperity; and enlightenment encompasses religious knowledge as well as philosophical knowledge of the workings of nature that can be applied for the benefit of humanity. Scholars who are determined to portray Bacon as an advocate of imperialism and colonization continue to overlook the Solomonic model of political order that is so obvious here and in other of Bacon's writings. Amy Boesky, for example, claims that ancient Rome was Bacon's prototype but that he modernized it by conjoining imperialism with the power of science (*Founding Fictions,* 63–65).

## Solomon's House and Bacon's Instauration

While Bacon uses biblical descriptions of Solomon's piety and charity to link Solamona's kingship with the Hebrew king, he significantly modifies the conventional notions of Solomonic wisdom. The famous biblical account of the judgment of Solomon accents his psychological insight that allowed him to understand his subjects and to rule them justly. In the *New Atlantis* Bacon associates Solomonic wisdom with his understanding of the workings of nature. The Governor claims that Bensalem possesses a copy of Solomon's *Natural History* and that Bensalem's ongoing work advances the knowledge contained in that book. There is, of course, no mention of this *Natural History* in the biblical accounts. Bacon makes the biblical connection by quoting fragments from the biblical description of Solomon's knowledge of the natural order: "of all plants, from the *cedar of Libanus* to the *moss that groweth out of the wall,* and of all *things that have life and motion.*" And, as we have seen, Bacon connects Solomonic knowledge to charity and piety: the work of Solomon's House brings relief to "man's estate" and demonstrates the love and mercy of the Creator.

The transformation of the attributes of Solomonic wisdom is complemented by the transformation of the Solomonic Temple into Solomon's House. Charles Whitney has provided the most penetrating study of this transformation and has shown how the references to the biblical Solomon and to the appropriation of the Solomonic Temple are tied to Bacon's concept of instauration.[12] As Whitney explains, the Vulgate edition of the Bible created a typology that centered on the apocalyptic motif of the rebuilding of the Temple of Jerusalem. The term used in the Vulgate for the rebuilding is *instauro,* which has the dual meaning of building up (construction) and rebuilding. The development of this apocalyptic motif centers on Josiah's rebuilding of the Temple of Jerusalem in the seventh century B.C. The Temple was originally built by Solomon in the eleventh century B.C. Because the Temple held the Ark of the Covenant, it stood as a symbol of God's presence among the Hebrews and associated the kingdom with religious piety and justice, and it identified the kingdom as the agency for both God's justice and his mercy. The kingdom reached its zenith during the reign of Solomon, when the Hebrews enjoyed unprecedented prosperity and freedom from religious or political interference by neighboring powers. After Solomon, however, the Hebrew nation was overrun and lost its political autonomy and religious freedom. Beginning in the eighth century B.C., Israel was constantly threatened with the loss of its political autonomy and with the loss of its religious freedom. In 624 B.C. pressure from neighboring powers waned, and the young king Josiah was able to institute political and religious reforms, including rebuilding of the Temple. During reconstruction, the Temple's Mosaic Law (the Deuteronomic Code) was rediscovered, and this crucial recovery was interpreted as the beginning of a renewed covenant with God. The biblical account makes it clear that the project of rebuilding was understood as providentially guided and signaled the restoration of God's relation to the people. Josiah's rebuilding is referred to in the Vulgate as an instauration. After Josiah's efforts at reconstruction, there was another loss of political autonomy and the people again were dispossessed. In subsequent years the rebuilding of the Temple became the prime symbol for the reestablishment of true religion and represented recovery of the people's relation with God after a period of suffering as a result of sin, ignorance, and error.

Whitney has demonstrated that Bacon uses the notion of instauration as no previous author had, making it the root symbol for his program. Moreover, according to Whitney, Bacon employs the connotation of building or rebuilding as edification or re-edification. The word *edifice* and its derivatives either can denote a structure or can refer to the building up or the construction of knowledge (edification). Bacon chooses to emphasize the latter. For him instauration depends upon a recovery of knowledge that clears away accumulated epistemological errors and reestablishes a proper foundation. This notion of instauration is developed in the *New Atlantis* by utilizing the dual meanings of edifice and edification. King Solamona builds an edifice—Solomon's House—that is responsible for rebuilding and advancing knowledge (edification).

According to Whitney, Bacon's emphasis on the revitalization of natural philosophy, that is, the rebuilding of Solomon's House, displaces the biblical notion of a spiritual recovery and advance represented by the apocalyptic motif of the rebuilding of Solomon's Temple. The *New Atlantis,* however, depicts Solomon's House, not as a displacement of Solomon's Temple, but as its complement. In the *New Atlantis* Bacon several times demonstrates the importance of purified religion as a spiritual basis for the well-being of the people and associates it with providential action on behalf of the people. So, Bacon does not dismiss or displace the idea of spiritual renewal.[13] He chooses, however, to emphasize what for him is an equally important part of recovery or rebuilding: to rebuild natural philosophy so human beings can recover the benefits God instilled in the Creation. The description of Solomon's House makes it clear that its first pursuit is light. Light as enlightenment is a basic religious motif, and Bacon never changes its religious connotation. At the same time, natural philosophy not only leads to reverence for God and God's Creation but also provides practical insights into how to relieve human suffering and improve the human condition. While others stress the need for spiritual regeneration, Bacon emphasizes the need for the complementary instauration of knowledge.

While the symbolic ties between Solomon's Temple and Solomon's House are the key to understanding Bacon's concept of instauration, they do not explain how Bacon's instauration of knowledge involves recovery and rebuilding in the way that the apocalyptic dream of rebuilding Solomon's Temple does. To adequately develop this concept requires an examination of the account by the Governor of the Strangers' House of the prehistory of Bensalem and Atlantis, an episode that has been largely ignored by most scholars. In this account the Governor tells the Europeans why Bensalem is the only ancient civilization to escape calamity, explains the role of Solomon's House in preserving and perpetuating the knowledge essential to Bensalem's utopian state, and clarifies why Solamona, the king who establishes Solomon's House, decided that it is necessary for Bensalem to remain hidden from other inferior civilizations.

Clarifying the significance of this account for Bacon's concept of instauration requires comparing the Governor's account to the Platonic myth of Atlantis, which Bacon draws upon, and then relating both the Governor's account and the Platonic myth to Bacon's description in his *Wisdom of the Ancients* of a pure, ancient philosophy that degenerated into the inferior and impotent philosophical systems of Plato and Aristotle. We can then compare the activities of Solomon's House, which is Bacon's model for the instauration of knowledge, to these mythic descriptions of a primordial state of excellence that has been lost but might be recovered through divine Providence and human effort.

## The Prehistory of Civilization

According to the Governor of the Strangers' House, Bensalem, Atlantis, and civilizations from the far-flung corners of the world carried out a mutual exchange of learning and material goods while living in peace. A series of cataclysms destroyed the other great civilizations and left most nations in an infantile state, having lost all records of their previous greatness and all ability to restore themselves to their former condition. Not only were the civilizations reduced to infancy and the memory of their own past greatness eclipsed, they forgot about the other great civilizations as well. Consequently, Bensalem, the only civilization to be spared, chooses to remain obscure because, as the Bensalemite official indicates, the country has nothing to be gained and much to be lost by making itself known in the rest of the world. As previously noted, the island does continue to monitor developments in other countries throughout the world and brings back any information that can be used by Bensalem. The most learned and incorruptible inhabitants of Bensalem, the members of Solomon's House, carry out these expeditions in secret, however.

In recounting these remarkable events, the Bensalemite official notes that the only records of the great primeval age available to the Europeans are the brief references in the work of "one of your philosophers." The allusion is to Plato's discussion of the golden age of Athens and to the demise of the great seagoing empire, Atlantis, found in the *Timaeus* and the *Critias*. The topic of the first of the two interrelated Platonic dialogues, the *Timaeus,* is the best form of society. At the beginning of the dialogue, Socrates specifically requests that the discussion move from speculation on the nature of an ideal society to accounts of the best societies that have actually existed. In response, the others agree that recounting the ancient, virtually unknown history of Athens will meet Socrates' request. Critias, who relates the story, explains that the account originated with Solon, who had learned it from a priest during a visit to Egypt. It is important that Solon is the source of the story because he is, of course, the great Athenian lawgiver. He was also a poet, and Critias claims that Solon's recounting of the episode was as great and memorable as the stories of Hesiod and Homer, and had he finished his poetic account, he would have joined the ranks of the greatest poets of Greece.[14] That the story comes from ancient Egypt is significant because the Greeks believed that Egypt was the most ancient civilization and the only one to have survived the floods and other natural catastrophes that decimated other civilizations. The account given to Solon by the Egyptian priest concerns the most dramatic period in Athenian history, one that deserved to be the most renowned of all, and yet it is one that was virtually lost. According to the priest, Athens and other countries suffer the same fate: "your people and the others are but newly equipped, every time, with letters and all such arts as civilized States require; and when, after the usual interval of years, like a plague, the flood from heaven comes sweeping down afresh upon your people, it leaves none of you but the unlettered and uncultured, so that you become young as ever, with no knowledge of all that happened in old times in this land or in your own."[15]

The priest tells Solon that Athens was once the most valiant in war and in all respects the best governed, and was actually a millennium older than Egypt. In its primordial golden age, Athens was a land whose inhabitants "were the offspring and nurslings of the gods." The wisdom inspired by the goddess Athena discovered "all the effects which the divine causes produce upon human life, down to divination and the art of medicine which aims at health, and by its mastery also of all the other subsidiary studies" (*Timaeus,* 39). Athens holds a special place in the memory of the Egyptians because it defeated the invading Atlantans, who attempted to enslave Greece, Egypt, and the rest of the world. Though Athens repels the Atlantans, Solon is told that "there occurred portentous earthquakes and floods, and one grievous day and night befell them, when the whole body of your warriors was swallowed up by the earth and the island of Atlantis in like manner was swallowed up by the sea and vanished; wherefore also the ocean at that spot has now become impassable and unsearchable, being blocked up by the shoal mud, which the island created in its settling down" (*Timaeus*, 14).[16] Socrates accepts this "true history" as an admirable response to his request. Critias then outlines subsequent topics to be discussed. Timaeus will speak first because he knows astronomy and can give an explanation of the formation of the cosmos and an account of humanity's original and true nature. Critias then is to give an account of the lost history of humanity, which will fill in the events from the beginning of the cosmos to the commonly known recent history.

In the *Critias* Athens and Atlantis are both portrayed as paradisiacal countries prospering from their respective patron deities, Athena and Poseidon. Critias begins his account by stating that order and harmony existed among the gods, and there was complete accord regarding the division of the world among them. Critias first turns to the creation of Athens by Athena and Hephaestus and indicates that the accounts of its founding have been lost or exist only in fragments. As a result, the laws and forms of government of the original great civilization have passed from memory. Critias then provides a fuller account of the founding of Atlantis. Poseidon created the island, giving it a topography and climate that produced an abundance of food and other natural comforts and protected the island from invasion. Poseidon mated with mortal women to create a race of demi-gods to inhabit the land. (The first born is Atlas; hence the name of the country.) These people were industrious and accomplished great feats of engineering and navigation. "For many generations, so long as the inherited nature of the God remained strong in them, they were submissive to the laws and kindly disposed to their divine kindred. For the intents of their hearts were true and in all ways noble, and they showed gentleness joined with wisdom in dealing with the changes and chances of life and in their dealings with one another" (*Critias* 303–5). Their nobility of character made them immune to the desire for vast wealth because they valued virtue and honor over material things. But this idyllic condition did not last "when the portion of divinity within them was now becoming faint and weak through being ofttimes blended with a large measure of mortality, whereas the human temper was becoming dominant . . . being unable to bear the burden of their possessions, and became ugly to look upon . . . filled as they were with lawless ambition and power" (*Critias* 305). The last important episode recorded in the *Critias* occurs when Zeus, the minister of justice and order in the cosmos and on earth, convenes a council of the gods to take corrective action to chasten and improve a once-honorable race that was in a woeful plight.[17]

The purpose of the Platonic accounts of the fate of Atlantis and of a golden age virtually lost from memory is made clear in the opening dialogue of the *Timaeus*. The participants in the dialogue are discussing the best form of society. Their intent is to limit the discussion to actually existing societies, not unattainable ideal states. The dialogue makes it clear, however, that the historical horizon has to be expanded beyond the immediate past. The age is not one in which humanity has realized its full potential. It is a period of iron, not gold. In the Platonic dialogues, it is evident that the primary difference between the primordial golden age and the current state of degeneration lies in the eclipse of knowledge of the divine and in the loss of the skills of divination, medicine, engineering, agriculture, and navigation. In the Platonic context, then, an essential requirement for recovering the capacity for human excellence clearly lies in reattaining the original, pure forms of knowledge. The two Platonic myths, taken together, give an account of the creation of the cosmos and the primordial age before human hubris caused corruption and degeneration to set in. After the cosmos is created, the gods amicably divide the territories. Athena, for example, becomes the patroness of Athens, and Poseidon becomes the patron of Atlantis. The human race that the gods create is a combination of divine spirit and matter. The gods' gifts to the human race include an idyllic world, and human beings have dominion over all terrestrial things. Using their god-given abilities, they are able to accomplish great feats of engineering and navigation. The Atlantans, as the children of Poseidon, were especially accomplished navigators. But the idyllic age is destroyed when the material aspect of human nature gained prominence. The predominance of the material leads to avarice and to the will to dominate and control, and Atlantis uses its navigational skills to subjugate other civilizations. According to the *Critias,* the hubris of Atlantis is brought to an end by the gods. Zeus, the god of justice, calls a council of the gods to decide on a proper punishment. This punishment must be severe enough to end Atlantis's marauding but not so severe as to annihilate it. The text states that Atlantis can be brought back again at some future date. White has incorrectly characterized this ending speech by Zeus as being about destruction (*Peace among the Willows,* 112–21). Zeus is the minister of justice and is responsible for the restoration of order. The Atlantans have violated their place in the order of things, and that order has to be restored by the gods. So the emphasis is not on destruction but on the restoration of order. Also, the punishment is not to be a total destruction. While order must be restored, Atlantis will have an opportunity to rise again.

This promise of restoration perhaps explains why Bacon chooses to call his text the *New Atlantis.* Since the name of the utopian island is Bensalem, this choice of title is curious and should have intrigued scholars more than it has. In fact, a surprising number of scholars have even used the two names interchangeably. Denise Albanese uses both Bensalem and New Atlantis to refer to the utopian island without explaining the dual use ("The *New Atlantis* and the Uses of Utopia," 508). Similarly, Howard White treats the names New Atlantis and Bensalem as interchangeable equivalents, saying, "the New Atlantis or Bensalem as the natives called it" (*Peace among the Willows,* 121). White also claims that there are only three civilizations discussed in the *New Atlantis:* the old Atlantis, the new Atlantis, and the Europe of the travelers (143). Amy Boesky even claims that Bensalem's King Altabin builds Bacon's New Atlantis to replace Atlantis (*Founding Fictions,* 20).

Perhaps Bacon uses the myth of Atlantis and the promise or restoration (instauration) to complement the prevalent apocalyptic theme in England of the reestablishing of Jerusalem. While James I exploited the political elements of the idea of a renewal of the Solomonic kingdom, the primary association was with religious renewal. As we have noted, Bacon regarded the renewal of natural philosophy, as portrayed in the work of Solomon's House, as the necessary complement to the religious renewal that was under way. Bacon apparently wishes to augment the apocalyptic religious images associated with the New Jerusalem with the prospects of the renewal of Atlantis. Atlantis was known for its engineering and navigation, and its great accomplishments in these areas reflected its wise use of the gifts the gods had provided. Atlantis declined only after it fell away from divine intent and became dominated by material concerns. Its renewal would be allowed by the gods, once Atlantis had come to recognize the errors of its ways and had returned to a spiritual state. Perhaps Bacon intends to suggest that

England's spiritual renewal coupled with his reform of knowledge will permit it to emulate the engineering and navigational feats of Atlantis; therefore, England can become the new Atlantis—and, of course, a chastened Atlantis would also greatly resemble Bensalem. If this is Bacon's intent, then it might also explain why Bacon leaves his story incomplete. Bacon is proposing that England continue its emphasis on religious recovery and begin recovery of natural philosophy. Whether this will be done or not is out of Bacon's hands. It will depend on whether or not James I is like Solomon and Solamona and will choose to implement the pious study of nature in order to draw from the Creation the benefits that God has provided.

Another important aspect of Bacon's concept of instauration is also found in Bacon's use of the Platonic myths of Atlantis and the primordial history of the world. In the *Critias* Socrates criticizes the intellectual and political state of his own age as infantile and impotent when compared to the attainments of the primordial past. In other writings Bacon criticizes the medieval and Renaissance reverence for Platonic and Aristotelean philosophy and offers a new organon, or method. In the *New Atlantis,* Bacon cleverly employs Plato to make the critique.

Significant differences exist, of course, between Bacon's uses of the myth of a primordial age of human excellence and those of Plato. The focus of the Platonic dialogue is on the development of right political order. Bacon's interest in political order and disorder is secondary. His utopia makes it clear that political order derives from right religion and the proper study of nature. One of the biggest obstructions to the recovery of right knowledge—in Bacon's view—is the misplaced reverence for Platonic and Aristotelian philosophy. As portrayed in the Platonic dialogues and in Bacon's own account of the prehistory of the world, the period of Greek civilization that is valued by the Europeans is not an age of wisdom and of high civilizational attainment but a period of infancy or childhood following on natural calamities. Most efforts by the Greeks of this period were necessarily devoted to subsistence living; and once a civilization was stable enough to devote itself to considerations of political order and justice or to the study of the natural order, it had little or no frame of reference, because the records of the great achievements of the past had been lost. Bacon makes this point in the *New Atlantis* by having the Governor of the House of Strangers tell the Europeans that some scriptures and ecclesiastical traditions are not available in Europe and that Bensalem possesses Solomon's natural history, which is unknown in Europe. Moreover, the activities of Solomon's House, as described by the Governor, clearly do not follow Platonic or Aristotelian methods of investigation and deduction. They are based upon more ancient and purer forms of philosophy. The significance of the ancient wisdom for the (re)building of knowledge is presented in Bacon's *Wisdom of the Ancients* of 1609, which augments the primordial history of Atlantis and Bensalem.[18] We now need to briefly examine key themes in this work in order to more fully understand Bacon's description of the work of Solomon's House and to more adequately understand how the recovery of ancient wisdom relates to Bacon's instauration of natural philosophy.

## Ancient Wisdom and the Instauration of Knowledge

In the preface to *Wisdom of the Ancients,* Bacon explains that the fables of Homer and Hesiod "must be regarded as neither being the inventions nor belonging to the age of the poets themselves, but as sacred relics and light airs breathing out of better times, that were caught from the traditions of more ancient nations and so received into the flutes and trumpets of the Greeks" (*WFB*, 6:697–98). The problem is that their true meaning has been lost, obscured, or distorted over time, and previous generations have been unqualified to interpret them. Bacon's purpose, therefore, is to re-present the fables and give them their proper interpretation. For the present purpose, our discussion can be confined to one of these fables; a more thorough analysis is conducted in chapter 4. For Bacon, the fable of Orpheus is the story of the decline of philosophy as it descends from the natural philosophy of the ancient wisemen to moral and civil philosophy and finally to a state of almost total disintegration. In its pristine state, according to Bacon, "natural philosophy proposes to itself as its noblest work of all, nothing less than the restitution and renovation [*instauratio*] of things corruptible, and (what is indeed the same thing in a lower degree) the conservation of bodies in the state in which they are, and the retardation of dissolution and putrefaction" (*WFB*, 6:721).[19] The effort at retardation, however, means arduous labor, and failure leads to frustration and to the adoption of the easier task—the management of human affairs through moral and civil philosophy. This stage of philosophy remains stable for a while, but it too declines with the passage of time, and moral and civil laws are put to silence. And if such troubles last, Bacon warns, "it is not for long before letters also and philosophy are so torn in pieces that no traces of them can be found but a few fragments, scattered here and there." When philosophy and civilization reach this low point, barbarism sets in and disorder prevails "until, according to the appointed vicissitude of things, they break out and issue forth again, perhaps among other nations, and not in the places where they were before" (*WFB*, 6: 722). Three elements of this Baconian fable are worthy of emphasis. The pure, original philosophy takes as its task the restitution and renovation of things corruptible. This God-given ability is lost through the lack of human effort and will. The decline, however, is not permanent. According to "the appointed vicissitude of things," i.e., providential intervention, true philosophy will return, and humanity will be restored to its primordial condition—but not necessarily in the place it originated.

With this brief discussion of Bacon's fable of the degeneration of the original, pure form of philosophy in mind, we can now better understand the activities of Solomon's House as the preservation and perpetuation of the original, pure form of natural philosophy. The Europeans are told that Solomon's House was created "for the finding out of the true nature of all things (whereby God might have the more glory in the workmanship of them, and men the more fruit in the use of them)" (*WFB*, 3: 146). The Bensalemite official further explains that the name Solomon's House was inspired by the Solomonic reputation for wisdom, which is known in Europe, but the name was chosen also because Bensalem had possession of Solomon's *Natural History*, a text that had been lost to the Europeans. This text held special knowledge of the workings of nature, which Solomon's House used as the guide for its own remarkable work. When the Europeans have an audience with a Father of Solomon's House, they are told: "The End of our Foundation is the knowledge of Causes, and secret motions of things" (*WFB*, 3:156). Their investigations produce new artificial metals, which are used for curing diseases, and blended mineral waters created by the brethren "for health and prolongation of life" (*WFB*, 3:158). The activities of Solomon's House are reminiscent of Bacon's accounts in *Wisdom of the Ancients* of the original, pure philosophy used to retard age, prolong life, and restore corruptible things to their original, pure state.[20] In addition, the reference to Solomon's *Natural History* seems to allude to a Jewish esoteric tradition in which Solomon not only was wise in the way described in the biblical accounts but also possessed a deep understanding of the mysteries of the Creation and was a magus. Several variations of this tradition were fairly widely known in the early modern period. In one, the original esoteric knowledge was given to Adam but was lost through the Fall. Another version has the knowledge given to Moses on Mount Sinai and placed in the Ark of the Tabernacle, where it was accessible only to the High Priest. The Ark and later Solomon's Temple became an omphalos or center for communing with the powers and principalities governing the world. The work of Solomon's House, then, is clearly in accord with both the "pagan" tradition of a pure ancient wisdom and the Jewish esoteric traditions associating Solomon and Solomon's Temple with cabalistic knowledge.[21]

Scholars have linked the activities of Solomon's House to the instauration of learning that Bacon hoped James I would have the Solomonic wisdom to support, and Sprat and others viewed Solomon's House as a model for the Royal Society. But the foregoing discussion indicates that in order to lay the foundations for the advancement of learning, philosophy must be restored to its original form and purpose. In other writings Bacon gives more stress to discovery rather than recovery, but these passages indicate that Bacon was convinced that a pure, natural philosophy existed in the past.

## The *New Atlantis* and the Dimensions of Instauration

This analysis shows that the *New Atlantis* presents a twofold view or description of instauration. One view is represented by Bensalem and involves a spiritual rejuvenation. The other is a recovery of natural philosophy represented by both the work of Solomon's House and by Atlantis before it became corrupted. Bacon chooses to stress the latter in his utopia because he was concerned that the recovery or instauration of natural philosophy was being overlooked. For Bacon, the instauration of knowledge or the building of Solomon's House was as important to creating a kingdom like that of Solomon's as was the religious recovery.

Recognizing the predominance of these religious motifs is important to understanding the full scope of Bacon's program for a great instauration through the advancement of learning. This program is not a secular or humanistic departure from traditional religion, and Solomon's House is not the prototype for a modern scientific think-tank. Careful reading of the full text demonstrates that the activities of Solomon's House cannot be separated from the underlying themes of providential salvation and deliverance. The link to Solomon's Temple and Solomon's House stresses the importance of the recovery and advance of knowledge as an integral part of the instauration or the rebuilding of man's relation to God and his recovery of the benefits God placed in nature for human beings to enjoy. It is also important to note that the work of Solomon's House is tied to the spiritual, as well as material, well-being of the people. Moreover, humanity must regain a reverence toward nature as God's Creation in order to derive the benefits from the Creation. The pious study of nature also guards against humanity's pride and its effort to create its own fantasy world.

As already noted, the *New Atlantis* explains why Bensalem's research institute is named Solomon's House. One key reason is that the members of Solomon's House possessed a copy of Solomon's *Natural History*, which revealed many of the secret benefits God had placed in the Creation for man to use. The association is more than a general linking of Solomon's reputation for wisdom with the wisdom of Bensalem's institute. The Solomonic wisdom alluded to is the wisdom of the workings of nature and the ability to use that knowledge for the benefit of humankind.

Bacon's emphasis on Solomon's House rather than on Solomon's Temple reveals the way in which Bacon's vision of renewal or instauration is unique, and it is important that this emphasis be properly understood. Charles Whitney has described Bacon's substitution of Solomon's House for Solomon's Temple as a symbolic dislocation in which the fundamental function of instauration is carried out in the new Temple—Solomon's House—by the new priests, the Brethren of the House.[22] But the work of Solomon's House is not a substitute for the work of the Temple; it is the complement to it. Bacon indicates in several passages in other writings that he believes religious reform is under way. What is not under way, and what is crucial, is the reform of natural philosophy. This is where Bacon directs his foremost attention. The biblical themes of instauration are reinforced by references to the prehistory of the world before human ignorance and error resulted in divine punishment. This primeval golden age offers another vision of what a well-ordered empire can be, with Atlantis serving as a proper symbol of Bacon's intent and as a complement to Bensalem. Atlantis also provides an object lesson regarding the need for right religion to guide the efforts of natural philosophy. If pride replaces piety, science and technology will become sterile or self-destructive.

That Bacon sees the two aspects of instauration as complementary is evident in other writings that will be analyzed in detail in subsequent chapters. In *The New Organon,* for example, Bacon says that "man by the fall fell at the same time from his state of innocency and from his dominion over creation. Both of these losses however can even in this life be in some part repaired; the former by religion and faith, the latter by arts and sciences" (*WFB,* 4:247–48). In *The Great Instauration* Bacon urges that "all trial should be made, whether that commerce between the mind of man and the nature of things . . . might by any means be restored to its perfect and original condition, [or at least] reduced to a better condition than that in which it now is" (*WFB,* 4:7). Bacon believed that the religious reform could be accomplished through the work of others. It was his duty to advance the reform of natural philosophy. Both were necessary for the complete instauration of man's relation to God and to his dominion over nature. The quotation from *The Great Instauration* indicates the full scope of Bacon's instauration. The complete instauration will overcome the ravages of Original Sin and restore humanity to its prelapsarian condition. The *New Atlantis,* then, offers a multilayered analysis of the disorder of the Europeans' society and prescribes necessary cures. The contrast between European nations and Bensalem points to the sources of order and disorder. Both Bensalem and Europe have the benefit of Christian religion. Bensalem's Christianity is a pure form of gospel Christianity, uncorrupted by human ignorance and error. Europe's Christianity by contrast has been distorted and is plagued by philosophical and theological squabbling. Bensalem and Europe also have schools of natural philosophy. Bensalem's school of natural philosophy is the House of Solomon, which investigates nature in a reverent attempt to discover the benefits placed in Creation by a loving God. Europe's natural philosophy has been marginalized and corrupted by Scholastic and philosophical bickering and is dominated by competing schools of thought no longer grounded in empirical investigation of nature.[23] England, nevertheless, has at its disposal the necessary means for utopian reform: a reformed and purified religion and, through Bacon's efforts, a reformed and revitalized natural philosophy. The two are complementary and each is indispensable for the restitution of humanity to its prelapsarian condition.

## Conclusion

Because Howard White and others have argued that Bacon's use of biblical images and religious themes is cynical and transforms a spiritual quest into a material hedonism, it is important to review how religious motifs actually function in the text. Contrary to White's interpretation, the emphasis on a transformation from preoccupation with material concerns to spiritual conversion is present from the beginning and constitutes the dramatic action in the *New Atlantis*. At the beginning of the story, the Europeans are concerned with being rescued from a storm, and they seek assistance for those who are ill. Almost from the beginning, however, the Europeans recognize the excellence of the island and are struck by its order and its religion. After the Europeans have been allowed to reside in the Strangers' House, the narrator urges his companions to conduct themselves so that they can earn the respect of the Bensalemites. The more they learn about Bensalem, the more they wish to become residents there. So while their initial concern was their physical rescue or well-being, their exposure to the quality of life in Bensalem makes them realize that they have been rescued from personal, social, political, and spiritual disorder and disorientation. Even Howard White acknowledges that the European travelers "not only wish to stay but are somehow made worthy of staying."[24]

That religious and spiritual thematics are central is reflected not only in the transformation of the Europeans but also in the persons with whom the Europeans have contact. The Bensalemite official, who boards the European ship, offers Christian charity in the form of provisions and medicines. The first interviews are provided by the Governor of the Strangers' House, a Christian priest, who responded warmly when the first question from the Europeans concerned the island's religion. The second set of interviews, given by Joabin, centers around matters of social order and morality and includes discussion of Judaeo-Christian dreams of installing the Kingdom of God on earth. The final interview is given by a Father of Solomon's House. He describes the physical and material benefits provided by Solomon's House, but he also emphasizes that their study is motivated by piety and stresses that the ability to discover useful information is dependent on piety and charity. The Governor of the Strangers' House also stresses piety and charity as the motivations for founding Solomon's House. In his account the Governor of the Strangers' House refers to the biblical episode in which Solomon is rewarded for his "large heart." As his reward, Solomon chooses to ask for knowledge in order to be able to meet the needs of his people. It is well known that Bacon repeatedly links the knowledge of nature with the ability to bring relief to man's estate. Most often this linking is associated with knowledge as power. What is often overlooked is Bacon's emphasis on charity as the motive for using the knowledge of nature for the benefit of humankind. It is wrong, therefore, to link Bacon to a Faustian exercise of egomaniacal power. The understanding of nature enables humanity to enjoy the blessings that God provides.

The manner in which Bacon refers to Solomon and equates Solomon's House with Solomon's Temple in the *New Atlantis* also has special apocalyptic and millenarian implications. The Temple in Jerusalem was the primary symbol of religious and political order. It housed the Ark of the Covenant, which was the symbol of divine election, and represented the making of the covenant between God and the Hebrews and the giving of the law as the basis for the covenant. One of the greatest instances of Israel's defeat and humiliation was the profanation of the Temple; and one of its greatest moments of rejuvenation occurred when King Josiah was able to reestablish political independence and to rebuild the Temple. Josiah's reform did not endure; Israel was again defeated and this time taken into captivity. During the post-exilic time, the apocalyptic yearning for restoration centered on the rebuilding of the Temple, and the Temple remained an apocalyptic symbol through the New Testament period to Bacon's age. The term used in the Vulgate edition of the Bible for Josiah's reform and for other messianic or apocalyptic revivals is *instauratio*. This term is, of course, a key symbol in Bacon's writings. He uses the term frequently and he includes it in the title of one of his major publications, *Instauratio Magna*.

When examined carefully, the *New Atlantis* is clearly seen to be an intricately constructed literary work permeated with religious themes, including providential deliverance (for both the Europeans and Bensalem), apocalyptic instauration of the Kingdom of God on earth, and the societal embodiment of the cardinal Christian virtues, especially charity. It is not a society of "pleasant things," as Howard White asserts in *Peace among the Willows* (106), nor is it the case, as Denise Albanese claims, that "the references to crosses and oblations, to piety and Christianity, which crowd the earlier pages, . . . virtually disappeared thereafter" ("The *New Atlantis* and the Uses of Utopia," 514). The primary religious motif of salvation and deliverance is evident from the outset. The European voyagers are tossed off course by a storm and are surrounded by darkness, but then are delivered—like Jonah—to safety. The Europeans describe the island of Bensalem as a land of angels or as the Kingdom of God on earth. The biblical imagery of election and salvation is predominant in subsequent episodes. The conversion of Bensalem is providential deliverance and is suffused with symbols of special election, including the Pillar of Cloud and the Ark of the Covenant. These themes are important to understanding Bacon's program of instauration, and this analysis prepares the way for an examination of these motifs in Bacon's other writings. The next chapter focuses on *The Great Instauration*.

# Chapter 2

## *The Great Instauration*

*The Great Instauration* was published in 1620 when Francis Bacon was lord chancellor and at the height of his political power. Originally, Bacon envisioned this work as a six-part *magnum opus*. The first part was to be an inventory of the scientific disciplines: those that were already complete, those currently under way, and those not yet begun. The second part was to provide a clear statement of the first principles of the true scientific method. The third was to be a natural history of phenomena to be studied by Bacon's new science in order to gain the fullest benefit for humankind. The fourth was to offer examples or paradigms for applying the new science to crucial fields of investigation. The fifth was to catalog Bacon's own contributions to research, and the sixth and final section was to provide a systematic statement of the "final goals and benefits of his new science." The text published in 1620 contains only a small portion of the project Bacon had envisioned, offering primarily an abbreviated statement of part two of the original program, that is, a statement of the first principles of a true, scientific method.[1] Bacon offers three reasons for publishing *The Great Instauration* in its abbreviated form. The first is that he wants to provide an outline of the kind of work that needs to be done so that it can be adopted by others and thereby create a communal effort to interpret nature and to advance the kingdom of man. His second justification is that Bacon regards his most important contributions to be identifying the primary flaws in natural philosophy as it presently exists and setting out the fundamental principles for a new philosophy of nature. Bacon's third explanation is that any effort at cataloging would be preliminary and could only suggest the projects to be undertaken. The published text, therefore, presents what Bacon regarded as his most essential contribution to launching the rehabilitation of knowledge.

The predominant scholarly interpretations of *The Great Instauration* have focused on Bacon's criticism of then-current epistemology and on his introduction of his inductive method. Frequently, these analyses characterize Bacon as a patriarch of modernity, who rejects traditional theology and philosophy and advances the cause of the new science. Jerry Weinberger offers a succinct statement of this stance in his edition of the *New Atlantis* and *The Great Instauration:*

> Along with Machiavelli, Hobbes, and Descartes, Francis Bacon was one of the founders of modern thought. These founders coupled realistic politics with a new science of nature in order to transform the age-old view of mankind's place in the world. They argued that once the efforts of the human intellect were directed from traditional concerns to new ones—from contemplation to action, from the account of what men ought to do to what they actually want to do, and from metaphysics to the scientific method for examining natural causes—the harsh inconveniences of nature and political life would be relieved or overcome. No longer to be revered or endured, the worlds of nature and society would become the objects of human control.
> Bacon called his enterprise "the great instauration."[2]

The problem with such an approach to *The Great Instauration* is similar to the problem with the prevailing interpretations of the *New Atlantis*. It ignores the materials that precede Bacon's epistemological critique and, thereby, ignores or distorts the context in which this epistemology is to be understood. Our analysis of the *New Atlantis* demonstrated that the presentation of the work of Solomon's House, which is a frequent focus of scholarly attention, is preceded by several episodes permeated with religious themes and images of providential salvation. These religious motifs are an integral part of Bacon's utopian vision of an instauration of the relation of humanity to nature and to God; and the work of Solomon's House cannot be properly understood apart from these religious motifs. In the analysis of *The Great Instauration* offered here a similar argument will be made. That is, attention will be given to the materials that precede Bacon's epistemological critique. These materials include the frontispiece, the proemium, and the dedicatory letter. These sections of the text are filled with themes of providential intervention and apocalyptic deliverance, just as the *New Atlantis* is permeated with similar motifs. Giving these opening sections proper consideration calls into question prevailing interpretations that present Bacon as a modernist who breaks completely with previous religious and philosophical traditions and reduces the human quest for meaning and purpose to a concern for material comfort. As we shall see, *The Great Instauration* provides further evidence that Bacon's instauration has as its primary aim the restitution of humanity to a prelapsarian relation with God and nature.

In order to allow these themes to unfold in the text, the analysis will closely examine how the opening sections establish a context for understanding the nature of Bacon's epistemological revolution and its intended consequences. In these compact, concentrated venues Bacon introduces the key image of the instauration of knowledge and establishes its connections to providential design.

## The Frontispiece

It was standard practice in Bacon's age to carefully plan the illustration for the frontispiece so that its iconography could serve as a visual statement of the contents of the book.[3] Moreover, we know that Bacon made special and frequent use of parables and allegory in the presentation of important issues. So, the general practice of encoding frontispieces and Bacon's practice of using myths and allegories indicate that the frontispiece deserves careful consideration.[4]

In the foreground of the frontispiece stand two columns (figure 1). A ship is sailing through the columns, and another moves toward the distant horizon. Script, which appears between the columns, identifies the author as Francis of Verulam and Lord Chancellor of all of England and also gives the title of the book, *Instauratio Magna*. Though the term *instauratio* was

Figure 1. *Instauratio Magna*

## The Great Instauration

not in common usage in Bacon's time, his readers, nevertheless, would know the term and recognize the context for its use. As noted in chapter 1, the term was used in the Vulgate as a root symbol for apocalyptic restoration and had specific association with the rebuilding of Solomon's Temple. This leitmotif received heightened attention during the reign of James I, who was frequently referred to as the new Solomon who would establish a new Jerusalem. So, this title, *Instauratio Magna,* would have signaled to Bacon's reader that this text concerned apocalyptic restoration and renewal.

Bacon's contemporaries would also be familiar with the combination of the two columns in the foreground and the ships sailing toward the distant horizon as a portrayal of the Pillars of Hercules.[5] In classical mythology the Pillars of Hercules represent the boundaries of the known world, the proper habitat of humans, and stand as markers against humanity transgressing its place in the order of things and venturing into the unknown and uninhabitable.[6] Illustrations employing this theme, therefore, frequently added an epigram, "non plus ultra," cautioning against venturing too far and pridefully transgressing humanity's allotted place. In the early modern period this classical symbolism and the motto were transformed when Spanish and Portuguese exploration opened the New World. King Charles V changed the motto from "non plus ultra" to "plus ultra" and thereby transformed it from a caution against going too far to a command to exceed the limits that had been erroneously imposed on the boundaries of the known world and on the territory suitable for humans to occupy.[7]

Bacon relies on this new, transformed meaning, but he transfers it from the terrestrial to the intellectual realm.[8] Bacon's image intends to invoke the benefits of breaking through the false limitations of the realm of knowledge, and this intent is conveyed in the epigram that Bacon sets in the lower foreground of the frontispiece. This inscription reads "multi pertransibunt et augebitur scientia" (many shall go forth and knowledge will be increased). Bacon's motto is a modification of the Vulgate version of Daniel 12:4, part of a prophetic vision in which the Archangel Michael reveals God's plan to deliver Israel and install the Kingdom of God on earth. Bacon preserves the apocalyptic thrust by relating it to the opening of the New World through the Columbian Voyages; but he transfers the focus.[9] The exploration of the earth's surface proved ancient geography false, and this profound attack on ancient authority signaled to Bacon the need for a thorough revaluation of the approach to the study of the natural world. The program of instauration offered in the body of the text, then, offers a criticism of the parameters of the current state of knowledge and argues that these boundaries are as false and inhibiting as the ancient prohibition against terrestrial exploration. Knowledge cannot be built upon these old foundations—they are as irrelevant as ancient geography. The foundations must be built fresh from the ground up.

The frontispiece, then, does indeed signal the subject matter of the text in three important ways. First, the opening of the New World undermines the authority of traditional knowledge by exposing its fundamental errors while also showing the extraordinary potential of new, unexpected discoveries. Second, the quotation from the book of Daniel indicates that the pursuit of new knowledge is divinely sanctioned; it is not an act of arrogance or of hubris. The exploration of the New World is not a prideful defiance of the warnings of the gods; it is the fulfillment of divine intent and links human effort to divine design. Third, Bacon uses the passage from Daniel to link the advance of knowledge to the religious and political meaning that the term *instauration* already had in Jacobean England.

While we are here concerned primarily with how the frontispiece functions in *The Great Instauration,* this study also addresses the function of instauration as the root concept for Bacon's vision of providential restoration of the proper relation of God, humanity, and nature. It is appropriate, therefore, to relate the frontispiece to other parts of Bacon's corpus that can reveal its fullest meaning and function in relation to Bacon's program. First, it is useful to consider the iconographic significance of sailing beyond the Pillars of Hercules to the accounts of the ancient history of Athens and Atlantis, which Bacon uses in the *New Atlantis*. Originally, great civilizations from the far corners of the world navigated the oceans and carried on peaceful commerce. Traversing the Pillars of Hercules became associated with hubris only after Atlantis lost its divine inspiration, became avaricious, and sailed toward Athens to conquer it. Consequently, according to the account in the *Timaeus,* the formation of a barrier to separate the Mediterranean world from the outer ocean occurred as a result of the cataclysm that destroyed ancient Athens and Atlantis. But the accounts indicate that the gods would allow civilizational excellence to be restored after humanity has been punished for its hubris. This same sense of the prospects of recovery or instauration occurs in Bacon's *Wisdom of the Ancients*. His recounting of the degeneration of philosophy ends with a reassurance that the state of barbarism is not permanent. The text says that pure philosophy will be restored "according to the appointed vicissitude of things... perhaps among other nations, and not in the places where they were before" (*WFB*, 6:722). The description of the pure state of knowledge and its restoration are consonant with Bacon's choice of the terms *instauro* and *instauratio*, which carry the twofold meaning of "building up" and "rebuilding."[10]

Another important connection between the instauration of knowledge and overseas expansion is presented in the frontispiece of Bacon's *Sylva Sylvarum* (figure 2), another text aimed at recovering and advancing knowledge.[11] Its iconography is similar to the frontispiece of *The Great Instauration*. Here again a pair of columns stands in the foreground with a wide expanse of sea receding toward the distant horizon. In this frontispiece, however, the columns are not the Pillars of Hercules; they are the columns of Solomon's Temple, an iconographic motif that appeared frequently in Tudor and Stuart art. The pillars of Solomon's Temple are found, for example, in Holbein's portrait of Henry VIII and were used frequently in masques and processions for James I. In this frontispiece, no ships sail toward the distant horizon; instead, a world globe is situated between the columns, and above the columns rays of light break through the clouds to illuminate the *mundus intellectualis*. If the Temple of Solomon is conceived in the traditional biblical sense, the meaning of this frontispiece remains unclear. The iconographic intent of the frontispiece does become intelligible, however, if it is considered in relation to the Jewish esoteric tradition associated with the Solomon's Temple and the description of the work of Solomon's House in the *New Atlantis*. As already noted, the Elders of Solomon's House use Solomon's *Natural History* to guide their study of nature. The Elders stress that the purpose of their ongoing investigation is not accumulation of wealth or material goods but rather to seek "God's first creature, which was *Light:* to have *light* (I say) of the growth of all parts of the world" (*WFB*, 3:147). This passage from the *New Atlantis* fits thematically with the frontispiece of the *Sylva Sylvarum*.[12] The *mundus intellectualis* is situated between the columns and is illuminated by divine

Figure 2. *Sylva Sylvarum* (1651). Courtesy of the University of Florida Libraries

Light from above. What is more, there is a caption just below the heavenly emanation: "Et vidit Deus lucem quod esset bona," which reinforces this thematic association. This frontispiece, therefore, seems to augment or complement Bacon's root concept of the instauration of learning requiring *re*covery of ancient wisdom as well as *dis*covery of new forms of knowledge. It would, then, also complement the interpretation of sailing beyond the Pillars of Hercules as an escape from degenerated forms of learning, which permits both the recovery of pure philosophy and the opening of new horizons of empirical investigation. This instauration of knowledge, in turn, holds the promise of restoring humanity to its primordial, prelapsarian state of excellence.

## The Proemium

The frontispiece is followed by Bacon's proemium. Its main theme is stated in the first sentence:

> Being convinced that the human intellect makes its own difficulties, not using the true helps which are at man's disposal soberly and judiciously; whence follows manifold ignorance of things, and by reason of that ignorance mischiefs innumerable; he thought all trial should be made, whether that commerce between the mind of man and the nature of things, which is more precious than anything on earth, or at least than anything that is of the earth, might by any means be restored to its perfect and original condition, or if that may not be, yet reduced to a better condition than that in which it now is. (*WFB*, 4:7)

In the very first phrase, Bacon contends that the human intellect is responsible for its ignorance and error because it refuses to utilize corrective resources at its disposal. In the next phrase Bacon explains why he has undertaken his present project: "He thought all trials should be made, whether that commerce between the mind of man and the nature of things... might by any means be restored to its perfect and original condition." The first important feature to note in this statement is the reference to restoration. According to this statement, Bacon intends to attempt to rebuild the correspondence between the human intellect and its proper object of study—the natural world—and the goal is to rebuild it to its "perfect and original condition."

This provocative opening statement sets up the principal themes Bacon addresses in the body of his text by at least implicitly posing three key questions: Why does knowledge become disoriented? Why does the intellect refuse to accept the corrective measures available to it? and How can the original and perfect condition in which there was a direct correspondence between human knowledge and nature itself be restored? Bacon provides a partial response to these questions when he asserts that the present disordered state cannot be corrected by using prevailing epistemological principles: "the primary notions of things which the mind readily and passively imbibes, stores up, and accumulates... are false, confused, and overhastily abstracted from the facts... [and as a result] the entire fabric of human reason which we employ in the inquisition of nature, is badly put together and built up, and like some magnificent structure without any foundation" (*WFB,* 4:7). Although this compact statement requires elaboration, the main point is clear. The errors that exist in human reasoning cannot be corrected by employing that system's method of reasoning; the system itself is causing the problems. For progress to be made, a new set of principles must be introduced that can lead away from learned ignorance and error toward truth.

The imagery that Bacon employs here, of an elaborate structure that lacks a proper foundation, is not a casual choice; rather, the selection has been carefully made and relates directly to Bacon's concept of instauration as a rebuilding or a re-edification. According to Bacon, the errors that had accumulated have reached such a pervasive state that no restitution can be accomplished without abandoning the current causes of disorder and replacing them with a new starting point or foundation. As Bacon puts it, "There was but one course left, therefore,—to try the whole thing anew upon a better plan, and to commence a total reconstruction of sciences, arts, and all human knowledge, raised upon the proper foundations" (*WFB,* 4:8). Bacon acknowledges that the challenge of restitution is daunting but contends that it is far better to attempt to move toward the truth than to continue in error. Moreover, Bacon adds there is reason to believe that the instauration can be successfully completed because some results or benefits have already been obtained. Getting the project of reconstruction under way is a matter of urgency, Bacon explains; therefore, he is attempting to set out first principles and provide some preliminary results. He hopes that his statement of theoretical principles, along with some empirical samples, will be sufficient to persuade others to abandon ignorance and to take up the pursuit of truth.

In the final paragraph of the proemium, Bacon explains why he has chosen to undertake this project. First, it falls to him because no other man seems ready to take on the task. Moreover, Bacon regards this as the most worthy legacy he could leave because it will provide the most benefit to the human race. Bacon is careful to point out, however, that he is motivated not by personal ambition but by the worthiness of the goal. Without a proper context to understand Bacon's juxtaposition of ambition to charitable service, this statement might seem to be little more than a literary convention that clothes his enterprise in formulaic modesty. But we have seen in the analysis of the *New Atlantis* that Bacon links natural philosophy with the Christian virtue of charity and makes the study of nature an act of worship of the Creator. The emphasis on God's mercy and on humanity's need for charitable concern for others is a theme also found in the dedicatory letter, the next section of *The Great Instauration* to be examined.

## Epistle Dedicatory

Bacon, who was lord chancellor when he wrote *The Great Instauration*, begins his dedication by telling his monarch that the king might feel that Bacon has been neglecting his responsibilities to the state while he has been working on this project. Bacon assures the king, however, that the work itself, which is something both "copied from a very ancient model" and "totally new," is a service both to the king and to the nation (*WFB*, 4: 11). While Bacon stresses the importance of the work, which is a suitable project to dedicate to a great king, he claims that the product is not the result of his own wit but is instead "a child of time." Such modesty might be attributed to stylistic convention; but as we have already noted, Bacon chooses to minimize his own role in order to accent the role of divine Providence. Here Bacon indicates that his book "may be ascribed to the infinite mercy and goodness of God, and to the felicity of your Majesty's times"

(*WFB*, 4:11). Bacon then adds that because God's hand is in the project, the work that he is dedicating to James I will make the king's reign "famous to prosperity" as "times of the wisest and most learned of kings" in which the "regeneration and restoration of the sciences occurred." Bacon then links the reign of James I to the recovery and advancement of learning by associating James with Solomon: "you who resemble Solomon in so many things" (*WFB*, 4:12).[13] Here we recognize that Bacon is not only emphasizing God's mercy rather than his own genius, but is also identifying the reign of James I with an apocalyptic moment that links God's new mercies to the restoration of knowledge through Bacon's program of instauration.

The themes and images of the dedication augment or reinforce symbols and motifs found in the earlier sections. The dedication, like the frontispiece, emphasizes apocalyptic opportunities for improving the human condition through the advancement of knowledge. The frontispiece contains the apocalyptic passage from Daniel, which stresses the increase of knowledge; and the dedication presents Bacon's instauration as a result of providential grace. Both the frontispiece and the dedication challenge the authority of received wisdom. The knowledge inherited from the classical tradition, rather than being the record of human excellence, is filled with ignorance and error that distort humanity's role in the natural order and cause humanity to suffer unnecessarily. The dedication and the proemium both minimize Bacon's role in setting out the program of instauration in order to heighten the sense of God's actions on behalf of humanity. In both the proemium and the dedication Bacon depicts himself as one who has been chosen by God to be the instrument for bringing relief to man's estate through his advancement of knowledge that will correct the ignorance and errors that have accumulated over the course of history. In both the proemium and the dedication Bacon emphasizes the twofold nature of the instauration as both discovery and recovery.

## The Preface

In the preface Bacon indicates that he intends to analyze why "the state of knowledge is not prosperous nor greatly advancing" (*WFB*, 4:13). Bacon identifies the first problem obstructing the advancement of knowledge as an undue reverence for the past. Because men have overestimated the value of the arts that they already possess, these arts have become "pillars of fate set in the path of knowledge; for men have neither desire nor hope to encourage them to penetrate further" (*WFB*, 4:13). The first task, then, is to break through the barriers that obstruct the advance of truth and prevent the mind's authority over nature. This language evokes the imagery of the frontispiece, where the Pillars of Hercules symbolize the false boundaries of the human realm. As already noted in the discussion of that image, Bacon is drawing on the associations with the advances through overseas exploration and his own program for expanding the frontiers of knowledge. As he continues his criticism of the undue reverence for classical learning, particularly of natural philosophy, Bacon introduces another memorable image when he likens classical philosophy to an adolescent boy: both are sterile and incapable of producing or generating. This is, of course, an inversion of the Renaissance reverence for the classical age as a period of maturity and excellence, which must be recovered and emulated if humanity is to advance. Bacon, by contrast, portrays the classical period as humanity's childhood and disparages his contemporaries, who hold such a vaulted opinion of the philosophy of Plato and Aristotle. According to Bacon, the wisdom "which we have derived principally from the Greeks is but like the boyhood of knowledge, and has the characteristic property of boys: it can talk, but it cannot generate" (*WFB*, 4:14). As we shall see, Bacon will repeat the association of true knowledge with productive knowledge and will contrast sterile, empty knowledge with utilitarian knowledge. But before developing this motif further, Bacon offers another vivid image to describe the present state of learning. Returning to nautical imagery, Bacon refers to the present impediments as being like Scylla, who obstructs navigation or prevents return to one's proper destination (*WFB*, 4:14).[14] This shift in imagery may at first seem abrupt, but Bacon has actually skillfully combined the images of adolescent boys with Scylla to highlight the theme of sterility and generation. Scylla is a monster, and monsters are misshapen creatures incapable of generation or of reproducing. Bacon has, therefore, used the image of the adolescence of philosophy and the impediments it poses to true learning to characterize the unproductive, sterile state of contemporary knowledge, and he juxtaposes this condition to the "true and lawful marriage" of the mind to nature, which can produce benefits for humanity.[15]

Bacon next contrasts the mechanical arts to the stagnant, nonproductive, nongenerative state of philosophy. After an inventor introduces a new tool or artifact, others seek to improve it and to apply it to new circumstances. The initial discovery, then, serves as the stimulus to further refinement and to new applications. Philosophy, on the other hand, flourishes "most in the hands of the first author, and afterwards degenerates" (*WFB*, 4:14). While artisans continue to perfect an invention, the followers of a few great original thinkers seek only to preserve or to embellish "those things which have been invented already" (*WFB*, 4:15). The disciples of the philosophical schools are so devoted to the founder of the school and to his method that they do not seek to advance beyond what the founder accomplished. Here again we have the contrast between sterility and productivity.[16]

After these images of the barriers obstructing knowledge, of the idolatrous worship of philosophical schools, of the childlike, unproductive systems of philosophy, Bacon introduces the image of the river of time to counter the Renaissance reverence for the past. Over its course, a river carries forward the light and the airy, while the heavy sinks and is lost. Bacon claims that not only has the present age been left without weighty, substantive philosophy, it has deluded itself into thinking that the limited knowledge it does possess exhausts the mind's capacities. The philosophy of the present age, rather than acknowledging its own frailties and shortcomings, "lay[s] the blame upon the common condition of men and nature [rather] than upon themselves. And then whatever any art fails to attain, they ever set it down upon the authority of that art itself as impossible of attainment" (*WFB*, 4:16). The deterioration of philosophy has been so prolonged and so thoroughgoing that it has come to be accepted as the permanent human condition. This profound delusion has to be exposed before any progress toward knowledge can be attained.[17]

After this dreary depiction of the present as an age of disorder, Bacon begins to introduce steps that can be taken to bring needed reform. The key for Bacon is to look first at the mechanical arts, which possess two features lacking in natural philosophy: the mechanical arts are directly involved with the investigation of nature and have as their purpose the production of knowledge and implements to improve the human condition. By looking to the mechanical arts, then, it will be possible to move from philosophical opinion, which is preoccupied with the constructs of the mind, toward "experience and facts of nature." But Bacon also indicates that the mechanical arts in their present form have limitations as well that must be overcome. While the mechanical arts work to refine an original, crude idea or implement, their attention to the immediate and utilitarian limits the scope of possibilities: "all industry in experimenting has begun with proposing to itself certain definite works to be accomplished, and has pursued them with premature and unseasonable eagerness; it has sought, I say, experiments of Fruit, not experiments of Light" (*WFB*, 4:17). So, the mechanical arts need to be enhanced by theoretical reasoning, which attempts to search out a broader range of applications. Bacon offers some explanation of what he means in the following passage:

> But as in former ages when men sailed only by observation of the stars, they could indeed coast along the shores of the old continent or cross a few small and mediterranean seas; but before the ocean could be traversed and the new world discovered, the use of the mariners needle, as a more faithful and certain guide, had to be found out; in like manner the discoveries which have been hitherto made in the arts and sciences are such as might be made by practice, meditation, observation, augmentation,—for they lay near to the senses, and immediately beneath common notions; but before we can reach the remoter and more hidden parts of nature, it is necessary that a more perfect use and application of the human mind and intellect be introduced. (*WFB*, 4:18)

This metaphor clearly evokes the iconography of the frontispiece; but the essential point here is that the mariner's needle is a highly creative development that is several steps removed from navigation by landmarks or by fixed stars. Bacon elaborates on this theme, especially in *The New Organon*, where he argues that each new discovery or invention—when it is fully exploited—opens up vistas that had been unimaginable before.

As Bacon reaches the end of his preface, he switches the tone of his narrative and offers a prayer that God will bless the work he is undertaking and through his hands God will "endow the human family with new mercies" (*WFB*, 4:20). This prayer recalls the dedication, where Bacon suggests that his work would provide great blessings for the human race because it is the work of Providence. While a petition to God to bless the work that is being offered and use it for some divine purpose is a common motif, the portion of Bacon's prayer that immediately follows is not so conventional. He prays that "things human may not interfere with things divine, and that from the opening of the ways of sense and the increase of natural light there may arise in our minds no incredulity or darkness with regard to the divine mysteries" (*WFB*, 4:20). It would be fairly standard to differentiate natural philosophy from theology or reason from revelation, but Bacon goes further. He is more directly concerned with the equation of knowledge with sin. In the medieval and early modern periods, Original Sin was frequently equated with pride and with rebellion against humanity's creatureliness. The temptation by Satan was to obtain the knowledge necessary to overcome dependence on God and be able to surpass the creature's debt to the Creator and, thereby, become like God.[18] Bacon takes pains to clarify or redefine the connection between Original Sin, pride, and knowledge by linking pride with seeking knowledge that is properly the province of God alone. Bacon specifically identifies this knowledge with the divine mystery of salvation and grace.

The second connection that Bacon makes between knowledge and sin is with human beings' infatuation with schools or systems of thought. As Bacon indicates in his preface, humans are prone to worship intellectual constructs rather than devoting themselves to the empirical study of nature, which is the one true object of human intellectual investigation. This devotion to intellectual systems upsets and dislocates the proper subject of knowledge and substitutes a man-made idol. Bacon emphasizes, however, that the desire for knowledge of the natural world is neither forbidden nor sinful. Moreover, according to Bacon, the proper remedy for sin is in directing the quest for knowledge to its proper subject and in utilizing human reason and art as God intended: "For it was not that pure and uncorrupted natural knowledge whereby Adam gave names to the creatures according to their propriety, which gave occasion to the fall. It was the ambitious and proud desire of moral knowledge to judge of good and evil, to the end that man may revolt from God and give laws to himself, which was the form and manner of the temptation" (*WFB*, 4:20). This compact statement is pregnant with meaning. It asserts that man's knowledge of nature is not sinful. God charged man with the duty and privilege of "naming" the lesser creatures. "Naming" means defining the essential

# The Great Instauration

traits of the created world in relation to human needs and concerns. This brief passage also contains a description of the proper task of natural knowledge. Human beings are to be actively involved in exploring the Creation, seeking out its characteristic traits, and putting them to use. After the Fall, however, human beings became full of pride, turned away from their God-given duties, and attempted to be autonomous, that is, self-governing.

This brief reference to the Fall and to Original Sin also helps to make clear why human beings have become disoriented and knowledge has become stagnant. Human beings have a propensity to become pridefully self-absorbed and turn away from God and from the Creation. They become fascinated with their own creations rather than with God's Creation. They indulge their fantasies and imaginations rather than their reason. This condition is precisely the condition that Bacon describes in the opening sections of the preface. Once this is realized, the full extent of Bacon's program of instauration becomes clear. Bacon wants to restore knowledge to its original condition before the Fall. He wants to return humanity to its duty of obtaining a true and uncorrupted knowledge of the Creation according to its God-given properties.

When the full scope of Bacon's instauration becomes evident, it also becomes clear why Bacon characterizes the state of disorientation and confusion as temporary. The present condition, which is the result of pride and vanity, prompts humans to claim that anything their own philosophical systems cannot understand is impossible to know. In making this assertion, arrogant and ignorant humans transform a temporary disorder into what they contend is a permanent part of the human condition. Further on, Bacon will argue that human beings cannot save themselves from the profound alienation they have caused. Humanity can be saved only if God grants mercy and offers guidance that can lead human beings back to their unalienated state. This is the context for understanding Bacon's project. In Bacon's view, God has chosen the present age for granting new mercies, and Bacon is his means.

After this prayer Bacon addresses himself to his readers:

> I would address one general admonition to all; that they consider what are the true ends of knowledge, and that they seek it not either for pleasure of the mind, or for contention, or for superiority to

others, or for profit, or fame, or power, or any of these inferior things; but for the benefit and use of life; and that they perfect it and govern it in charity. For it was from lust of power that the angels fell, from lust of knowledge that man fell; but of charity there can be no excess, neither did angel or man ever come in danger by it. (*WFB*, 4: 20–21)

This passage is followed by an exhortation for others to join the instauration of the foundations of true knowledge, and this is followed by a further contrast between human errors and the true knowledge of nature that Bacon is going to set on its proper course. Then Bacon urges his reader to have hope and to expect dramatic results, though the full realization will not be accomplished in Bacon's lifetime. So, the preface concludes with the same emphasis on hope and apocalyptic expectation that is present in the other parts of *The Great Instauration* that we have examined thus far.

## The Plan of the Work

The preface is followed by a brief description of the plan of the work, which is to have six parts: the divisions of the sciences; the new organon, or directions concerning the interpretation of nature; the phenomena of the universe, or a natural and experimental history for the foundation of philosophy; the ladder of the intellect; the forerunners, or anticipation to the new philosophy; and the new philosophy, or active science. This listing is followed by a few paragraphs containing "arguments for the several parts." Bacon explains that part 1 will be a catalog of received wisdom with some enhancements. While this part was never published, *The Advancement of Learning* is recognized as its preliminary statement. Part 2 was to contain a new methodology for conducting natural philosophy. This section also was never fully completed, but Bacon indicates that he offers a compact statement of this in an aphoristic style in *The New Organon*, which was bound together with *The Great Instauration*. The title, *The New Organon*, is taken from Aristotle, who referred to his methodology as an "organon." Bacon is clearly offering his own method as a correction and substitute for Aristotle's. According to Bacon, the new organon differs from and surpasses the old Aristotelian one in three ways. The first major difference is in the goal. The aim of *The New Organon* is not the invention of arguments but the creation of arts; that is, the aim is to provide knowledge that produces works. This, of course, is consistent with Bacon's preceding statements and criticisms. He has repeatedly indicated that the problem with current philosophical methods is their stagnation and sterility, and he has warned that progress can only occur if natural philosophy is combined with the mechanical arts to produce new benefits for humankind. The second key difference between the old and new organon is what Bacon calls "the order of demonstration." By this he means a rejection of the syllogism and its replacement by induction. The syllogism is a system of internal logic, which is effective only if its starting premise is grounded in fact. But the system cannot critically assess its starting principles. In Bacon's words, "if the very notions of the mind (which are as the soul of words and the basis of the whole structure) be improperly and overhastily abstracted from facts... the whole edifice tumbles" (*WFB*, 4:24). Induction, on the other hand, begins with empirical analysis and, therefore, has an objective reference for testing and correcting theories extrapolated from its empirical base.

In describing the faults in the current method of philosophy Bacon repeats his criticism of both the human intellect and human senses; but he also explains that these faults are not permanent: restoration is possible through arduous effort. Bacon explains that it will become obvious that his method is on the right track because human arts will begin to tap nature's potential and there will be advances in knowledge and improvements in the human condition.

Part 3 of the project is to be a natural history that "may serve as foundation to build philosophy upon." Here Bacon again emphasizes that nature is the source of truth, not man's imagination. Bacon also adds that a full catalog of natural history must include the results of human art, which produce new operations from nature. Two times in this brief discussion Bacon stresses the need to "vex" nature, that is, labor and effort are needed in order to bring new results to light.[19] In order to obtain results, however, the reconstruction of knowledge must move away from intellectual speculation to penetrate "the Cardinal virtues in nature," that is, the essential components to be explored for human benefit. Bacon describes these essential elements as the letters of the alphabet of nature. He implicitly contrasts the alphabet and language of nature to the fantasies of the human mind, which names phantoms and creates idols. Bacon is arguing that human beings in the present condition do not have direct access to the language of nature. Their alphabets and language are full of human fantasy, which have to be purged before the true elements of nature reveal themselves. In this discussion Bacon also makes reference to the wedding of human art with nature in order to generate new creations (*WFB*, 3:27–29). This by now is a familiar theme that Bacon uses repeatedly in *The Great Instauration*.

Of the six parts described in this section, only one of them is offered in conjunction with *The Great Instauration,* and it is in abbreviated form. It is important to emphasize that Bacon thought these parts deserved to be published immediately because they pointed to the essential problems and sketched the remedies, and he believed he had an obligation to set the new enterprise in motion. As we have seen, Bacon was convinced that the time was right and that divine Providence was working through him to bring about reform.

## The Instauration of Knowledge

Bacon's stress on the providential and apocalyptic elements of instauration draws upon familiar elements of Christian belief in his age. As we have seen, the term itself is drawn from an apocalyptic typology of recovery and rebuilding associated with political and religious renewal. Bacon's instauration is distinctive in two aspects, however. First and foremost, Bacon identifies recovery of the knowledge of nature as an integral element of religious and political renewal. The second distinctive feature, which is closely connected to the first, is that Bacon links the instauration of knowledge to the restoration of humanity to its prelapsarian state. In order to make his case, Bacon has to provide a nuanced interpretation of the Fall that distinguishes sinful from legitimate knowledge. As we have seen, Bacon equates sin with a prideful rebellion against God in an effort to know the divine mysteries of grace and salvation and in the arrogant attempt to be independent from God and autonomous. The ironic punishment for this sin is to have the wish granted. God permits humans to create their imaginary worlds and allows them to make do with their own devices. The result is the disorder and suffering that pervades the world.

Knowledge of nature, God's Creation, on the other hand, is not prohibited by God. On the contrary, it is one of God's gifts to humanity and is intrinsic to its well-being. Bacon's emphasis on recovery and renewal is grounded in his conviction that God provides guidance that permits restitution. Bacon is persuaded that God is actively opening new vistas in his own age, and he has been chosen to help point the way toward recovery.

In framing his concept of instauration this way, Bacon is moving away from a common understanding of Original Sin. This is evident in the fact that he takes care to redefine the Fall by differentiating between the two types of knowledge. By pointing to this distinctive aspect of Bacon's instauration, there is no intent to portray Bacon as unorthodox or as a disingenuous believer. Bacon's emphasis on the recovery of the knowledge of nature as a vital element of instauration is distinctive, but it is not unique or idiosyncratic. Many Christian thinkers in Bacon's age sought a restoration of true religion by drawing upon other forms of religion and natural philosophy, including Hermeticism and Neoplatonism, which were revived in the Renaissance as part of the recovery of ancient wisdom.[20] The most notable is the Florentine Neoplatonist Marsilio Ficino, whose Platonism was highly synthetic and was intent on showing the essential links in a single *prisca theologia* tradition. Ficino understood his work as a complement to Christian theology that could correct accumulated errors and could revitalize true devotion to God.[21] In his *Theologia Platonica,* Ficino explains that he is attempting to restore the principles of natural philosophy in order to turn humanity's mind toward a reverence for God, the Creator. In similar fashion, Bacon says that he hopes God will bless his work and that his natural philosophy will become a means for inspiring worship. Pico della Mirandola is also worthy of note because of the importance of his retelling of the Creation myth in his *Oration on Human Dignity,* which has strong affinities with Bacon's interpretation of Adam's creation and fall. Because of the importance of Bacon's reinterpretation, it will be useful, therefore, to look briefly at parallels with Pico's.[22] As we shall see, these materials fit well with Bacon's references to the instauration of learning, especially to his description of his project as very new and at the same time quite old.

Pico's *Oration* was prepared as an introduction to his 900 Theses, which he believed could overcome the fragmentation of knowledge, end bitter doctrinal disputes in philosophy and theology, and lead to a deeper understanding of nature. This, in turn, would inspire devotion to God, the Creator. Because of the prevailing confusion in philosophy and theology, Pico felt it necessary to pose the most basic question of why human beings were created by God. Pico begins by retelling the story of the Creation. After God had already created the terrestrial world, the celestial realm, and the super celestial region, "the Divine Artificer still longed for some creature which might comprehend the meaning of so vast an achievement, which might be moved with love at its beauty and smitten with awe at its grandeur. When, consequently all else had been completed (as both Moses and Timaeus testify), in the very last place, He bethought Himself of bringing forth man."[23] In order that humanity might to be able to understand the totality of reality, God mixed parts of all three worlds—the terrestrial, celestial, and super celestial—together in the human soul.[24] Also, because God wanted humanity to love him freely, God gave man free will. "We have made you a creature neither of heaven nor of earth, neither mortal nor immortal, in order that you may, as the free and proud shaper of your own being, fashion yourself in the form you may prefer" (*Oration*, 7). The gift of free will, however, comes with a risk. If perverted, it can be transformed "from a saving to a damning gift" (*Oration*, 12). Humans can turn away from God and the Creation and become preoccupied with material pursuits or with a second reality made up by "the empty forms of the imagination, as by the wiles of Calypso, and through their alluding solicitations made a slave to [their] own senses" (*Oration*, 10). In this degenerated or fallen state the human mind has been left in "a vertiginous whirl" (*Oration*, 33), and though "born to a high position, we failed to appreciate it, but fell instead to the estate of brutes and uncomprehending beasts of burden" (*Oration*, 12). It is because of the abuse of free will that both philosophy and theology are currently in such a state of disarray.

After reminding the fathers of the true human condition, Pico explains how humanity can be restored to its original, prelapsarian state: "Let a certain saving ambition invade our souls so that, impatient of mediocrity, we pant after the highest things and (since, if we will, we can) bend all our efforts to their attainment" (*Oration*, 12). For Pico, ancient wisdom provides the guide toward the needed reorientation of the mind and the restoration of natural philosophy. "Since it is not granted to us, flesh as we are and knowledgeable only of the things of the earth, to attain such knowledge by our own efforts, let us have recourse to the ancient fathers" (*Oration*, 15). The sources Pico cites include the early church fathers, classical philosophers, the wise men of the Old Testament and the *prisci theologi*—Pythagoras, Zoroaster, and Hermes Trismegistus. The reorientation of humanity requires a process of purging or purifying the lower elements of the soul so that the intelligence can devote itself fully to the contemplation of the Creation and of God. This process of purification not only prepares the mind to comprehend nature but also strips away the pursuit of material gain and preoccupation with the self.

> We, therefore, imitating the life of the Cherubim here on earth, by refraining the impulses of our passions through moral science, by dissipating the darkness of reason by dialectic—thus, washing away, so to speak, the filth of ignorance and vice—may likewise purify our souls, so that the passions may never run rampant, nor reason, lacking restraint, range beyond its natural limits. Then may we suffuse our purified souls with the light of natural philosophy, bringing it to final perfection by knowledge of divine things. (*Oration*, 16)

In describing the process of ascent Pico makes specific reference to aspiring to the realms of the cherubim and the seraphim. "The Seraphim burns with the fire of charity; from the Cherubim flashes forth the splendor of intelligence," and if we meditate upon the Creator and his Creation, "we shall be resplendent with the light of the Cherubim. If we burn with love for the Creator only, His consuming fire will quickly transform us into the flaming likeness of the Seraphim" (*Oration*, 13–14). Pico also makes reference to Jacob's Ladder as a process of purification that purges the mind of conflict and the soul of its terrestrial preoccupations so that it is able to focus on love of God and understanding of the Creation (*Oration*, 12–17).

When the soul is properly prepared, it can be reunited with God:

> when the soul, by means of moral philosophy and dialectic shall have purged herself of her uncleanness, adorned herself with the many disciplines of philosophy as with the raiment of a prince's court and crowned the pediments of her doors with the garlands of theology,

the King of Glory may descend and, coming with the Father, take up his abode with her. If she prove worthy of so great a guest, she will, through his boundless clemency, arrayed in the golden vesture of the many sciences as in a nuptial gown, receive him, not as a guest merely, but as a spouse. (*Oration*, 23)

When the soul has been purified by the arts, "which we call expiatory, moral philosophy and dialectic," it will be admitted to "the interpretation of an occult nature by means of philosophy" (*Oration*, 25). Pico identifies two forms of occult science that represent "the highest form of philosophy." The first is magic, which calls forth "from their hiding places into the light the powers which the largess of God has sown and planted in the world." Pico stresses, however, that magic does not itself work miracles, so much as sedulously serve nature as she works her wonders (*Oration*, 57). Magic "draws forth into public notice the miracles which lie hidden in the recesses of the world, in the womb of nature, in the storehouses and secret vaults of God" (*Oration*, 57). And, Pico notes, magic excites "an admiration for the works of God which flowers naturally into charity, faith and hope" (*Oration*, 58). The other occult science is the Cabala, which was given to Moses when he was on Mount Sinai. "In addition to the law of the five books which he handed down to posterity, [Moses] receive[d] from God a more secret and true explanation of the law" (*Oration*, 59). This Cabala was not made public but was kept by the high priests of the tabernacle. After the Babylonian captivity, however, when the Temple was restored by Zarubabel, it was decided that the Cabala should be written down so that it would not be lost forever.[25] Pico explains that the Cabala has been made available to Christians and been shown to contain the mysteries of the Christian faith. For Pico, this is the true form of Judaism and "there is no point of controversy between the Hebrews and ourselves on which the Hebrews cannot be confuted and convinced out of the cabalistic writings" (*Oration*, 65).[26]

Pico explains that he has had the opportunity to study the ancient writings, including the occult sciences of magic and Cabala, and he has distilled the essential truths contained in these writings and is able to show their commensurability with Christian theology. He is, therefore, proposing both a restoration of ancient truth, which had been lost, and the institution of the new philosophy that was superior to anything available in the past.

This brief description of Pico's *Oration* makes affinities with Bacon evident. Both Pico and Bacon affirm that God intends for humanity to know and to understand Creation; knowledge is not a source of Original Sin. In fact, knowledge of nature leads to love of God. Both Pico and Bacon maintain that philosophy and theology in their current states are in disarray and that humanity will remain alienated from its true nature and from God until natural philosophy can be restored. Both Pico and Bacon see the process as a restoration and an advance. Pico makes more explicit reference to the *prisca theologia* and to magic and Cabala, but Bacon's writings, especially the *New Atlantis* and *Wisdom of the Ancients,* clearly indicate that the recovery of the highest form of natural philosophy provides the ability to penetrate the secrets of nature and reveal the miracles planted in the womb of nature by God. Both also indicate that the restoration of natural philosophy to its true subject matter, namely, God and God's Creation, sets this stage for recovery and for a return to true religion.[27] Finally, both link the recovery of knowledge with a spiritual purification that purges away selfish, material concerns and leads to loving devotion to God and to charitable actions on behalf of humanity.

Before concluding this comparison, it is important to again emphasize that the intent is not to claim that Bacon derives his views directly from Pico. The point being made is that Bacon, like many of his contemporaries, drew upon Neoplatonic and Hermetic materials as complements to Christian theology. In Bacon's case, these ancient wisdom writings directly affect his interpretation of scripture and his understanding of God's providential design.

## Conclusion

This analysis demonstrates the inadequacies of interpretations that focus only on Bacon's epistemological critique or the presentation of his own new epistemology. The setting in which these epistemological principles are presented is one of providential intervention that creates an apocalyptic hope of restoring humanity to its proper relation to nature and to God. The root motif of this text is exactly what the title indicates—an instauration. This instauration is more than the rebuilding of knowledge; it is also a spiritual rejuvenation and restoration initiated by God's providential action and by humanity's response to the apocalyptic opportunity that Providence provides.

This analysis also demonstrates that while Bacon's epistemology is new and while it is a break from the Aristotelian and Scholastic epistemology, it is also a restoration of the inquiry into nature that began with Adam and continued through the esoteric Jewish tradition and "pagan" traditions of a *prisca theologia*. So, it is wrong to characterize Bacon as a modern who is rejecting traditional modes of inquiry. Bacon is rejecting degenerated, deteriorated modes of inquiry that begin with Plato and Aristotle and continue into the Scholastic tradition. For Bacon these forms of philosophy are characterized by system building and human speculation that are too far removed from an empirical investigation of nature. The result of this divorce between nature and human intellectual activity is sterility and impotence. The cause of this degenerated condition is human pride, which privileges the human imagination and human speculation over the investigation of God's Creation.

The purpose of the demonstration of parallels between Bacon's epistemology and the epistemological principles found in the Neoplatonic and Hermetic traditions is to demonstrate the full meaning of the concept of instauration. Bacon understands his contribution to be a return of humanity to the condition that God intended. In this condition humanity lives in harmony with nature, derives benefits from nature through investigation of the Creation, and learns of God's love and mercy through the discovery of the benefits God provides in the Creation. So, in linking Bacon to the *prisca theologia* tradition, this analysis demonstrates that Bacon shared the Neoplatonic view that there is a profound difference between the prevailing impotent, sterile state of humanity and the original state as God created humanity. He also shares the conviction that alienation from both God and nature can be overcome.

Analysis of *The Great Instauration* has also shown that it is permeated with apocalyptic references. Bacon is convinced that God is acting to create the conditions under which humanity can be restored to its prelapsarian condition. Bacon is clear that only God can create this opportunity; humanity cannot save itself. On the other hand, the instauration requires humanity to be actively involved in the restoration. This active involvement requires a spiritual regeneration that will cleanse humanity of its arrogance and pride. And the instauration requires "good works"—that is, humanity must be directly involved in the restoration of nature. An important element of Bacon's understanding of the apocalyptic moment is Bacon's stress on the importance of humility and charity as the motivation for the study of nature. Other scholars have focused on the mastery of nature and depicted Bacon as a secular man determined to exploit nature. *The Great Instauration* makes it clear that the purpose of knowledge is to provide relief for humanity's estate. Bacon, as the person most responsible for introducing the instauration, repeatedly characterizes his effort as a charitable act. This contrast between a prideful attempt to dominate nature and the reverent study of nature is expressed in the frontispiece, where Bacon replaces the prideful "plus ultra" with a quote from the apocalyptic book of Daniel. The extraordinary deeds that are under way are under providential guidance and are part of an apocalyptic fulfillment.

Identifying these themes establishes a substantial correspondence with the *New Atlantis*. *The Great Instauration* sets out the epistemological principles necessary for the two aspects of instauration, and the description of the work of Solomon's House in the *New Atlantis* demonstrates the benefits to be derived. The *New Atlantis*'s account of the prehistory of civilization presents a picture of what human existence is intended to be. Bensalem never faced the calamities other civilizations endured because it maintained its piety. *The Great Instauration* offers the hope that the period of darkness and sterility is coming to an end and humanity will be able to regain what it has lost.

As we shall see, these themes of apocalyptic deliverance and instauration permeate *The New Organon*.

# Chapter 3

## *The New Organon*

*The New Organon,* which was published as the second part of Bacon's *Great Instauration,* consists of a preface and two collections of aphorisms. Both sets are entitled "Aphorisms Concerning the Interpretation of Nature and the Kingdom of Man." The second of these offers detailed analyses of the flaws in Aristotelian and Scholastic philosophy and sets out the principles for Bacon's new method; it is more of what is to be expected in a treatise on epistemological principles. The first collection of aphorisms, on the other hand, is more concerned with identifying the primary problems that necessitate rethinking epistemological issues and providing some reassurance that the present state of disorder and confusion can be overcome. In this regard, the first collection has affinities with key elements of the preface to *The Great Instauration.*

The analysis offered here concentrates on the first set of aphorisms and examines how the religious dimensions of Bacon's enterprise serve as the foundation for both his analysis of the current state of disorder and his assessment of the prospects for instauration. The investigation of *The New Organon* will follow the same procedure used with the *New Atlantis* and *The Great Instauration.* That is, it will provide a close textual reading, seeking to identify key terms, symbols, and images that Bacon employs to make his case. This method is particularly appropriate for *The New Organon* because Bacon carefully constructs each aphorism to provoke the reader

*The New Organon* 73

to reflect on key terms and phrases and to freely associate them with other settings in which they occur. Moreover, in some of the aphorisms it is as important to recognize what Bacon leaves unsaid as it is to pay attention to what and how he actually says what he does. Before turning to the aphorisms, however, it is important to first give brief attention to the title and the preface.

## Title and Preface

This title is an obvious and direct reference to Aristotle's organon. It signals Bacon's intent to set out new epistemological and methodological principles and conveys at least an implicit criticism of Aristotle; otherwise, a new epistemology would be unnecessary.

In the opening of the preface Bacon asserts that some men have overestimated and others underestimated the accomplishments of reason and the mechanical arts. Those who overestimated unduly value the things that have been discovered and have concluded that nothing more can be obtained. Those who undervalue the human faculties assert that there is no direct link between reason and nature that can produce any beneficial results. Bacon identifies these two stances as those of the rationalists and of the skeptics and claims that both have prevented the advancement of science and have done philosophy "a great injury" (*WFB*, 4:39). To counter the deleterious effect of both positions, Bacon proposes to introduce a method that establishes a proper correspondence between the operations of the intellect and its subject, the natural world.

While he claims that his method is new, Bacon also indicates that there is precedent to be found in pre-Socratic philosophy. Bacon says that the ancient Greeks, "whose writings have been lost," avoided the predicaments of the present schools and were able to advance knowledge. They "took up with better judgment a position between these two extremes—between the presumption of pronouncing on everything and the despair of comprehending anything" (*WFB*, 4:39). Although they admit the difficulty of the task of attaining truth, they nevertheless follow up "their object and engage with Nature; thinking (it seems) that this very question,—viz. whether or no anything can be known,—was to be settled not by arguing, but by trying. And yet they too, trusting entirely to the force of their understanding, applied no rule, but made everything turn upon hard thinking and perpetual working and exercise of the mind" (*WFB*, 4:39). This attitude and method of the pre-Socratics, Bacon adds, is closer to "the native and spontaneous processes of the mind." A bit further on Bacon adds that he will take this pre-Socratic perspective and will refine it in order to provide "recovery of a sound and healthy condition" (*WFB*, 4:40) of the mind and its relation to nature. The position Bacon takes in the first two paragraphs of this preface is, therefore, similar to his description of his enterprise in *The Great Instauration*, where he claims that his epistemology would reestablish the mind's authority over nature. By this claim he means that the study of nature will produce beneficial results and not simply build intellectual constructs. Bacon adds that these results will, themselves, provide proof of the validity of his method.

Bacon next warns that his new epistemology does not simply offer refinements on present modes of investigation; it requires a completely different foundation. Because this is the case, his program will not be welcomed by many of the intellectual elite who are too enamored with their present systems. Moreover, not all men are capable of contributing to the exploration of the intellectual horizon. In spite of this array of impediments, Bacon indicates that he is optimistic that progress will be made. Given Bacon's list of impediments to progress, the reason for his optimism is worthy of attention. Bacon begins by explaining that he is merely "a guide to point out the road; an office of small authority, and depending more upon a kind of luck than upon any ability or excellency" (*WFB*, 4:41). This oblique statement would be insignificant in and of itself, but we have seen elsewhere Bacon's use of similar language to minimize his role in order to emphasize the operation of Providence. As we shall see, the last third of the aphorisms in this section takes as their principal subject the reasons that humankind should be hopeful, and the principal explanation is that Providence is at work.

## Aphorisms: Book 1

The first collection contains 128 aphorisms, which are organized in the following manner: aphorisms 1–10 describe humanity's vocation as the interpreter and minister of nature and contrast this calling to the sterility of the existing sciences that make it impossible to carry out this vocation. Aphorisms 11–17 attribute the present sterility to the inutility of logic. Aphorisms 18–37 contrast two types of knowledge, which Bacon describes as "anticipation of nature" and "the interpretation of nature." Aphorisms 38–70 present the famous discussion of the Idols of the Mind. Aphorisms 71–115 point out the causes of the present errors, which impede progress, and then offer grounds for hope for the future. Aphorisms 116–128 contain Bacon's anticipations of and replies to "potential objections" to his program.

This brief listing reveals the structure and the movement of Bacon's argument. He begins by describing humanity's true vocation and identifying impediments to carrying out that calling. Bacon then moves from an analysis of the present state of disorder to an identification of reasons to expect that these conditions can and will be changed so that humanity will have its proper vocation restored. We now need to examine the aphorisms in detail.

### Aphorisms 1–10: The Interruption of the True Correspondence between the Mind and Nature

The first several aphorisms contrast humanity's true vocation as the interpreter of nature with the present condition, in which humanity is preoccupied with its own intellectual constructs and is incapable of understanding nature, advancing knowledge, or improving the human condition. While this is a familiar theme, there are subtleties to Bacon's expression of it that are important to develop. Aphorism 1, which is a statement of the proper relationship of reason, art, and nature, asserts that humanity can understand the workings of nature only if its understanding is grounded in facts or in careful reflection and interpretation based upon the observation of nature. The second aphorism succinctly characterizes how and why human understanding becomes confused and unproductive: "Neither the naked hand nor the understanding left to itself can effect much." Both faculties need "instruments and helps" if productive work is to be done (*WFB*, 4:47). This brief statement introduces what becomes more fully developed later. First, it asserts the necessary interplay of the mind and the hand, or the intellect and the applied arts. While this is now a familiar theme, Bacon adds a new element. Not only must the mind and art work in concert, they must take advantage of every tool or resource appropriate to each to augment the capabilities of the other. As Bacon puts it, "the instruments of the hand either give motion or guide it, so the instruments of the mind supply either suggestions for the understanding or cautions" (*WFB*, 4:47). The third aphorism also stresses the necessary collaboration between "human knowledge and human power" and adds that the starting point for human intellectual endeavor is nature itself. In Bacon's phrasing, nature must be obeyed in order to be commanded. That is, human reasoning will not be productive if intellectual endeavor is not grounded in empirical study. The fourth aphorism repeats this theme by asserting that "all that man can do is to put together or put asunder natural bodies" (*WFB*, 4:47). This concept is central to Bacon's program; it affirms that everything beneficial to humanity is contained within nature itself and can only be brought to light by a combination of empirical investigation and inductive reasoning. This key idea, only briefly alluded to in this aphorism, is made more conspicuous in later aphorisms; and it will become clear that it is central to understanding the religious premises undergirding Bacon's project of instauration. Aphorism 5 points to previous work that has been successful in producing results but has not been as efficient as it might be. Bacon's reference is to "the mechanic, the mathematician, the physician, the alchemist, and the magician" (*WFB*, 4:48). It is noteworthy that Bacon includes magic and alchemy among the applied sciences. While he does indicate that their results have not been as substantial as they might be, he makes the same charge against mathematics and medicine.

In aphorisms 6 and 7 Bacon asserts that present methods are indicted by their lack of success. This lack of success sometimes is obscured because there are large library collections that seem to suggest encyclopedic or comprehensive knowledge. But this is misleading; these volumes contained multiple, repetitive statements of the same limited results. When these results are measured against the enormous span of time involved in their development, it becomes evident that much of what has been achieved is the result of accident not method; and much more has been left unexplored because human beings have been too content with the limited results. Moreover, the present epistemological systems offer no means for further advancement; instead they memorialize the limited, accidental success of the past. These statements are followed in aphorism 9 by the accusation that the present state of science idolizes the intellectual systems of the past and this adulation prevents inquiry into the workings of nature: "The cause and root of nearly all evils in the sciences is this—that while we falsely admire and extol the powers of the human mind we neglect to seek for its true helps" (*WFB*, 4:48). This brief statement is a prelude to the extended description of the Idols of the Mind found in aphorisms 38–70. Aphorism 10 augments aphorism 9 by referring to the fantasies created by the human mind removed from the study of nature as a form of madness. These two aphorisms are followed by a more extended criticism of the present philosophical system's inability to correct itself and return to a sound epistemological foundation.

Aphorisms 1–10, then, begin with an assertion of the true correspondence between intelligence and nature, which leads to truth and to the improvement of the human condition. This true science, that is, the interpretation of nature, once existed but has been lost and has been replaced by spurious science based on speculation. This rupture in the grounding of reason in direct investigation of nature has had two results. The first is stagnation in the interpretation of nature and in advancing the kingdom of man. The second is the preoccupation of the mind with its own creations rather than God's Creation. In accounting for the second of these two derailments, Bacon explains that early on the applied arts had achieved accidental success and subsequent generations have produced imitators rather than more innovators. So, not only has the advance of truth been derailed, sycophants have memorialized the erroneous methods of the past and have become oblivious to the accomplishments of ancient, natural philosophers, whose achievements are now almost lost from memory.

### Aphorisms 11–37: The Problems of the Syllogism and the Prospects for the Recovery of the Correspondence between the Mind and Nature

Aphorisms 11–15 attribute the derailment of philosophy to logic and to the syllogism. The problem, Bacon explains, is that the logic and order of these systems are internal and do not have any method of correcting their starting principles. As a result, their terminology has lost direct grounding in nature and refers to human constructs rather than to actually existing phenomena. In aphorism 19 Bacon again asserts that progress can only be made if the new foundation is established:

> There are and can be only two ways of searching into and discovering truth. The one flies from the senses and particulars to the most general axioms, and from these principles, the truth of which it takes for settled and immoveable, proceeds to judgment and to the discovery of middle axioms. And this way is now in fashion. The other derives axioms from the senses and particulars, rising by a gradual and unbroken ascent, so that it arrives at the most general axioms last of all. This is the true way, but as yet untried. (*WFB*, 4:50)

In aphorism 20 Bacon explains that this latter method is not utilized because it involves hard work, which is contrary to the mind's "natural" tendency to rush to conclusions rather than work arduously. At this point, Bacon does not explain why this condition obtains; but his explanation becomes clear further on. Bacon considers humans to have two natures. The first is the prelapsarian condition, and the other is the condition of the mind and the senses after the Fall.

Aphorisms 21–25 begin a transition from Bacon's description of epistemological disorder to his presentation of reasons to believe recovery is possible. In aphorism 21 Bacon notes that not all minds fall victim to prevailing errors; some are capable of making an effort in the proper direction. Unfortunately, a willingness to work vigorously is not enough. These willing minds need guidance, that is, a proper method to aid in the search. While Bacon does not say it here, he has already said elsewhere that he is providing precisely the guidance that is needed. Aphorism 23 introduces a key contrast between the natural world, which is humanity's proper object of study, and the mind's imaginary constructs, which have become its primary preoccupation. This aphorism juxtaposes the fictions and idols (*idola*) of the mind to the true signatures and marks set upon the works of Creation. This language anticipates the discussion of the Idols of the Mind and draws a distinction between the language of nature (the signatures set upon the works of Creation by God) and the verbal constructs of man. The signatures are the proper object of study, but the present system substitutes false appearances for reality. Before humanity can return to the proper study of knowledge, the false constructs have to be cleared away. As noted in previous discussions, this is one of the primary meanings of Bacon's term *instauration*.

Before moving to the next set of aphorisms, one further point needs to be made with regard to the introduction of the language of idols. Scholars have correctly pointed out that the term *idolum* primarily means false or illusionary.[1] This meaning certainly fits in the context of this aphorism, because Bacon is faulting the creation of man-made abstractions that separate the mind from its true object of study, nature. But scholars who choose to stress this meaning of the term usually do so in order to caution against misunderstanding the term *idol* in the religious sense of false objects of worship. This contrast seems inappropriate in Bacon's case. Bacon is arguing that humanity is guilty of focusing on its own creations or fantasies and that this prevents the study of God's Creation. For Bacon this is an idolatrous worship of man-made, false gods. This meaning fits this aphorism and is consistent with Bacon's broader criticism of the human condition. In *The Great Instauration* and elsewhere Bacon identifies the principal sins of humanity as the sin of pride, the effort to be like God, and the sin of vanity, that is, worshiping itself or its own creations. This meaning is underscored in the second sentence of aphorism 23, which contrasts "empty dogmas, and the true signatures and marks set upon the works of creation as they are found in nature" (*WFB*, 4:51).[2] This understanding of idol/idolum relates Bacon's work to another familiar early modern theme as well. The Neoplatonic, alchemical, Hermetic, and Cabalistic traditions all maintained that God had imprinted a code on nature that humanity could use to reveal nature's benefits for humanity. According to these traditions, humanity would gain control of nature and could use it for human benefit, if it properly understood God's design in the Creation. Bacon shares with these various traditions the fundamental conviction that the true understanding of nature produces useful knowledge. The theme that Bacon is presenting in this aphorism is the theme of the disparity or the discrepancy between knowledge of nature that generates benefits for humanity and the sterile, empty speculations that create only idols, that is, illusions and fantasies. This contrast between the empty words of philosophy and true knowledge was addressed in aphorisms 14 and 15.

As we shall see, Bacon is introducing in these several instances the contrast between humanity's present state and its prelapsarian condition in which humanity had mastery over nature. Before the Fall a direct correspondence existed between the nature of the Creation and humanity's language or the words that humanity used to designate nature according to its human usefulness. This theme is in turn related to the idea of instauration. The false constructs of the mind have to be cleared away in order that a real epistemology can begin to produce useful knowledge through the direct study of nature.

Aphorisms 26 through 36 continue the contrast between the disordered state of knowledge and Bacon's new organon. Aphorism 26 develops the contrast between true knowledge—that is, the interpretation of nature—and prevailing opinion—that is, anticipations of nature. Bacon explains that "anticipations" build from vulgar, common-sense assumptions rather than from rigorous, empirical investigation. While vulgar assumptions are to be expected among the common people, philosophers are supposed to pursue truth. The fact that the vulgar dominates what passes for philosophy is one of the symptomatic features of the present age. In aphorisms 35 and 36 Bacon again stresses the need for a new foundation that can clear away ignorance and opinion and provide knowledge. Bacon warns, however, that not everyone will be able to follow these new directions, and Bacon again identifies his role as "guide" for the instauration of the edifice of learning.

### Aphorisms 38–70: The Idols of the Mind

Aphorism 38 begins Bacon's discussion of the Idols of the Mind. The first of the four sets of idols to be avoided is that of the Idols of the Tribe, or the flaws in the human race, which make it impossible for man to be "the measure of all things" (*WFB*, 4:53). This phrase, of course, is the famous pre-Socratic description of humanity and a main theme renewed by Renaissance humanism. Bacon cautions that the human senses are flawed and that "the human understanding is like a false mirror, which, receiving rays irregularly, distorts and discolours the nature of things by mingling its own nature with it" (*WFB*, 4:54). The Idols of the Cave are flaws in the individual. By this Bacon means the particularities each individual has with regard to native intelligence, education, and the circumstances into which he is born. The Idols of the Market Place refers to popular opinions that form the basis of social and intellectual intercourse. Here again he is alluding to commonplace, vulgar notions that have to be transcended if real knowledge is to be obtained. Bacon is also challenging the idea of a correspondence between human language and truth or reality. In prevailing opinions, words do not name things; they are products of the human imagination and not of reality. As a result "words are imposed according to the apprehension of the vulgar... but words plainly force and overrule the understanding, and throw all into confusion, and lead men away into numberless, empty controversies and idle fancies" (*WFB*, 4:55). The Idols of the Theater are the distortions of various philosophical schools, which are to some degree better than vulgar opinions but are opinions, nevertheless. Bacon refers to these as Idols of the Theater because to him the philosophical schools are the same imaginary products as those created by the playwright in his fantasy world. The philosophers, like the playwright, are creating a second reality; they are not accurately portraying the first. Aphorisms 45 through 70 continue to develop the various attributes of the four forms of idolatry.

### Aphorisms 71–91: Bacon's New Method

Aphorisms 71 through 85 turn from a description of the problems of the present to the benefits to be derived from the new organon. Bacon's epistemology brings discipline to the senses and to the intellect, and this discipline produces both "Experiments of Light" and "Experiments of Fruit." This language is similar to that found in the *New Atlantis,* where the Brethren of Solomon's House explain that they are seeking, not material rewards, but the "Light." As we have seen in our discussion of that text, *light* means the divine illumination of God's Creation. This divine illumination opens the investigation of nature to reveal the benefits to be exploited by humanity. These benefits are "the fruits." Here in *The New Organon* Bacon maintains it is the fruits, that is, the benefits, that serve as the test of the intellectual principles being applied; or, as Bacon phrases it in aphorism 73, the fruits are "the sponsors and sureties for the truth of philosophies" (cf. *WFB,* 4: 73–74). In discussing the benefits of his approach, Bacon once again notes that his methodology only appears to be new because humanity has lost memory of anything but the philosophical systems that have come down from Plato and Aristotle through to the present. In this discussion Bacon employs the image of time being like a river that is also found in *The Great Instauration:* "Time, like a river, bringing down to us things which are light and [on top], but letting weighty matters sink." In the same aphorism Bacon also describes the wisdom of Plato and Aristotle as childlike or infantile, as he did in *The Great Instauration.* In making this allusion, Bacon adds: "nor should we omit that judgment, or rather divination, which was given concerning the Greeks by the Egyptian priest,—that 'they were always boys, without antiquity of knowledge or knowledge of antiquity'" (*WFB,* 4:73). This phrase, quoted from Plato's *Timaeus,*[3] relates to his previous juxtaposition of mature knowledge, which can generate benefits, to the sterile system of boys, which cannot. The reference to Plato's *Timaeus* also reminds us of its broader use in the *New Atlantis* to describe an age of excellence that has since been lost from memory. Here again we have the notion of instauration as building or rebuilding repeated through an allusion to Bacon's organon as a recovery of the ancient, true method.

Aphorism 72 repeats Bacon's charge that the Greeks had no history worthy of being called history "but only fables or rumors of antiquity." He also criticizes their limited understanding of geography: "the travels of Democritas, Plato, and Pythagoras, which were rather suburban excursions than distant journeys, were talked of as something great. In our times on the other hand many parts of the New World and the limits on every side of the Old World are known, and our stock of experience has increased to an infinite amount" (*WFB,* 4:73). This passage parallels the frontispiece of *The Great Instauration,* where a ship sails beyond the Pillars of Hercules, which represent the boundaries of the known world in the classical age.

Aphorisms 73 and 74 turn to the merits of the mechanical arts, which are to be valued more than the sterile philosophical systems because, even in their imperfect forms, they produce something of use. The reason for their productivity is that they begin with empirical investigation of nature, something now foreign to philosophy. Beginning with aphorism 75, Bacon argues that current philosophy is not only sterile but causes despair of ever being able to improve the relation between the intellect and nature. Aphorism 75 also asserts that the arrogance of the founders and followers of the philosophical schools is such that, "not content to speak for themselves, whatever is beyond their own or their master's knowledge or reach they set down as beyond the bounds of possibility, and pronounce, as if on the authority of their art, that it cannot be known or done; thus most presumptuously and invidiously turning the weakness of their own discoveries into a calumny on nature itself, and the despair of the rest of the world" (*WFB*, 4:75). In aphorism 77 Bacon indicates that there is no corrective for the arrogant claims of the philosophical schools to represent all that can be known about the human condition, because alternative philosophical approaches have been lost or obscured. Continuing this analysis, Bacon states that there is an assumption that once the Aristotelian system was fully developed, the old philosophical systems died away. The implication is that they died away because the Aristotelian system was superior to and a perfection of those previous efforts. Bacon argues, however, that the old systems did not die away just because the Aristotelian system suddenly appeared. "For long afterwards, down even to the times of Cicero and subsequent ages, the works of the old philosophers still remained." Bacon then employs his river simile yet again, adding that "when on the inundation of barbarians into the Roman Empire human learning had suffered shipwreck, then the systems of Aristotle and Plato, like planks of lighter and less solid material, floated on the waves of time, and were preserved" (*WFB*, 4:76).

Aphorisms 78 and 79 develop the idea of instauration as both something new and something old. Bacon asks his reader how it is that the wrong traditions have carried over from ancient times. The first explanation, he says, is that only "three revolutions and periods of learning can properly be reckoned; one among the Greeks, the second among the Romans, and the last among us, that is to say, the nations of Western Europe" (*WFB*, 4:77). So, the first answer that Bacon gives is that the periods of productivity have actually been quite brief in comparison to the periods of sterility. The problem is further complicated by the fact that even in these brief periods of productivity, little attention has been given to the study of nature; other subjects dominated and prevented further progress in natural philosophy. "Again the age in which natural philosophy was seen to flourish most among the Greeks, was but a brief particle of time; for in early ages the Seven Wise Men, as they were called, (all except

Thales) applied themselves to morals and politics; and in later times, when Socrates had drawn down philosophy from heaven to earth, moral philosophy became more fashionable than ever, and diverted the minds of men from the philosophy of nature" (*WFB*, 4:78). Aphorism 81 adds that little progress has been made in natural philosophy because humankind has lost sight of "the true and lawful goal of the sciences." The true goal, "that human life be endowed with new discoveries and powers," has been replaced by the vain philosophizing of the system builders. Bacon concludes this aphorism: "If then the end of the sciences has not as yet been well placed, it is not strange that men have erred as to the means" (*WFB*, 4: 79–80). Aphorisms 82–91 enumerate reasons for the derailment of philosophy, including the denigration of experiment, complacency regarding past achievements, and a misplaced concern that natural philosophy might subvert the authority of religion.

### Aphorisms 92–119: Reasons for Despair, Reasons for Hope

Aphorisms 92–119 contain Bacon's discussion of the factors that cause humans to despair of any improvement to the human condition and then offer his assurances that there are reasons for hope. In aphorism 92 Bacon concedes that there are valid reasons to be skeptical and distrustful of any claims made regarding a method to advance the sciences out of their long period of stagnation. These include "the obscurity of nature, the shortness of life, the deceitfulness of the senses, the weakness of the judgment, the difficulty of experiment" (*WFB*, 4:90). Nevertheless, Bacon confidently affirms that he is capable of offering hope and explains that the basis for hope is in the catalog of advances and discoveries, that is, in the empirical evidence of progress in science. "[The] strongest means of inspiring hope will be to bring men to particulars, especially to particulars digested and arranged in my Tables of Discovery (the subject partly of the second, but much more of the fourth part of my Instauration), since this is not merely the promise of the thing but the thing itself" (*WFB*, 4:91). By following this procedure, Bacon explains, it will be possible to inspire hope in the minds of men and thereby provide proper preparation for the intellectual quest that must be undertaken. Bacon then likens himself to Columbus. Before Columbus's expeditions opened the geographical world, his project and his reasons were met with skepticism by the great majority of his contemporaries; but once his voyage was successful, Columbus's evidence was validated and many others rushed to follow his lead and to benefit from his pioneering work. Similarly, Bacon's project, which challenges the prevailing beliefs and promises productive benefits from a bold, new departure, will be met with skepticism. Nevertheless, once the benefits of the new method are apparent, others will readily join in and follow Bacon just as many joined in to follow Columbus. The parallels Bacon makes here between the opening of the terrestrial and the intellectual worlds call to mind the frontispiece of *The Great Instauration* and build upon earlier aphorisms in which Bacon criticized humanity's clinging to the familiar intellectual terrain. Beginning in aphorism 93, Bacon links the opening of the terrestrial and the intellectual worlds with Providence: "The beginning is from God: for the business which is in hand, having the character of good so strongly impressed upon it, appears manifestly to proceed from God, who is the author of good, and the Father of Light." Furthermore, Bacon adds, God works in mysterious ways: "everything glides on smoothly and noiselessly, and the work is fairly going on before men are aware that it has begun" (*WFB*, 4:91–92). Bacon then adds that the prophecy of Daniel, touching the last stages of the world, should not be forgotten: "Many shall go to and fro, and knowledge shall be increased." Bacon remarks that this passage clearly intimates "that the thorough passage of the world (which now by so many distant voyages seems to be accomplished, or in course of accomplishment), and the advancement of the sciences, are destined by fate, that is, by Divine Providence, to meet in the same age" (*WFB*, 4:92).

These three sentences offer a compact statement of Bacon's deepest conviction about the remarkable events of his time and about his role at this momentous stage in history. Providence guides the pivotal events in human history. Human beings are the actors that God uses to unfold his plan, but divine purpose sets them in motion. Quite often human beings are not aware that anything remarkable is under way. The changes may come slowly and subtly or they may be disregarded because, at the outset, they appear to be marginal to or even contradictory to the opinions and practices of the age. Overseas expansion and exploration, which have transformed the world for the good of humanity, are acts of Providence and are key elements of "the business that is at hand" (cf. *WFB*, 4:92–93). Then using the phrase "God, who is the author of good, and the Father of Light," Bacon makes intellectual breakthroughs the complement to overseas expansion. Bacon's previous discussion of "light" symbolism makes the reference clear here. True knowledge comes through divine illumination and occurs when the human mind is properly attuned to its subject, which is God's Creation.[4] In other words, Bacon's new epistemology establishes the procedures for enlightenment. These references make clear the reasons that Bacon compares himself to Columbus in the previous aphorism. This brief passage also gives full weight to Bacon's use of the passage from the book of Daniel, making it part of his own apocalyptic vision. Bacon's statements make it clear that he understands that the overseas exploration is virtually complete—it is something accomplished in a relatively brief period within his lifetime. Bacon is convinced that the intellectual advances, the exploration of the uncharted regions of intellectual territory, can be accomplished in a similarly small span of time. If many join in and follow Bacon in this enterprise, as terrestrial explorers joined Columbus, their collaborative efforts will advance the new learning at a rapid pace. In some passages Bacon states that the project will not likely be accomplished in his lifetime, but he seems to think that it will be finished by the next generation. These statements make clear how well the frontispiece of *The Great Instauration* conveys the main themes at the heart of Bacon's enterprise. They also help explain Bacon's references to his role as "an accident of time" or as the result of fate in *The Great Instauration* and in *The New Organon*.[5] In the concluding phrase quoted above, Bacon identifies or equates fate with Providence, and earlier, in aphorism 40, he lists Fortune as one of the "fantasies" that the human mind had constructed.

When the apocalyptic themes contained in these passages are placed in the broader context of Bacon's statements in the *New Atlantis, The Great Instauration,* and in other aphorisms in *The New Organon,* it becomes evident that he sees his own age as the beginning of the restoration of humanity to its prelapsarian condition. The context includes the obvious references to humanity's present state in comparison to humanity's original condition, and it also includes his descriptions of the protracted period of ignorance and error that characterizes human history. In earlier aphorisms Bacon has stressed how little humanity has accomplished in its recorded history. Among the explanations he gives for so little progress is the vanity and pride of the human race, which are characteristic of Original Sin. Bacon also attributes the lack of progress to the mind's tendency toward error and to the unreliability of the senses. In *The Great Instauration* Bacon made it clear that these are not permanent conditions; it is possible for humanity to recover its original condition, a theme Bacon takes up beginning with aphorism 94. So, Bacon is offering humanity hope not just for greater prosperity and relief from suffering. Bacon hopes for and urges humanity to hope for restoration to paradise. As noted at the beginning of this discussion, the theme of hope now dominates the remainder of the aphorisms. Aphorism 92 and 93 set out the basis for that hope in no uncertain terms. Humanity can have hope because it is now evident that Providence has been at work and that a monumental change in the human condition is under way.

In light of these monumental happenings, Bacon indicates that it is necessary to reconsider the reasons for a lack of progress throughout most of human history. He begins this reconsideration in aphorism 94, where he asks if the lack of progress is something fixed and inalterable in nature and in the human condition or if it is something that is temporal and correctable. As Bacon puts it, if misfortunes "are owing, not to the force of circumstances, but to [human] errors, you may hope that by dismissing or correcting these errors, a great change may be made for the better" (*WFB*, 4:92). In this same vein, Bacon adds that there is a profound difference between presuming that humans have diligently and laboriously dedicated themselves to the study of nature and have only produced modest results and realizing that human beings have made little or no progress because they have been going about their efforts the wrong way.

> If during so long a course of years men had kept in the true road for discovery and cultivating sciences, and had yet been unable to make further progress therein, bold doubtless and rash would be the opinion that further progress is possible. But if the road itself has been mistaken, and men's labour spent on unfit objects, it follows that the difficulty has its rise not in things themselves, which are not in our power, but in the human understanding, and the use and application thereof, which admits of remedy and medicine. (*WFB*, 4:92)

Aphorism 95 contends that a further impediment to progress is that knowledge has been bifurcated: "Those who have handled sciences have been either men of experiment or men of dogmas" (*WFB*, 4:92). Men of experiment are then likened to the ant: they only collect or use what they find readily available. The men of reason, on the other hand, are like spiders, because they spin their intellectual systems out of their own substance just as a spider spins its web out of material it generates. For knowledge to be restored and for humanity to be able to benefit from its knowledge of nature, the men of science must become like the bee, which

> gathers its material from the flowers of the garden and of the field, but transforms and digests it by a power of its own. Not unlike this is the true business of philosophy; for it neither relies solely or chiefly on the powers of the mind, nor does it take the matter which it gathers from natural history and mechanical experiments and lay it up in the memory whole, as it finds it; but lays it up in the understanding altered and digested. Therefore from a closer and purer league between these two faculties, the experimental and the rational, (such as has never yet been made) much may be hoped. (*WFB*, 4:93)

This phrase "never yet" in the last sentence is noteworthy because it introduces another apocalyptic term or phrase that is repeated in the next several aphorisms. This phrasing, coupled with the repeated stress on a valid reason for hope, reinforces the sense that the dramatic change is imminent, especially when the means for effecting change has been identified. The next several aphorisms link this sense of a monumental shift to the shift in epistemology. According to aphorism 96, "From a natural philosophy pure and unmixed, better things are to be expected"; and aphorism 97 contends that "better hopes may be entertained" if natural philosophy is attempted by a man with a well-purged mind (*WFB*, 4:93–94). The essential task in restoring knowledge is that of building up from experience and applying art to nature in order to draw out what is beneath the obvious. This latter statement compares to Bacon's reference to the bee. The bee not only uses what is available in nature but also takes it into its own system and reconfigures it to produce something original. This notion of investigating the hidden levels of nature is one repeated in several of the aphorisms in the remainder of this section of *The New Organon*.

Aphorism 97 also resumes the list of reasons for despair that Bacon had identified in aphorism 92, but here Bacon offers assurances that these impediments are conditional and can be corrected by rebuilding the foundations of knowledge. This rebuilding requires both the proper object of study and the proper method. According to Bacon, the new science must have two dimensions: a thoroughgoing analysis of the structures of nature and a creative ordering and utilization of nature's building blocks. "The secrets of nature reveal themselves more readily under the vexations of art than when they do their own way" (*WFB*, 4:94). Two aspects of this statement are worth underscoring. First there is an emphasis on humanity's creative involvement. While some discoveries are ready-made in nature and can be easily found, many more require laborious digging and then must be refined and developed to be made useful. The second aspect to note is Bacon's emphasis on the necessity of human labor. An important ingredient in Bacon's biblical perspective on the human condition is his conviction that "man must till the soil" as a result of Original Sin. Hard work is both the punishment for and the means of recovery from Original Sin. This labor is a form of penance that God requires; but in requiring it, God also transforms the penance into a form of beneficence. Having emphasized the importance of the mechanical arts in aphorism 98, Bacon gives equal stress to the importance of augmenting the mechanical arts through systematic theoretical and philosophical analysis. Bacon clarifies his point in aphorism 99 by again using his reference to experiments that produce fruit and experiments that produce light.

> But then only will there be good ground of hope for the further advance of knowledge, when there shall be received and gathered together into natural history a variety of experiments, which are of no use in themselves, but simply serve to discover causes and axioms; which I call "*Experimenta lucifera*," experiments of *light*, to distinguish them from those which I call "*fructifera*," experiments of fruit.
>
> Now experiments of this kind have one admirable property and condition; they never miss or fail. For since they are applied, not for the purpose of producing any particular effect, but only of discovering that natural cause of some effect, they answer the end equally well whichever way they turn out; for they settle the question. (*WFB*, 4:95)

Bacon continues to develop the relationship between theoretical and applied science in aphorisms 100–105. The combination of the two establishes the means for steady progress to replace the haphazard hit-and-miss techniques that dominated for so long.

> But not only is a greater abundance of experiments to be sought for and procured, and that too of a different kind from those hitherto tried; an entirely different method, order, and process for carrying on and advancing experience must also be introduced. For experience, when it wanders in its own track, is, as I have already remarked, mere groping in the dark, and confounds men rather than instructs them. But when it shall proceed in accordance with a fixed law, in regular order, and without interruption, then may better things be hoped of knowledge. (*WFB*, 4:95)

Here Bacon is again employing familiar imagery, contrasting the darkness and ignorance of present methods to the illumination that will be provided by his new organon.

Aphorism 101 asserts that progress in knowledge cannot be accomplished by abstract reasoning divorced from empirical investigation and again contrasts the words of philosophy to the alphabet of nature: "experience has not yet learned her letters. Now no course of invention can be satisfactory unless it be carried on in writing. But when this is brought into use, and experience has been taught to read and write, better things may be hoped" (*WFB*, 4:96). Aphorism 103 continues the language of reading and writing from nature, and Bacon asserts that his method will make men literate. In the next several aphorisms Bacon repeatedly uses the language of hope and contrasts current philosophy, which was based on illusion and fantasy, to his method, which is based in empirical investigation that breaks nature down into its constituent parts, that is, into the letters of the alphabet. These letters of the alphabet of nature become the tools that enable humans to learn to read and write. To read means to be able to investigate, to decipher the structure of nature as it really is. To write means to be able to take these constituent parts and through human creativity form them into new things that will be useful to humanity. In other words, humanity will again be literate. As noted in previous discussions, Bacon obviously has in mind Adam's naming of the animals as the

*The New Organon*                                                                 91

process in which humanity comes to know and to use nature. As we have seen, he is clearly contrasting this primordial state to the empty language of philosophy.[6] Aphorisms 107 and 108 assert that the key cause of despair has been identified and the appropriate remedy found. "So much then for the removing of despair and the raising of hope through the dismissal... of the errors of past time" (cf. *WFB*, 4:98–99).

Aphorism 108 also argues that the many benefits that have accrued to humanity from accidental discovery and through flawed methods should give men of his age both hope and confidence that a systematic application of the proper method will greatly accelerate the benefits to be gained. Aphorism 109 claims that each new discovery is a gateway opening up a wide range of possibility.

> Another argument for hope may be drawn from this,—that some of the inventions already known are such as before they were discovered it could hardly have entered any man's head to think of; they would have been simply set aside as impossible. For in conjecturing what may be men set before them the example of what has been, and divine of the new with an imagination preoccupied and coloured by the old. (*WFB*, 4:99)

To support his stance, Bacon identifies three recent, unexpected inventions that fundamentally transformed human circumstance—gunpowder, the magnet, and silk. While each is developed from naturally occurring substances, human ingenuity transforms the substance into something so unexpected and remarkable as to defy logic and common sense. Silk, for example, is light and soft yet has exceptional strength. Bacon then adds, "There is therefore much ground for hoping that there are still laid up in the womb of nature many secrets of excellent use having no affinity or parallelism with any thing that is now known.... They too no doubt will some time or other, in the course and revolution of many ages, come to light of themselves, just as the others did; only by the method of which we are now treating they can be speedily and suddenly and simultaneously presented and anticipated" (*WFB*, 4:100). This is an intriguing statement. The reference to the womb evokes Bacon's comparison and contrast to sterility and productivity. The material of the natural world provides the substance, and God provides the generative ideas that give nature its form.

God placed everything in nature that humanity requires for a productive, comfortable life. The phrase "no doubt some will come to light themselves just as others did" suggests that God provides for humanity even when humans cannot provide for themselves.

Aphorism 112 expresses Bacon's conviction that collaborative effort will make possible "the discovery of all causes" and that the work of science will be completed in "but a few years" (*WFB*, 4:102). Aphorism 113 suggests that Bacon's own experience and his contribution to the advancement of science can serve as a model for what to expect. Even though he has been preoccupied with many other duties and has been in ill health, he has been able to set down the foundations for the new learning and point others in the proper direction. If this much can be accomplished by the limited efforts of one person, one can have great hope for the extraordinary accomplishments of a concerted effort. Aphorism 114 reiterates Bacon's claim that the exploration of the New World serves as a basis for hope. Before the discovery, it was impossible to imagine what existed; but once the initial discovery was made, many were able to follow and in relatively short time complete the exploration. Bacon has already indicated in a previous aphorism that the exploration of the intellectual terrain can occur just as quickly, if the same model is utilized. In aphorism 118 Bacon introduces another important theme when he indicates that he has undertaken this program of instauration "with religious care" (*WFB*, 4:105). This imagery and Bacon's sense of vocation are developed more fully in aphorism 120.

### Aphorisms 120–130: Natural Philosophy and Religion

In aphorism 120 Bacon says, "And for myself, I am not raising a capitol or pyramid to the pride of man, but laying a foundation in the human understanding for a holy temple after the model of the world. That model therefore I follow. For whatever deserves to exist deserves also to be known, for knowledge is like the image of existence; and things mean and splendid exist alike" (*WFB*, 4:106–7). This statement is followed in aphorism 121 by Bacon's claim that he is "seeking for experiments of light, not for experiments of fruit [at the present moment]; following therein, as I have often said, the example of the divine creation; which on the first day produced light only, and assigned to it alone one entire day, nor mixed up with it on that day any material work" (*WFB*, 4:107). These statements make a close tie between natural philosophy and religion. They also have a direct relation to the description of the work of Solomon's House in the *New Atlantis*. The Brethren of Solomon's House study the work of God's Creation. In fact, Solomon's House is also referred to as the College of the Six Days Works. Bacon's reference to building a temple has obvious ties to "Solomon's House" in the *New Atlantis,* which serves as the complement to Solomon's Temple. These connections help to explain Bacon's description, in aphorism 118, of his efforts being undertaken with "religious care." These references and images also augment Bacon's root notion of instauration. When Bacon uses this term to refer to building, rebuilding, or re-edification, he means it to refer to the restoration of knowledge on its proper foundation. This restoration carries humanity back to its study of nature as God's Creation. By studying nature human beings realize God's plan for Creation and for humanity, and this inspires man with the love of God. This is why Bacon frequently says there is no conflict between religion and natural philosophy. Religion is based on God's words and revelations; natural philosophy is based in God's works, the natural world. And just as there are priests and prophets of God's word, there need to be priests of God's work, that is, priests of nature. The reference to building a temple occurs in a phrase that contrasts this appropriate religious endeavor to an idolatrous building of a temple to human pride. Set in this context, the pyramid to human pride recalls the famous biblical episode of the building of the Tower of Babel. This image in turn relates to Bacon's references to the alphabet of nature and to the empty words of man that refer to illusionary fantasies. When human beings are prideful and self-absorbed, they forget God and try to become divine themselves. This is unnatural and sinful and alienates humanity from God and from the Creation. Bacon sees the myth of the Tower of Babel as a parable explaining why human language no longer refers directly to creation and reality. When Bacon says he is building a new temple, he means he is tearing down the edifice that man has created and replacing it with an epistemology that ties the human mind directly to the investigation of nature so the investigation can produce benefits to humanity. Thus the references to the temple are related to references to experiments of light in aphorism 121. Part of Bacon's statement regarding light may be puzzling because he seems to downplay the search for practical application by saying he is searching for light and not for fruit, but his statement is not contradictory or confusing when read in context. Here and elsewhere, Bacon stresses the importance of penetrating the basic structures of nature and not stopping until the probing has reached the most fundamental levels. Only when this deep level has been reached can all of the benefits be exploited. This statement is comparable to the Father's declaration that Solomon's House seeks Light. It is also conveyed in the frontispiece of Bacon's *Sylva Sylvarum,* which shows divine light radiating down to the pillars of the Temple of Solomon and onto the natural world.[7]

Aphorisms 122–130 focus on the benefits of Bacon's new method, and the language in which Bacon presents the merits of his case is revealing. In aphorism 122 he begins by acknowledging that many will be skeptical of his method because it is new and does not attempt to follow current fashion. Bacon urges his contemporaries to judge his method by the results produced. Then he makes an intriguing statement:

> But for my part, relying on the evidence and truth of things, I reject all forms of fiction and imposture; nor do I think that it matters any more to the business in hand, whether the discoveries that shall now be made were long ago known to the ancients, and have their settings and their risings according to the vicissitude of things and course of ages, than it matters to mankind whether the new world be that island of Atlantis with which the ancients were acquainted, or now discovered for the first time. For new discoveries must be sought from the light of nature, not fetched back out of the darkness of antiquity. (*WFB,* 4:108–9)

This statement is interesting for the purpose of this analysis because of the reference to the legend of Atlantis. One of the ideas that circulated in Europe during Bacon's time was that the Americas were the ancient civilization of Atlantis after it had been destroyed, a notion also found in the *New Atlantis.* It also fits Bacon's several references to navigation and to sailing beyond the false confines of the Pillars of Hercules. At the practical level, it does not matter whether Bacon is building something completely new or whether he is rebuilding from the ancient past. His emphasis in

*The New Organon*

this aphorism is on testing the merits of the system by the results it produces, not by its pedigree.

In the final paragraph of this aphorism Bacon indicates that his method does not depend on the genius or creativity of any one person, including himself; the process, not the individual, is most important. Using his empirical method, the results can be tested and exploited by several different persons. But there is another reason for diminishing the importance of individual wit. Bacon attributes his part, "as I have often said, rather to good luck than to ability, and account it a birth of time rather than of wit. For certainly chance has something to do with men's thoughts, as well as with their works and deeds" (*WFB*, 4:109). As we have seen from previous analysis, the references to luck and to chance are ultimately to be read as references to Providence. So, here again Bacon is emphasizing, not his intelligence, but rather his calling by God to help usher in the new age of peace, harmony, and prosperity. Aphorism 123 seems to interrupt the reference to Providence with a curious reference to the difference between water and wine. "Now other men . . . have in the matter of sciences drunk a crude liquor like water. . . . Whereas I pledge mankind in a liquor strained from countless grapes, from grapes ripe and fully seasoned, . . . then squeezed in the press, and finally purified and clarified in the vat" (*WFB*, 4:109–10). Spedding cites a reference to Philocrates as a source for the water-to-wine comparison.[8] Given the broad biblical references throughout *The New Organon*, however, another reference comes more readily to mind: the wedding at Cana, where Jesus transforms water into wine.[9] According to the Gospel of John, this is Jesus' first miracle and the first sign of his divinity. Given the several occasions where Bacon minimizes his own importance, it is not likely that his purpose is to compare himself to Jesus. Instead, he is employing a central biblical motif of deliverance or rescue that is divinely provided. This reference, therefore, continues broad apocalyptic themes in *The New Organon* and fits the previous aphorism, where Bacon diminishes his role in order to accentuate that of God. In a similar way, it could be said that the conversion of water to wine does not depend on the person Jesus. What is important is God's use of him to provide deliverance for humanity. In aphorism 124 Bacon again juxtaposes his view of knowledge to the conventional view, which holds contemplative knowledge to be the highest and the practical arts to be inferior. Bacon, on the other hand, contends that philosophy is too often speculative and too far removed from nature to be able to produce benefits for humanity. Bacon's statement is worth quoting at length:

> For I am building in the human understanding a true model of the world, such as it is in fact, not such as a man's own reason would have it to be; a thing which cannot be done without a very diligent dissection and anatomy of the world. But I say that those foolish and apish images of the worlds which the fancies of men have created in philosophical systems, must be utterly scattered to the winds. Be it known then how vast a difference there is (as I said above) between the Idols of the human mind and the Ideas of the divine. The former are nothing more than arbitrary abstractions; the latter are the creator's own stamp upon creation, impressed and defined in matter by true and exquisite lines. Truth therefore and utility are here the very same things and works themselves are of greater value as pledges of truth than as contributing to the comforts of life. (*WFB*, 4:110)

In aphorism 128 Bacon warns again that his method needs to be tried because no progress is coming from methods currently used, and aphorisms 129 and 130 stress the reasons to hope that progress will occur. Bacon again cites the unprecedented advances made in recent times. He says that printing, gunpowder, and the magnet have "changed the whole face and state of things throughout the world; the first in literature, the second in warfare, the third in navigation; whence have followed innumerable changes; insomuch that no empire, no sect, no star seems to have exerted greater power and influence in human affairs" (*WFB*, 4:114). Earlier Bacon had noted that such discoveries are the highest thing that humanity can attain, because "discoveries are as it were new creations, and imitations of God's works" (*WFB*, 4:113) In other words, humanity comes closest to fulfilling its potential when it exerts creative control over nature, becomes a co-creator with God, and is able to provide benefits to humanity. Bacon then juxtaposes the exercise of power over nature to three inferior forms of human aspiration.

> The first is of those who desire to extend their own power in their native country; which kind is vulgar and degenerate. The second is of those who labour to extend the power of their country and its

dominion among men. This certainly has more dignity, though not less covetousness. But if a man endeavour to establish and extend the power and dominion of the human race itself over the universe, his ambition (if ambition it can be called) is without doubt both a more wholesome thing and more noble than the other two. (*WFB*, 4:114)

Here again Bacon is drawing an essential distinction between selfish ambition and charity. Bacon next turns to the ancient tradition of giving divine honors to inventors and honoring them more than those who rendered service to the state, and he asks: "if men have thought so much of some one particular discovery as to regard him as more than man who has been able by some benefit to make the whole human race his debtor, how much higher a thing to discover that by means of which all things else shall be discovered with ease" (*WFB*, 4:115). It is hard to reconcile Bacon's professed modesty and humility with the evident claim that his contribution is more than any one single invention; it is the means to master nature totally. Should he not then receive the highest imaginable honors from humanity? Bacon concludes this aphorism by stating again that the mastery of nature, the expanding of human dominion, is God-given. "Only let the human race recover that right over nature which belongs to it by divine bequest, and let power be given it; the exercise thereof will be governed by sound reason and true religion" (*WFB*, 4:115). This statement also is curious. Bacon has over the last several paragraphs discussed pride and ambition. He has spoken of some ambitions being more noble than others, but he has given little or no evidence that humanity is capable of selfless generosity and charity. In fact, immediately before the lines just quoted, Bacon acknowledges that human talents can be debased and used for wickedness and for material gain. Why, then, does Bacon expect humanity suddenly to have a change of heart? Bacon provides little by way of explanation. He simply asserts that the benefits he will bring to humankind will have such a transforming effect that human life will be governed by reason and by true religion. If we try to determine the basis of Bacon's optimism regarding this transformation of human behavior, there does not seem to be any explanation other than a millenarian hope and expectation. This dimension of Bacon's philosophy is its most extraordinary and can only be understood in relation to his religious conviction that true religion and a proper understanding of nature will overcome the sins of pride and vanity and restore humanity to its prelapsarian purity. The *New Atlantis* portrays the utopian order that will result.

In many ways aphorism 129 is the real conclusion to book 1 of *The New Organon*. Aphorism 130 moves from his vision of the reform that is possible to a transition in which he concedes that his findings are preliminary and provisional.

## The Second Book of Aphorisms

The second book of aphorisms does not need to be examined in as much detail as the first. Most of its aphorisms compare and contrast the primary principles of Bacon's epistemology to Plato's and Aristotle's systems of philosophy.[10] While this element of Bacon's work obviously is crucial, our interest is more in Bacon's vision of what can be accomplished by his method than with the method itself. One key element presented in book 2, however, needs to be at least briefly considered: Bacon's discussion of forms as the ordering structure that God gives to matter. The human mind, in order to understand nature and be able to exploit it, must investigate material substances, but the real search is for the forms contained within matter. This part of Bacon's epistemology follows traditional idealism. Aphorism 15, however, contains a passage that is crucial for understanding Bacon's instauration or re-edification: "To God, truly, the Giver and Architect of Forms, and it may be to the angels and higher intelligences, it belongs to have an affirmative knowledge of forms immediately and from the first contemplation. But this assuredly is more than man can do, to whom it is granted only to proceed at first by negatives, and at last to end in affirmatives, after exclusion has been exhausted" (*WFB*, 4:145). Two aspects of this process need comment. First, Bacon says this method of proceeding by both negatives and positives is necessary because the human mind is prone to false constructions. Unless it is firmly grounded in empirical analysis, the mind is inclined to fantasy. If we were to pause to ask why this is so, we would not find a direct answer; but if we recall the several instances when Bacon contrasts the prelapsarian condition to the present state of disorder, we understand. Because of the sin of pride, humanity is inclined to build Towers of Babel; and because humanity sinned against God and had to be punished, humanity has to labor diligently to gain any benefit from nature. This is why Bacon says direct knowledge of forms is accessible to God but not to man. Humanity is capable of coming to know the structure of the natural world in the same way that God knows it or as fully as God knows it, but humans cannot do it through rational speculation. They must pay their dues and work laboriously.

Aphorism 26 describes this process of investigation and compares it to fire as a means of refining and purifying. This is a fairly obvious alchemical reference, and aphorism 51 cites instances of magic in a positive way because magic does produce useful knowledge, though its means of attaining such knowledge are flawed. Aphorism 52 departs from Bacon's technical discussion of his epistemology to restate the goal and benefit. Bacon says that he is handing over to humanity "their fortunes" now that their understanding has been emancipated and has come of age. It has been emancipated from the Idols of the Mind, has matured, and is now capable of generating (cf. *WFB*, 4:246–48). By now this contrast between sterility and productivity is a familiar theme. These changes, Bacon says, cannot but improve man's estate and enlarge his power over nature. On the surface, there is no necessary connection between correcting epistemological errors and improving the human condition; but by now, it is evident in Bacon's writings that he equates true knowledge with instrumental power over nature, and he asserts an inevitable connection between right knowledge and an improvement of the human condition. The frame of reference for understanding these assumptions is made clear in this aphorism when Bacon says:

> For man by the fall fell at the same time from his state of innocency and from his dominion over creation. Both of these losses however can even in this life be in some part repaired; the former by religion and faith, the latter by arts and sciences. For creation was not by the curse made altogether and for ever a rebel, but in virtue of that charter "in the sweat of thy face shalt thou eat bread," it is now by various labours (not certainly by disputations or idle magical ceremonies, but by various labours) at length and in some measure subdued to the supplying of man with bread; that is, to the uses of human life. (*WFB*, 4:247–48)

This passage not only is the last sentence of the last aphorism of book 2; it is the climax, the end, which integrates the various elements of Bacon's program for rebuilding.

## Conclusion

While Bacon centers his complaints on philosophical and epistemological problems, his ultimate concern is with the source of disorder and confusion that is the primary impediment to human well-being. He begins by faulting philosophical schools for clinging to the engendering ideas of a major philosopher and enshrining his ideas in a sterile system. From this critique of the Western philosophical tradition Bacon moves to a more general problem in human nature: the tendency to pride and self-infatuation. Bacon says the human mind is inclined to build elaborate intellectual systems and then take pride in its ingenuity. When Bacon explains the source of these human faults, his ultimate reference is the biblical account of Adam's creation and fall. Adam fell through pride, that is, he fell through a rejection of the duties that God gave him and in the attempt to create a second reality out of his own fantasies. The punishment for humanity's rebellion was the loss of Paradise and the loss of dominion over nature. But of course the biblical account does not end here. While humanity is punished for its sin by being forced to work hard to produce benefits from the natural world, the account promises that humanity will not forever be alienated from God and from its rightful place in Creation. At a time when God chooses, he will begin to restore humanity to its rightful place.

It is against the backdrop of this biblical account that Bacon interprets his own age. The disorder that permeates the world is the result of continuing sin based on pride and on laziness. In the aphorisms Bacon makes it clear that humanity is so far removed from any hope that God has once again intervened on humanity's behalf to provide "new mercies." God has done this by providing humanity with startling, unexpected breakthroughs that undercut some of the most deeply held convictions about what can be known and what can be done in the natural world. The most frequently cited example is the discovery of the New World, which, for

Bacon, is emblematic of the faults with the knowledge systems of the past. Geography and other natural sciences inherited from the ancients are fragmentary, limited, and incomplete. Rather than being encyclopedic collections of the wisdom of the past, they are records of human ignorance transmitted from generation to generation. The ignorance and the error of these traditions are exposed through the dramatic discoveries that opened the New World. In the aphorisms Bacon also mentions other recent discoveries—the magnetic compass, for example, which made the wisdom of the past look foolish. But it took these dramatic breakthroughs in order to get human beings to abandon the Idols of the Mind. As we have seen, Bacon contends that these events are so unprecedented that they can rightly be regarded as miracles. The apocalyptic shift from darkness to light is grounded, therefore, in the opening of the New World and other discoveries and inventions that have transformed human experience. For Bacon these works are due to Providence. This attribution is made clear as Bacon moves through the various aphorisms. At the outset Bacon uses words like *accident, luck,* and *happenstance;* but in aphorism 93 Bacon indicates that among the errors that humans have made is the error of calling divine Providence fate.

These elements of Bacon's religion are essential to understanding Bacon's program of instauration. Without them, there is no basis for confidence in the instauration. We pointed to the key example of this in the preceding analysis. In aphorism 126 Bacon concedes that inventions have led to luxury and to a preoccupation with material things; but he insists that pride and greed will not dominate if his method is employed. Humanity's base impulses will be corrected by reason and by true religion. This assertion—not any evidence to counter his protracted discussion and criticism of human sin, pride, greed, and ambition—is all that Bacon offers. And it is worth noting that Bacon, an otherwise practical man, offers no description or program for introducing his system into the social and political structures. Even the *New Atlantis* offers no description of political organization. The only mention made of political order is in giving credit to King Salomona for helping found the House of Solomon. While Plato, in the *Republic,* provides a detailed program for re-education, Bacon does not find it necessary to discuss plans for correcting and overcoming the deeply ingrained human sins of pride, laziness, and ambition. He simply portrays a utopian order that escapes disorder and corruption through right reason and true religion.

These biblical and apocalyptic themes are also crucial to Bacon's understanding of his role in the instauration. Bacon has a heightened sense of vocation or special calling that parallels that of the Old Testament judges, priests, or prophets. Like Moses, he believes he is chosen to deliver the people from bondage and into their Promised Land. In other contexts, Bacon aligns himself closer to the Old Testament prophets. He even names one of them—Daniel—several times. Daniel was a visionary, who saw how disorder would be destroyed and the new order installed. Another example is the eighth-century prophet Amos, who criticized the worship of idols and urged people to return to the true God. This biblical sense of vocation stands in sharp contrast to modern scholarship's depiction of Bacon as a modernist and a secularist.

This analysis has shown that scholars who concentrate their analyses of *The New Organon* on Bacon's epistemological critique often ignore the apocalyptic and biblical themes that provide the context for understanding Bacon's reform or instauration of knowledge. Bacon's instauration is not the project of a secular modernist; it is a program for returning humanity to its prelapsarian condition. That this is the case is clear in Bacon's repeated references to the relation of Adam to God and to the Creation prior to the Fall and in his description of the consequences of the sin of pride that alienates man from God and makes his intellect sterile. It is also evident in the general tone and structure of *The New Organon*. Like a biblical prophet, Bacon condemns the ignorance and error that have alienated humanity from God and then presents signs and reasons for believing that God is at work to repair the rupture and allow humanity to return to its true condition. This apocalyptic tone has to be recognized in order to understand how Bacon can believe that the wretched state of affairs can be corrected.

# Chapter 4

## Themes and Images in Bacon's Early Writings

We began this study with the *New Atlantis* (1626) because it offered the fullest vision of Bacon's instauration and because the principal religious themes in Bacon's writings are found in it. We then looked at two of his major philosophical texts, *The Great Instauration* and *The New Organon*, which were published in 1620, to show the centrality of religion to Bacon's description of his instauration. This chapter will examine five of Bacon's earliest philosophical works, including *The Advancement of Learning* (1605) and *Wisdom of the Ancients* (1609). The other three are manuscripts that were not published but were circulated by Bacon to a close network of philosophers, theologians, and biblical scholars and church officials.[1] These works include *The Masculine Birth of Time* (1603), *Thoughts and Conclusions* (1607), and *The Refutation of Philosophies* (1608).[2] The purpose is to demonstrate that the religious motifs examined thus far were present in Bacon's early writings as well. More specifically, this analysis will show:

- The notion of the instauration of both natural philosophy and religion is a primary preoccupation of Bacon's from the outset.

- Bacon's sense of providential action in his own age provides the impetus for the wholesale instauration, but the evidence of this providential renewal and regeneration requires that humanity participate actively in the restoration of philosophy and religion. Such action is necessary to reorient humanity from the original sin of pride and to establish a prelapsarian reunion of humanity with God and with nature.

- Bacon relates his effort to establish a new philosophy to ancient traditions of learning that operated, however briefly, before Plato and Aristotle deformed Western philosophy.
- Bacon emphasizes the reintegration of theoretical and practical knowledge. He cites magic and alchemy as imperfect examples. While he clearly indicates that both are flawed in their present form, they are, nevertheless, part of a pre-Socratic ancient wisdom and point the way toward the reintegration of theoretical and practical knowledge for the present age.
- Bacon's understanding of himself as an instrument of Providence is present from his earliest writings through to the last.

The examination of these five texts will not be as thoroughgoing as the analysis of the three analyzed thus far. The focus will be more selective and will highlight key themes, images, and motifs in these works that correspond to the themes found in *The Great Instauration*, *The New Organon*, and the *New Atlantis*.

## *The Masculine Birth of Time*

Bacon's Latin text, as it appears in *WFB*, 3:521–34, has a title page and twelve pages of text, which are divided into three sections, or books, and discuss the proper interpretation of nature. The title page carries the principal title *Temporis Partus Masculus* (The Masculine Birth of Time) and the subtitle *Instauratio magna imperii humani in universum* (The Great Instauration of the Dominion of Man over the Universe). The title itself is highly symbolic. The phrase "masculine birth" underscores the emphasis on productivity and fecundity. In the *New Atlantis* the Feast of the Family ceremony, honoring the patriarch of the family, associates masculinity with productivity, while the feminine is associated with nurturing. So a masculine birth of time would be an age of potency and productivity. The image is, therefore, a corollary to Bacon's frequent use of the image of "the marriage of the mind to nature" and to his emphasis on the generative properties of true philosophy, which he contrasts to the sterility of false philosophy. The subtitle of this early work contains Bacon's leitmotif of instauration. While the instauration being discussed in the text is restoration of philosophy, the full title, *The Great Instauration of the Dominion of Man over the Universe,* is clearly taken from Genesis 1:26, where God gives humanity dominion over nature. The biblical context of the discussion of the renewal of philosophy is reinforced by the prayer on the title page:

> To God the Father
>
> God the Word, God the Spirit, we pour out our humble and burning prayers, that mindful of the miseries of the human race and this our mortal pilgrimage in which we wear out evil days and few, they would send down upon us new streams from the fountains of their mercy for the relief of our distress; and this too we would ask, that our human interests may not stand in the way of the divine, nor from the unlocking of the paths of sense and the enkindling of a greater light in nature may any unbelief or darkness arise in our minds to shut out the knowledge of the divine mysteries; but rather that the intellect made clean and pure from all vain fancies, and subjecting itself in voluntary submission to the divine oracles, may render to faith the things that belong to faith. (*PFB*, 59)

This prayer has obvious similarities to the prayer in the preface to *The Great Instauration,* where Bacon prays for relief from the misery of the human condition and associates this relief with a recovery of the right knowledge of the Creation that would restore humanity to its dominion over nature. Here the prayer is addressed to a trinitarian God: God the Father, God the Word, and God the Spirit. In Christian theology God the Father is associated with the creation of the universe; and God the Spirit is associated with the presence of God or with providential guidance. The reference to God as the Word or the "logos" appears in the Gospel of John, which is aimed at Greco-Roman philosophers searching for the knowledge (logos) of the structure of reality and the source of its order, beauty, and harmony. Bacon appears to be using the term in its philosophical meaning and, perhaps, also drawing upon the dual meaning of the Hebrew term *dabar,* which means both to speak and to act. In Genesis, for example, God brings the world into being by speaking. Bacon's prayer seems to be invoking this notion as well. For philosophy to be properly restored and for humanity to have dominion over nature, humanity must come to know God's language of creation. Bacon makes this point again in *The New Organon,* as we have already seen. The prayer also establishes a juxtaposition between right knowledge grounded in an understanding of nature and the sterile fantasies of the human imagination. This again is a main motif in both *The Great Instauration* and *The New Organon.* So, this title page embodies several motifs that are fundamental elements of Bacon's later writings. The central symbol of instauration is prominent, and its association with a recovery of the prelapsarian relation of humanity to God and to nature is established.

While this early work shares these general themes with two of Bacon's major texts, significant differences of tone and emphasis can be noted. The body of the text takes the form of a lecture or discourse by a wise man to a young man seeking initiation into philosophy.[3] The title of the first chapter, "The Legitimate Mode of Handing on the Torch of Science," indicates that the speaker is someone who has been able to escape the ignorance and errors that plague his age and is now willing to impart that knowledge to those who are willing to learn. While this title indicates that the knowledge being passed is science, its oracular mode is more common in esoteric philosophy or mystery religion. This mode of presentation is found, for example, in the *Corpus Hermeticum,* where the divine messenger, Pimander, reveals the mysteries of the divine Creation to Hermes Trismegistus. The reference to "the torch of science" in the title invites comparison to the images of light that play a prominent role in Bacon's later writings, especially in the *New Atlantis* and *The New Organon,* where Bacon links light with the right knowledge of nature. The meaning of the phrase "legitimate mode" is not immediately clear; but it becomes evident in the body of the text that Bacon is focusing on the stem of this word—*legis,* or law. The legitimate mode of passing on or renewing the torch of science is to ground it again in the laws of nature rather than in the sterile speculations of the human imagination. In the third paragraph of the text, he contrasts legitimate knowledge grounded in the study of nature to the "idols" of the human imagination.

> My intention is to impart to you, not the figments of my own brain, nor the shadows thrown by words, nor a mixture of religion and science, nor a few commonplace observations or notorious experiments tricked out to make a composition as fanciful as a stage-play. No; I am come in very truth leading to you Nature with all her children to bind her to your service and make her your slave. Does it seem to you then that I bear in my hands a subject of instruction which I can risk defiling by any fault in my handling of it, whether springing from pretence or incompetence? So may it go with me, my son; so may I succeed in my only earthly wish, namely to stretch the deplorably narrow limits of man's dominion over the universe to their promised bounds; as I shall hand on to you, with the most loyal faith, out of the profoundest care for the future of which I am capable, after prolonged examination both of the state of nature and the state of the human mind, by the most legitimate method, the instruction I have to convey. (*PFB*, 62)

Four paragraphs later the speaker's juxtaposition of the legitimate study of nature to the idols of the mind continues when he contends that Plato must be summoned before the bar, where he will be accused of teaching philosophers "to turn our mind's eye inward and grovel before our own blind and confused idols under the name of contemplative philosophy" (*PFB*, 64). This reference to a legal summons clarifies Bacon's use of *legitimate* as a legal motif.

The wise man (speaker) attacks Aristotle and Plato as well as Galen, Hippocrates, and their current disciples, who have derailed philosophy from the investigation of nature to the creation and perpetuation of an idolatrous worship of schools and systems of thought. While there is a difference in the charges brought against each of the schools, the common thread is that they perpetuate a philosophical system that has moved away from the empirical investigation of nature and, therefore, not only do not produce useful knowledge but have the arrogance to claim that such knowledge is not accessible. Anticipating a possible objection to his wholesale indictment of ancient philosophies, the wise man acknowledges that some insights have been gained and some relief of man's estate has occurred; but, according to the narrator, these results are due, not to the method used, but to accidental discovery. Because the discovery is not the result of the method, it does not generate any further advances in knowledge. Further on the speaker likens these discoveries to "the man who understands only his own vernacular" who is given a text in an unknown tongue.

> He picks out a few words here and there which sound like, or are spelled like, words in his own tongue. With complete confidence he jumps to the conclusion that their meaning is the same, though as a rule this is very far from true. Then, on the basis of this resemblance, he proceeds to guess the sense of the rest of the document with great mental exertion and equal licence. This is a true image of these interpreters of nature. For each man brings his own idols—I am not now speaking of those of the stage, but particularly of those of the market-place and the cave—and applies them, like his own vernacular, to the interpretation of nature, snatching at any facts which fit in with his preconceptions and forcing everything else into harmony with them. (*PFB*, 69–70)

In this compact statement we see several of Bacon's primary themes. In *The New Organon* Bacon speaks of the language of nature and maintains that human beings must learn its alphabet—the basic building blocks of the language of nature—in order to understand nature and reap the benefits. In this text Bacon begins on the title page with the prayer to "God the Word" that human pride can be overcome so that divine mercy can be granted to ease the human condition. In the passage just quoted Bacon again is likening even the best philosophical systems that had been transmitted from the past to a man who forces an unknown text to fit his own vocabulary. In some instances this arbitrary linking of human language to the language of nature produces a correspondence and some benefit is gained; but such gains are partial and fragmentary and misrepresent the whole of nature.

Having pointed to the state of disorder and cited examples from each of the sciences, Bacon concludes this text with the declaration that the principal task at hand is not a critical attack on prevailing philosophies. "The need is to set up in the midst one bright and radiant light of truth, shedding its beams in all directions and dispelling all errors in a moment. It is pointless to light pale candles and carry them about to every nook and cranny of error and falsehood" (*PFB,* 70). This brief text, however, does not contain the new epistemology.

How, then, is the text to be understood? Like Bacon's later writings, *The Masculine Birth of Time* places the most weight on the effort to get others to recognize the current state of disorder and to begin looking for an alternative. More than anything, these are efforts to make potential disciples realize that the current state of disorder is not natural or inalterable. The present condition is a result of human rebellion against both God and nature. Humanity attempted to be its own god and create its own world out of its imagination. The way back to a prelapsarian state is to recognize the nature of the sin and attempt to overcome it. The first important step is to abandon idle philosophical speculation and return to a study of nature. To accomplish this, a new beginning is necessary. The various philosophical schools—even if they have produced some positive results—need to be cleared away so that a new beginning can occur. The proof that the new philosophy is on the right track is the positive benefit gained from such searches. That is, right knowledge will provide the new mercies to relieve the human condition—as the opening prayer indicates.

Having pointed to similarities between this early text and Bacon's later writings, it is important to note a significant difference. This text is presented in an oracular mode in which a mature wise man offers to initiate a young disciple into the truth. As already noted, this mode is more typical of the forms used in esoteric religions rather than in schools of philosophy. It is found, for example, in the Gnostic text "The Hymn of the Pearl." In that text a divine messenger is sent to awaken one of the sons of God, who has fallen into the ignorance and error of worldly ways. It is also reminiscent of text of the *Corpus Hermeticum,* which laments the disordered state of the present world and promises that God will renew the world and restore humanity to its proper state. Bacon's text shares with the Gnostic and Hermetic texts this sense that initiation depends on a state of worthiness of the initiate. This is ironic because in some of his later writings, Bacon criticizes esoteric philosophies like alchemy or magic for placing too much emphasis on the special spiritual state of its practitioners. Here, however, Bacon presents himself as a wise man who has attained the truth and is seeking to initiate a select few. One possible explanation might be that Bacon is convinced that a spiritual awakening is already under way and that there are worthy disciples capable of restoring humanity's dominion over nature. As we have already seen, recovery of religious truth is for Bacon only one part of instauration. Religious reform is incomplete without a restoration of an adequate philosophy of nature.

As already noted, little is known about the circulation of this text. Unlike Bacon's later published writings, which are dedicated to the king or are obviously prepared for a general audience, this text seems to be for a privileged few who Bacon hopes will join him in ushering in the new age of peace, harmony, and prosperity. The success of the text depends on the intellectual and spiritual state of its reader and the reader's ability to recognize the kernel of truth it contains.

## *Thoughts and Conclusions*

*Thoughts and Conclusions,* which is almost three times as long as *The Masculine Birth of Time,* presents a series of meditations on the contemporary disarray in natural philosophy; the need for a method of induction, which could move the stagnant sciences forward; and the merits of cataloging recent advances in the sciences and practical arts, which could give hope that humanity is entering the new age of peace, harmony, and prosperity that would restore humanity to its proper relation to nature and to God. The first thirteen of these meditations take up the first topic—an analysis of the present state of disorder. The last six weave together a brief description of the proper method of induction with reasons for hope that progress can be made.[4] In its structure, then, *Thoughts and Conclusions* anticipates the structure of Bacon's *New Organon.* The two works also share similar themes and descriptions of Bacon's indictment against current philosophy and his description of the basis for hope. The opening meditation catalogs the stagnant state of medicine, alchemy, and the mechanical arts and attributes to random chance the few breakthroughs that have been made by the sciences. The second meditation criticizes the history of philosophy for not recognizing how little has been accomplished by the sciences, given the broad span of almost 2500 years. Lamentably, humanity has enshrined these few discoveries and has concluded that further advance is impossible. In Bacon's words, the philosophers boast "that whatever has not yet been discovered is indiscoverable" (*PFB*, 74). Meditations 4, 5, and 6 attribute the lack of success to philosophical system builders, who do not ground their systems in the study of nature; to an error in the definition of the goal of science, which should be steadily enriching the human race through new works and powers; and to the neglect of natural philosophy. According to Bacon, there has only been one brief interval in the history of humanity—the pre-Socratic period—in which natural philosophy flourished.

Meditations 8 through 11 blame the degeneration of natural philosophy on three sources: "the bad organization of cultural institutions," the damaging effects of public opinion, and the limitations of language. In these sections Bacon is criticizing the philosophy taught in universities; a general climate of opinion (the opinion that the present age has no great heroes like those who made discoveries in the past); and the imprecise use of language by both scholars and a general public, which perpetuates "vulgar opinions" and "popular notions" rather than careful analysis and the discovery of the truth of nature. As a result of these various adverse influences, barriers have been erected to the recovery and pursuit of truth. In describing these barriers, Bacon uses the familiar image of pillars that create a false barrier to expansion of knowledge or create a sterile state of affairs that does not permit generation of productive knowledge (*PFB*, 79–82). In describing this sterile state in meditation 13, Bacon invokes the legend of Scylla, which he also uses in *The Great Instauration*. "That lady had the face and countenance of a maiden, but her loins were girt about with yelping hounds. So these doctrines present at first view a charming face, but the rash wooer who should essay the generative parts in hope of offspring, is blessed only with shrill disputes and arguments" (*PFB*, 86). Bacon also stresses that the philosophy that has come down from the Greeks not only presents a sterile, unproductive mode of inquiry but also obscures earlier, more productive modes. Here, again, Bacon has in mind the inquiries of the pre-Socratics; but he adds, as he did in *The Masculine Birth of Time* and in *The New Organon*, that the effort to recover the truth from the fragments preserved from a distant, remote form of philosophy is less productive than attempting to study nature directly.

> He reserved the right to an opinion of his own about those distant ages, but thought it must not be allowed to influence the business in hand. Whether or not discoveries now made had been known to the ancients and the knowledge had been extinguished and rekindled with the changes of human fortune, is a matter of no moment, just as it matters not at all whether the New World is the old Atlantis or is now discovered for the first time. For truth must be sought from the light of nature, not recovered from the darkness of antiquity. (*PFB*, 87)

In meditations 14 and 15 Bacon introduces his method of induction and calls for a philosophy of invention. Before discussing induction Bacon points to the sterility of Aristotelian philosophy and of the syllogism. The alternative mode of philosophical investigation is induction, but Bacon warns that induction up to now has been limited and flawed. The difference between induction as it has been used and Bacon's new method is as different, Bacon claims, as the experience of the water drinker and the wine drinker. Ordinary induction is like "drinking an intellectual beverage which either flows from a natural source or has been raised with slight labor from some well." That is, it is a method that draws the benefit directly from nature, or it applies only a little human effort to acquire what is naturally available. Bacon's induction, on the other hand, is like the wine drinker who "prefers a draught prepared from innumerable grapes, grapes matured and plucked in due season from selected clusters, crushed in the press, purged and clarified in the vat; a draught moreover which has been so treated as to qualify its powers of inebriating, since he is resolved to owe nothing to the heady fumes of vain imaginings" (*PFB*, 90). The obvious thrust of this allegorical comparison is that Bacon's method requires detailed investigation and repeated efforts to perfect the stage of the process in order to produce the greatest benefit from the potential present in natural things.[5] In the meditation on the need for a philosophy of invention Bacon asserts that the way in which investigations into nature have been conducted must be reformed because they are not firmly grounded in the investigation of nature itself but are based more on the systematic procedures born out of the fantasies of philosophers. True invention requires a detailed study of nature and a rigorous effort to employ the benefits of nature for the human good.

The remaining four sections (16 through 19) shift from an indictment of the present state of disorder to an affirmation of the potential for dramatic advances. Meditation 16 is titled "The Time is Come for a Fresh Start." Here Bacon focuses on recent developments that have altered humanity's understanding of nature and presented unanticipated potential for the mastery of nature. The three that he mentions are printing, gunpowder, and the nautical (magnetic) needle.[6] Each of these is an example of combining induction with the mechanical arts and of moving from a fairly simplistic human invention to a highly sophisticated one that opened unimagined potential. But, Bacon adds, they have been discovered more or less in isolation. As important as they are, they only signal in a small way the enormous advances that can occur if a proper method is developed and a concerted effort is made by many scientists. In meditation 17 Bacon returns to the point made earlier when he claimed that there has been only one brief period in which natural philosophy held prominence and then only for a short time. He intimates that a new period is beginning that holds the prospects of far more results. The brighter prospect is due to what Bacon regards as stable political conditions but also, and more important, the prospects are brighter because Bacon is pointing the way to the appropriate method. Once it is spelled out and several devoted scientists join the call, tremendous advances can be expected. In meditation 18 Bacon briefly outlines the procedure for advancing the state of learning. The first step is to catalog all available data or facts that are the result of proper investigation of nature. These become a starting point for the application of Bacon's method of induction, which can exploit these and produce far greater results. Bacon continues this proposal in meditation 19, where he proposes creating tables of data that can serve as a guide. Bacon indicates that he will only communicate these tables to a few select men. Even though what he is proposing is an empirical method that should convince any rational human being, Bacon is persuaded that the disorder is so profound that he must select very carefully his first corps of disciples.

This early work contains many of the images and symbols at the heart of Bacon's later published writings. In meditation 13, for example, Bacon inverts the typical Renaissance idea that Greek philosophy represents a high point in human knowledge and says that the period of the Greeks "must rank only as the childhood of science. It has what is proper to boys. It is a great chatter-box and is too immature to breed" (*PFB*, 83). At several points Bacon refers to human fantasies as idols or as stage plays, that is, as fictions borne out of the mind that have little or nothing to do with reality. We have already noted his use of the idea of pillars as barriers to knowledge and his use of the legend of Scylla, and we have mentioned that the organization of this essay is similar to that of *The New Organon*. It begins with a stinging indictment of the disordered state of knowledge of the sciences, then offers reasons for hope that this state of affairs can be changed for the better. The hope for improvement is linked both to Bacon's discovery of a method and to providential action by God to renew the world and restore humanity to its rightful place.

Both *The Masculine Birth of Time* and *Thoughts and Conclusions* show that Bacon was convinced from early on that his own age was one in which an instauration was possible. While the previous 2500 years of human history are primarily a record of human ignorance and error, his own age would usher in a new beginning or renewal. The two works are permeated by a sense of apocalyptic expectation because Bacon believes Providence is at work renewing the world and creating new opportunities for humanity to regain dominion over nature. In each work the source of intellectual disorder and of unnecessary human suffering is traced to the sin of intellectual pride. Humanity becomes fascinated with its own intellectual constructions and stops devoting its attention to the study of nature. The result is that humanity can no longer discover in nature all of the benefits God intended. Therefore, Bacon associates the recovery from this original sin of pride with major improvements to the human condition. In these two works, in one fashion or another, it becomes evident that Bacon understands himself as an agent for restoration or renewal. In later works this theme will be more pronounced, but it is clearly evident here. It is also clear in both works that Bacon regards the opening of the New World, which is accomplished through technological innovation and what Bacon calls either chance or Providence, as a signal indicating that the barriers that have prevented humanity from regaining dominion over the world are being torn down and that progress is now possible. As noted above, these main themes are communicated in what become the primary images and symbols of the later works. He refers to the age of Greek philosophy as a stage of adolescence and not of maturity, of sterility rather than productivity. He uses his metaphor of time being like a river, which brings forward only what is light rather than substantial. He describes human creation as idols—that is, false objects of human worship, a form of self worship that interferes with the worship of God the Creator and his Creation.[7]

## *The Refutation of Philosophies*

The third of Bacon's early writings to be examined here is *The Refutation of Philosophies*. In the opening paragraph the narrator, presumably Bacon, explains that he is in the process of preparing a refutation of prevailing philosophies but finds the learned ignorance of the age to be so thoroughgoing that he despairs of finding an appropriate means of breaking through.[8] Under the circumstances, the only effective way to open a new perspective and to advance learning is to point to certain signs, that is, objective evidence that demonstrates the sterility of the current philosophies and offers hope that advances can be made. While he is in the midst of his work and vacillating between despair and hope, he receives a visit from a friend who has just returned from Paris and brings with him an account of a meeting in which a learned man spoke to a receptive audience about the very things with which Bacon himself is concerned.

This mode of presentation of Bacon's main themes, namely, the criticism of prevailing philosophies, the introduction of a better method, and the marshaling of evidence that progress can occur, appears to be yet another search for a venue that will allow him to present his argument in a way that will gain him the audience he needs. This particular mode of presentation has affinities with both Thomas More's *Utopia* and the dialogues of Plato. More's *Utopia* begins in a distant metropolitan city where several prominent political and intellectual elite gather to benefit from the knowledge of the foreign visitor renowned for his vast learning. Bacon's opening also resembles Platonic dialogues in which an observer reports to a friend of hearing Socrates discuss an important topic or to move knowledge out of the confusion of the Sophists to a deeper level of truth. But there is an important difference between Bacon's narrative and the other two. In More's

*Utopia*, the wise man, Hythloday, is questioned and challenged by prominent proponents of prevailing points of view. Through the interaction between Hythloday and his opponents, the critique of the present state of affairs develops and alternatives emerge. The Platonic dialogues also center around debate between a man of learning and those who hold the prevailing opinions of the day. Bacon's text, on the other hand, describes the gathering and the speaker in the following way:

> There were some fifty men there, all of mature years, not a young man among them, all bearing the stamp of dignity and probity. He picked out among them officers of state, senators, distinguished churchmen, people from all ranks of life, and foreigners from various nations. At his entry they were chatting easily among themselves but sitting in rows as if expecting somebody. Not long after there entered to them a man of peaceful and serene air, save that his face had become habituated to the expression of pity. They all stood up in his honour. (*PFB*, 104)

In Bacon's setting the men are talking casually among themselves until the honored speaker arrives; then they take their seats and wait for him to address them. Although these men are described as mature and of high standing, the speaker addresses them as his sons. In this setting Bacon obviously is not interested in creating a situation in which dialogue can occur. In the opening sections and in the body of the text, Bacon dismisses the value of any attempt to try to engage in debate with those who hold the prevailing points of view. Their opinions are so ingrained, they cannot be changed. What offers hope to Bacon, however, is that there are a few men in England and in other parts of Europe who have recognized the bankruptcy of the prevailing Aristotelian philosophy and are willing to consider an alternative. Structured this way, *The Refutation of Philosophies* is similar to the format of *The Masculine Birth of Time*, where a wise man promised to initiate a young seeker of the truth into the true philosophy. It is also the mode of address of the Elders in the *New Atlantis*.

The body of the text recounts the address given by the stranger to those who are gathered in Paris. This opening statement is a declaration of humanity's true nature, which stands at odds with humanity's present condition.

> We are agreed, my sons, that you are men. That means, as I think, that you are not animals on their hind legs, but mortal gods. God, the creator of the universe and of you, gave you souls capable of understanding the world but not to be satisfied with it alone. He reserved for himself your faith, but gave the world over to your senses. Neither of these oracles did he wish to be clear, but wrapped in obscurity. Yet have you no ground for complaint that he makes you exert yourselves. Your reward is to know the excellence of things. Now, so far as the things of God are concerned, I have the best hopes for you; but as regards human things I fear you are wrapped in eternal night. If I am not mistaken you are convinced that the state of your sciences is sound and flourishing. For my part I warn you not to over-estimate the abundance or utility of what you have. It does not mark the pinnacle of your attainment, it does not give you mastery of your desires, it does not mean the end of your task. (*PFB*, 106)

In order that they might awaken from this darkness of the night the speaker asks his audience to look hard at the current state of philosophy. At first glance it appears to be very rich and luxurious; but on closer examination the whole of contemporary philosophy is based on a few fragments of Greek philosophy. More specifically, it is narrowly based on Aristotle and ignores other Greek philosophers. Moreover, it is now evident that the Greeks had limited experience on which to base their views of the natural world and of human history. Greek philosophy took its rise "in an age that bordered on fables, was poor in historical knowledge, was little informed or enlightened by travel and knowledge of the earth, lacked both the respect for antiquity and the wealth of our modern times, and was deficient in dignity and precedent." While the paucity of the Greeks' knowledge should be clear in present times, it was also evident in ancient times as well. "We must not shut our ears to the words of the Egyptian priest, spoken to a distinguished Greek statesmen and recorded by a famous Greek author. For he spoke like a true Oracle when he said: 'You Greeks are always children'" (*PFB*, 109).[9] The narrator then says they were childlike not only in their knowledge of the past but even more in their natural philosophy. What can be more childish than a philosophy prompting chatter and argument but incapable of producing beneficial results?

In spite of the obvious limitations and flaws of contemporary philosophy and its foundation in Greek thought, it is so ingrained in public opinion and in university learning that it is difficult to move beyond. Nevertheless, the speaker urges his audience to not give up hope. "Undoubtedly, sons, there is in the human soul some portion of our understanding, however preoccupied and beset, which welcomes truth" (*PFB,* 109). So despite the enormous power of the present disordered state, something in the human soul resonates to truth and offers the hope that the present disorder can be overcome. The speaker maintains, however, that his purpose is not to engage in a detailed criticism of prevailing philosophies. Ultimately, this produces no positive result. His intent, instead, is to offer "signs" or empirical evidence that any rational person will accept as evidence of the flaws of the present system, the need for a new method, and prospects that the present age is ushering in an age of progress. The speaker then indicates that the first sign to be considered is that of "fruit" or productivity. "There is no 'sign' more certain and more noble than that from fruits. In religion we are warned that faith be shown by works. It is altogether right to apply the same test to philosophy. If it be barren let it be set at naught" (*PFB,* 123–24). The second sign, "abundant harvest," seems to be the obverse of this. "I say that your philosophy—and it is a field which has been tilled and cultivated for ages—has not yielded one achievement tending to enrich and relieve man's estate, which can truthfully be set down to the credit of its speculations" (*PFB,* 125). The third sign is "progress," and for the last 2000 years the state of philosophy has remained virtually unchanged. The fourth sign is the testimony of the major philosophers themselves who claimed that "whatever in the sciences is unknown by them or untouched by their masters, should be firmly declared to be beyond the limits of the possible.... These pronouncements have no other sense or purpose than to promote a deliberate and artificial despair both as regards the acquisition of knowledge and the possibility of action" (*PFB,* 127). The speaker then begins to investigate the reason philosophy has been so unproductive. The concise answer is that the workings of the speculative system are not grounded in the study of nature. "Man looks down and studies nature as if from some remote and lofty tower." In fact, there is a prejudice against the laborious investigation of nature, and abstract speculation is considered the highest form of philosophy. As long as this attitude prevails, no progress can be expected. The speaker then advises that progress and productive results can be achieved only through a proper joining of the mind and nature, and he employs the now familiar marriage imagery.

> Let us establish a chaste and lawful marriage between Mind and Nature, with the divine mercy as bridewoman. And let us pray God, the Father of men and nature as well as of lights and consolations, by Whose power and will these things are done, that from that marriage may issue, not monsters of the imagination, but a race of heroes to subdue and extinguish such monsters, that is to say, wholesome and useful inventions to war against our human necessities and, so far as may be, to bring relief therefrom. (*PFB*, 131)

To further explain the proper relation of the mind and nature, the speaker likens true philosophy to the bee. While ants simply gather and consume what is readily available from nature, and spiders weave webs out of themselves, "the Bee adopts the middle course, drawing her material from the flowers of the garden or the field, but transforming it by a faculty peculiar to herself. Such should be the activity of a genuine philosophy. It should draw its material from natural history and mechanical experience, but not take it unaltered into the memory, but digest and assimilate it for storing in the understanding" (*PFB*, 131). If the mind and nature are properly joined, progress can be made and the poverty of ancient philosophy and its contemporary form will become evident. To illustrate, the speaker compares the recent discovery of the New World to the understanding of geography and the natural world that existed for more than 2000 years. While ancient exploration was limited by the warning "non plus ultra," or go no farther, recent inventions changed this warning into a mandate to "plus ultra," or to go farther still. What is now needed is to transform the new discoveries into productive gain for humanity.

> It would disgrace us, now that the wide spaces of the material globe, the lands and seas, have been broached and explored, if the limits of the intellectual globe should be set by the narrow discoveries of the ancients. Nor are those two enterprises, the opening up of the earth

and the opening up of the sciences, linked and yoked together in any trivial way. Distant voyages and travels have brought to light many things in nature, which may throw fresh light on human philosophy and science and correct by experience the opinions and conjectures of the ancients. Not only reason but prophecy connects the two. What else can the prophet mean who, in speaking about the last times, says: Many will pass through and knowledge will be multiplied? Does he not imply that the passing through or perambulation of the round earth and the increase or multiplication of science were destined to the same age and century? (*PFB*, 131–32)

Here the speaker links the opening of the world to providential intent. New opportunities for humanity have been created by God, but as the speaker noted at the very beginning of his speech, humanity must work hard to uncover the mysteries of nature and reap the benefits that God intends. The prophecy from the book of Daniel indicates, however, that God intends that both the opening of the New World and the opening of the intellectual world be accomplished in the same age—the current age.

In the final paragraph of this text, the speaker urges his audience to take full account of the progress that has been made, of the new opportunities, of the benefits gained from recent inventions and the providential opening of the world, and to take courage to undertake the difficult task at hand: to throw off sterile philosophy and engage directly in the productive marriage of the mind with nature. The reaction of the audience was that they "talked to one another saying that they were like men who had come suddenly out of the thick shade into the open light and were for the moment dazzled, but carried with them a sure and happy augury of better sight to come" (*PFB*, 133).[10]

This examination shows that *The Refutation of Philosophies* is another text in which Bacon sets out his three primary objectives. The first makes the case that there is considerable reason to hope and to expect great advances in the relief of man's estate. The reason for this confidence is the providential opening of the New World and its obvious proof that the old philosophy was sterile and imposed false limitations on the investigation of nature's bounty. To develop his arguments, Bacon employs what now are familiar themes and images: he uses the metaphor of the ants, spiders, and bees; he inverts the usual understanding of the Greeks and makes theirs an age of adolescence rather than a golden age of maturity; he alludes to the epigram "non plus ultra" and to the prophecy found in the book of Daniel; and he associates Aristotelian philosophy with the sin of pride.

This mode of presentation, however, is not retained. In order to reach a broader audience, the later published writings drop the style of a teacher instructing an elite group of initiates.[11]

## *Wisdom of the Ancients*

When Bacon published *Wisdom of the Ancients* in 1609, classical mythology was a subject of high interest; and his book, like Comes's *Mythologia* (1551), was highly successful. Bacon, like Comes, upon whose work he drew heavily, was persuaded that many ancient fables contained compact, allegorical accounts of philosophical insights into "the difficulties of life and the secrets of science."[12] The true meaning of the fables, however, had been lost or distorted by subsequent philosophical schools—particularly those of Plato and Aristotle. These fables, therefore, needed to be reinterpreted. For Bacon, the resources for providing a proper reading of these parables was the widening and deepening insights into ancient thought provided by the recovery of ancient texts. These materials included the natural philosophy of the pre-Socratics, the *prisca theologia* tradition, and new resources for studying biblical texts. This recovery of ancient learning was complemented by Bacon's advances in natural philosophy. So while Bacon's interpretations sometimes depart from the predominant understanding of individual fables, he did not regard his interpretations as arbitrary. He believed he was reestablishing their true meaning, which had been lost. *Wisdom of the Ancients* is, therefore, a project of instauration. It is a recovery of ancient truth that had been lost or obscured, and it is an advancement of learning through Bacon's own epistemological efforts.

This analysis will focus on four of the fables dealing with natural philosophy and human nature: the four fables of Orpheus, Prometheus, Pentheus, and Pan. This is, admittedly, a relatively small sample, since the *Widsom of the Ancients* deals with thirty-one fables covering ethics, politics, human nature, and the sciences. Our purpose, however, is not to provide a thorough interpretation of the *Wisdom of the Ancients* but to offer a sample of the themes found in Bacon's analysis of the fables that relate to the main themes we have already analyzed.

### Orpheus

We have already discussed the fable of Orpheus in the analysis of the prehistory of civilization in chapter 1; therefore we will only briefly summarize the main themes. For Bacon, the fable of Orpheus is the story of the decline of philosophy as it descends from the natural philosophy of the ancient wise men to moral and civil philosophy and finally to a state of almost total disintegration. In its pristine state, according to Bacon, "natural philosophy proposes to itself, as its noblest work of all, nothing less than the restitution and renovation of things corruptible, and (what is indeed the same thing in a lower degree) the conservation of bodies in the state in which they are, and the retardation of dissolution and putrefaction" (*WFB*, 6:721). The effort at retardation, however, means arduous labor, and failure leads to frustration and to the adoption of the easier task—the management of human affairs through moral and civil philosophy. This stage of philosophy remains stable for a while, but it too declines with the passage of time, and moral and civil laws are put to silence. If such troubles last, Bacon warns, "it is not long before letters also and philosophy are so torn in pieces that no traces of them can be found but a few fragments, scattered here and there." When philosophy and civilization reach this low point, barbarism sets in and disorder prevails "until, according to the appointed vicissitude of things, they break out and issue forth again, perhaps among other nations, and not in the places where they were before" (*WFB*, 6:722). Three elements of this Baconian fable are worthy of emphasis. The pure, original philosophy takes as its task the restitution and renovation of things corruptible. This God-given ability is lost through the lack of human effort and will. The decline, however, is not permanent. According to "the appointed vicissitude of things," that is, providential intervention, true philosophy will return and humanity will be restored to its primordial condition—but not necessarily in the place it originated.

## Prometheus

The story of Prometheus is a fable about the human condition; and many interpreters of the myth present him as a secular hero who provides humanity with the instrumental means (fire) to become more self-sufficient and, therefore, less dependent on the gods. As punishment, Jupiter chains Prometheus to a rock and an eagle eternally tears away at his liver. In order to follow Bacon's reinterpretation, it is necessary to briefly summarize his presentation of the fable.

> Tradition says that Man was made by Prometheus, and made of clay; only that Prometheus took particles from different animals and mixed them in. He, desiring to benefit and protect his own work, and to be regarded not as the founder only but also as the amplifier and enlarger of the human race, stole up to heaven ... [and] brought fire to the earth and presented it to mankind. (*WFB*, 6:745)

Surprisingly, humans were not grateful to Prometheus; instead they "conspired together and impeached him and his invention before Jupiter." Because they rejected Prometheus and turned again to Jupiter, the gods were pleased and presented humanity with a new gift "of all others most agreeable and desirable,—perpetual youth." But humanity did not keep possession of this wonderful gift for very long because the foolish people loaded their gift on the back of an ass.

> The ass on his way home, being troubled with extreme thirst, came to a fountain; but a serpent, that was set to guard it, would not let him drink unless he gave in payment whatever it was that he carried on his back. The poor ass accepted the condition; and so for a mouthful of water the power of renewing youth was transferred from men to serpents. (*WFB*, 6:745)

After this tragedy, Prometheus made up his quarrel with human beings but retained his malice toward Jupiter and offered a deceitful sacrifice. "Having slain (it is said) two bulls, he stuffed the hide of one of them with the flesh and fat of both, and bringing them to the altar, with an air of devotion and benignity offered Jupiter his choice" (*WFB*, 6:745). Jupiter recognized the deceit and decided to punish both Prometheus and the human race, which Prometheus so dearly loved. Jupiter accomplished this by having Vulcan make a lovely woman, who was given gifts by each of the gods so that she was named Pandora. Then they gave her an elegant vase, which contained Hope at the very bottom, and the rest was filled with all mischief and misfortune. When Pandora offered her gift to Prometheus, he refused. She then went to Prometheus's brother Epimetheus, who opened it without hesitation. When he realized its contents, he attempted to close the jar but only succeeded in trapping Hope inside. Jupiter then seized Prometheus and charged him with stealing fire, making a deceitful sacrifice, and attempting to rape Minerva. As punishment, Jupiter had Prometheus bound to a column on Mount Caucasus and had an eagle tear at his liver by day. At night the liver was renewed so that the torture would never end. It did end, however, when Hercules sailed across the ocean in a cup that was given to him by the Sun. Hercules shot the eagle and set Prometheus free. Subsequently, Prometheus was honored by some nations in games called torch races, "in which the runners carry the lighted torches in their hands; and if any went out the bearer stood aside, leaving the victory to those that followed; and the first who reached the goal with his torch still burning received the prize" (*WFB*, 6:746).

After this recounting of the story, Bacon observes that this "fable carries in it many true and great speculations both on the surface and underneath. For there are some things in it that have been long ago observed, others have never been touched at all" (*WFB*, 6:746). Bacon then offers his exposition of the fable, which brings to light some truths never before revealed. First Bacon states that Prometheus "clearly and expressly signifies Providence: and the one thing singled out by the ancients as the special and peculiar work of Providence was the creation and constitution of Man" (*WFB*, 6:746–47). One reason that Providence was associated with human nature was that "the nature of man includes mind and intellect, which is the seat of providence" (*WFB*, 6:747), and since there is not a logical way to derive the unique properties of the mind and reason "from principles brutal and irrational . . . it follows almost necessarily that the human spirit was endued with providence not without the precedent and intention and warrant of the greater providence" (*WFB*, 6:747).[13] So, for Bacon, humanity is a unique product of divine Creation, and the human mind is evidence of divine Providence. While Bacon does not explicitly say so, it is evident that knowledge is intended to be used to improve the human condition, because this is the primary contribution of Providence (Prometheus).[14] Bacon then asserts that "the chief aim of the parable" is to affirm that humanity is the center of the world and "insomuch that if man were taken away from the world, the rest would seem to be all astray, without aim or purpose.... For the whole world works together in the service of man; and there is nothing from which he does not derive use and fruit" (*WFB*, 6:747). It is important to note that Bacon's anthropocentric view of the cosmos is grounded in the conviction that the humanity's place in nature is providentially designed. The benefits to be derived from the Creation, which are put there by divine Providence, are of two kinds: those that are obvious gifts and those that have to be drawn out through human providence or ingenuity. Bacon then turns to the section of the fable which states that Prometheus made man from clay and from "particles from different animals." Bacon says this part of the fable means that humanity's powers and faculties to understand and draw benefits from nature are reflected in his composite nature, which joins the material world with aspects of the divine intellect (*WFB*, 6:747).[15]

Bacon then turns to the most "remarkable part of the parable." Instead of being grateful to Prometheus for the gift of fire, humanity complained to Jupiter; and Jupiter is pleased with humanity and provides a new gift— eternal youth. The meaning of this section of the allegory, according to Bacon, is that human beings have to resist the temptation to assume that the discoveries made by foresight (the literal meaning of Prometheus) are full and complete discoveries of all the benefits to be founded in nature. This attitude is a reflection of human laziness, and it is ultimately blasphemous, because it turns humanity's devotion toward its own discoveries and to the work of a few men rather than toward devotion to God and to the pious study of other benefits placed in nature by God. According to Bacon, humanity's complaint and Jupiter's response can only make sense when it is recognized that the complaint reflects the realization by humanity that its own insight and its own practical arts are both limited and flawed and that God is the only source of the goodness that humanity derives from nature.

> The meaning of the allegory is, that the accusation and arraignment by men both of their own nature and of art, proceeds from an excellent condition of mind and issues in good; whereas the contrary is hated by the gods, and unlucky. For they who extravagantly extol human nature as it is and the arts as received; who spend themselves in admiration of what they already possess, and hold up as perfect the sciences which are professed and cultivated; are wanting, first, in reverence to the divine nature, with a perfection of which they almost presume to compare, and next in usefulness towards man; as thinking that they have already reached the summit of things and finished their work, and therefore need seek no further. (*WFB*, 6:748)

This attitude leads to complacency and is an offense to God. Those who recognize it as prideful and blasphemous escape these errors and are able to continue to advance human discoveries and to bring relief to man's estate. At this point, Bacon maintains that this insight was one of the truths stressed by the pre-Socratics and, subsequently, was lost by system builders like Aristotle and Plato. Bacon concludes this portion of his interpretation with the following statement: "let them know that conceit of plenty is one of the principal causes of want" (*WFB*, 6:749). This is, of course, a familiar theme in Bacon's other writings. Speculative philosophy has been sterile and unproductive; it must be displaced by return to the study of nature reflected in the work of the pre-Socratics and the *prisca theologia* tradition. This form of natural philosophy combines theoretical insight into nature with the development of the practical arts.

Bacon then turns to the gift of perpetual youth and its subsequent loss. This part of the allegory "seems to show that methods and medicines for the retardation of age and the prolongation of life were by the ancients not despaired of, but reckoned rather among those things which men once had and by sloth and negligence let slip, than among those which were wholly denied or never offered" (*WFB*, 6:749). The reference to the retardation of age and the prolongation of life is similar to the passage in the fable of Orpheus. The citation there and also the references in the *New Atlantis* make it clear that Bacon regards these skills as a fundamental part of the ancient learning that was lost. Bacon then considers how this loss occurred. The problem is in the slow pace of empirical investigation and with human impatience. Experience, represented as an ass, "seems stupid and full of delay... [and this] gave birth to the ancient complaint that *life is short and art is long*" (*WFB*, 6:749–50, emphasis in original). Bacon uses this as an opening to call for collaborative research that can accelerate the pace with which discoveries can be made. But before doing so, Bacon again criticizes the retreat from experience into sterile philosophical speculation. As a result, little progress has been made throughout the course of history. Bacon then returns to the question of the reconciliation between humanity and Prometheus, which Bacon interprets as further confirmation that humanity constantly gives up because the work is hard and falls back on its previous accomplishments rather than keeping to hard work and pursuing new discoveries.

Bacon interprets the deceitful sacrifice by Prometheus as a parable on religion. The sacrifice of the meat and the fat of the two bulls represents the true religious attitude on the part of man, and the offering of the empty skin represents hypocrisy. The religious man offers God his proper portion, that is, affection and devotion; and love of God manifests itself in charity. In the hypocrite, however, nothing is found "but dry and bare bones, with which the skin is stuffed out till it looks like a fair and noble victim: whereby are signified those external and empty rites and ceremonies with which men overload and inflate the service of religion: things rather got up for ostentation than conducing to piety" (*WFB*, 6:750–51).

The section on Pandora is a parable about the "morals and the conditions of human life," in which Pandora represents "pleasure and sensual appetite; which after the introduction of civil arts and culture and luxury, is kindled up as it were by the gift of fire" (*WFB*, 6:751). The material benefits gained through the work of divine and human providence become sources of complacency and even become the standard for measuring the quality of a society or a civilization. This materialism, which begins as pleasure, soon unleashes all kinds of misfortune, including "wars and civil disturbances and tyrannies." The response of Epimetheus represents those humans who are "improvident, who take no care for the future but think only of what is pleasant at the time... [;] they indulge their genius and amuse their minds moreover, as their ignorance allows them to do, with many empty hopes, in which they take delight as in pleasant dreams, and so sweeten the miseries of life" (*WFB*, 6:751). Prometheus, on the other hand, represents "the wise and fore-thoughtful class of men" who succeed in avoiding some of the misfortunes in life but in doing so "they stint themselves of many pleasures and of the various agreeableness of life, and cross their genius, and (what is far worse) torment and wear themselves away with cares and solicitude and inward fears. For being bound to the column of Necessity, they are troubled with innumerable thoughts" (*WFB*, 6:751). Few humans are able to escape from these conditions. "Very few therefore are they to whom the benefit of both portions falls,—to retain the advantages of providence and yet free themselves from the evils of solicitude and perturbation" (*WFB*, 6:752). The only way that such a balance can be attained is through external help, represented by Hercules. Hercules represents "fortitude and constancy of mind, which being prepared for all events and equal to any fortune, foresees without fear, enjoys without fastidiousness, and bears without impatience." Bacon states that this harmonizing is "not a thing which any inborn or natural fortitude can attain" (*WFB*, 6:752). It is something that is "adventitious"—a word in Bacon that alludes to divine Providence or grace, a point that Bacon returns to toward the end of his analysis where he makes an association with Hercules and Christ. But Bacon first turns to the assault on the chastity of Minerva, who represents divine wisdom. Bacon interprets this section of the fable as a wrongful effort by man to "bring the divine wisdom itself under the dominion of sense and reason" (*WFB*, 6:752–53). This is again a familiar theme. Bacon carefully distinguishes between divine and human knowledge and is careful to limit the pursuit of knowledge to the natural world. Divine truth is not accessible to man except through the scriptures and through divine revelation. Man must, therefore, "soberly and modestly distinguish between things divine and human, between the oracles of sense and of faith; unless they mean to have at once a heretical religion and a fabulous philosophy" (*WFB*, 6:753).

The penultimate paragraph returns to urge collaborative efforts to study nature and draw the benefits provided. Bacon introduces this point by returning to the section of the parable that describes the ceremonies instituted to honor Prometheus. According to Bacon, "fire in memory and celebration of which these games was instituted, alludes to arts and sciences, and carries in it a very wise admonition, to this effect—that the perfection of the sciences is to be looked for not from the swiftness or ability of any one inquirer, but from a succession" (*WFB*, 6:753). The more serious problem at present is that the "ceremonies," that is, the pursuit of theoretical knowledge and useful arts, have for the most part been abandoned altogether. Instead of advancing the arts and sciences, contemporary natural philosophy has stagnated into reverence for the pioneering work of ancient thinkers like Aristotle, Galen, Euclid, and Ptolemy. For science to advance and for the human condition to improve, the pursuit of arts and sciences must be revived, and for real progress to be made, the efforts must be collaborative. "Therefore men should be advised to rouse themselves, and try each his own strength and the chance of his own turn, and not to stake the whole venture upon the spirits and brains of a few persons" (*WFB*, 6:753).

In the final paragraph Bacon returns to the rescue by Hercules. "The voyage of Hercules especially, sailing in a pitcher to set Prometheus free, seems to present an image of God the Word hastening in the frail vessel of the flesh to redeem the human race" (*WFB*, 6:753). Bacon does not pursue this analogy further, however. To do so would violate his caution against attempting to use human reason to explore the mysteries of the divine. Such an effort is likely to produce blasphemy and insult God. Bacon concludes by saying, "I purposely refrain myself from all licence of speculation in this kind, lest peradventure I bring strange fire to the altar of the Lord" (*WFB*, 6:753).

We find familiar themes in Bacon's interpretation of this parable. Bacon regards the myth of Prometheus as being primarily about the interplay of divine Providence and human action. Bacon also contrasts humanity's prelapsarian condition to its fallen state. Prior to the Fall, there was a coincidence between divine and human providence; humanity was placed by God at the center of the world, and nature was intended for humanity's use. Because of pride and laziness, humanity lost this direct correspondence and has had to struggle to obtain the few benefits acquired over the course of history. Deliverance from this disordered state is possible, and has been possible from the outset. God intends humanity to be at the center of the universe and for nature to provide for all of humanity's needs. The defect is in humanity, which has lost sight of its divine vocation. As a result, it has created idols and worships them rather than

God. The remedy, however, can now be recognized, humanity can resume its proper relation with God, and rapid success will be possible, if humanity joins in the collaborative effort to advance the true philosophy of nature.

### Pentheus

The fable of Pentheus and Actaeon is a parable about curiosity and the unhealthy appetite of man for the discovery of secrets. Actaeon, as Bacon interprets the fable, represents a caution against attempting to know the secrets of princes and of kingdoms; the fable of Pentheus, which is our interest, is a warning against attempting to discover the secrets of divinity. According to the fable, Pentheus attempted to discover the secrets of Bacchus and was driven mad as punishment. As a result, Pentheus thought that he saw everything double, unable to tell fact from fantasy. When he attempted to return home, he could never arrive at his destination because he saw a double image and kept wandering between the two. Bacon interprets this as a warning against humanity overstepping its boundaries. The result is a confusion of the intellect that prevents an accurate vision of nature and leaves humanity wandering about in a state of confusion, which thwarts taking any decisive action with regard to divinity, nature, or morality. This brief interpretation underscores Bacon's several warnings against attempting to move from the study of nature into the study of divine mystery. In other contexts Bacon identifies this with Original Sin. The result of overstepping the boundary between the natural and the divine is to have truth in both realms obscured and to be left in a fantasy world of the mind's construction.

### Pan

Bacon interprets the fable of Pan as an elaborate description of universal nature, including both the terrestrial and the celestial realms. In summarizing the fable Bacon begins with the question of Pan's parentage, noting that speculations about his genealogy are of three kinds. "Some call him the son of Mercury; [others say] he was the offspring of a promiscuous intercourse between Penelope and all her suitors" (*WFB,* 6:707); and the third account says Pan is a son of Jupiter and Hubris (insolence). Despite these variations, all accounts agree that the Fates are the sisters of Pan. They also agree on the description of Pan. In appearance he is "human in the upper parts, the other half brute; ending in the feet of a goat" (*WFB*, 6:708). His body is shaggy, and he has a long beard. He also has horns, which are tapered and point toward heaven. He is cloaked in a panther's skin and carries a pipe made of seven reeds and a shepherd's staff that is crooked at the top. "The powers and offices assigned to him are these,— he is the god of hunters, of shepherds, and generally of dwellers in the country: also he presides over mountains; and is (next to Mercury) the messenger of the gods. He was accounted moreover the captain and commander of the nymphs, who were always dancing and frisking about him" (*WFB*, 6:708). Pan also possesses the power to cause sudden terror (panic). According to Bacon, an unusual aspect of the fable—in comparison to those about other gods—is that there are few accounts of his amorous escapades, and few offspring are attributed to him.

> The only thing imputed to him of this kind is a passion for Echo, who was also accounted his wife; and for one nymph called Syringa, with love of whom he was smitten by Cupid in anger and revenge because of his presumption in challenging him to wrestle. Nor had he any issue ... except one daughter, a little serving woman named Iambe, who used to amuse guests with ridiculous stories. (*WFB*, 6:708–9)

Not many adventures are attributed to Pan. There is the wrestling match with Cupid alluded to above, and this he lost. He also competed with Apollo in music and was judged the victor by Midas, "for which judgment Midas had to wear the ears of an ass, but not so as to be seen." He is also said to have entangled the giant Typhon in a net; and when the gods were searching for Ceres he found her by accident, while he was out hunting.

This fable, Bacon says, is "big almost to the bursting with the secrets and mysteries of Nature." The speculations about the origins of nature can be reduced to two. "Nature is either the offspring of Mercury—that is of the Divine Word (an opinion which the Scriptures establish beyond question, and which was entertained by all the more divine philosophers); or else of the seeds of things mixed and confused together [the results of promiscuous intercourse between Penelope and all her suitors]" (*WFB*, 6:709). This latter interpretation lends itself to a materialist explanation, which Bacon dismisses. Pan is one of the oldest gods and existed long before the time of Ulysses and Penelope. Moreover, Penelope was renowned for her chastity. So this account is spurious and was added as a gloss by some later, misguided authors. Bacon believes that the third account of the generation of Pan—that is, that he is the result of the union between Jupiter and Hubris—might have reached the Greeks through the Egyptians and reflects a "Hebrew mystery." This account explains the fallen state of nature, not its primordial condition. "It applies to the state of the world, not at its very birth, but as it was after the fall of Adam, subject to death and corruption. For that state was the offspring of God and Sin, [hubris]—and so remains" (*WFB*, 6:709). Bacon also finds the linking of nature to fate or destiny to be a true insight. "For natural causes are the chain which draws after it the births and durations and deaths of all things... in short all the fates that can befall them" (*WFB*, 6:709–10).

Bacon then turns to the physical description of Pan. He sees in the description of his horns the truth that

> the whole frame of nature rises to a point like a pyramid. For individuals are infinite: these are collected into species, which are themselves also very numerous; the species are gathered up into genera, and these again into genera of a higher stage; till nature, contracting as it rises, seems to meet at last in one point... [with the tip of Pan's horns touching] heaven; since the summits, or universal forms, of nature do in a manner reach up to God; the passage from metaphysic to natural theology being ready and short. (*WFB*, 6:710)

Bacon also finds truth in the description of the body of nature as being biform "on account of the difference between the bodies of the upper and lower world." Moreover, Bacon observes that all created things have a dual nature—one deriving from the celestial realm and the other from the terrestrial. Turning to the implements that Pan carries with him, Bacon interprets the pipe with seven reeds as representing the harmony and discord created by the motions of the seven planets. The shepherd's hook is curved toward the top "because all the works of Divine Providence in the world are wrought by winding and roundabout ways—where one thing seems to be doing, and another is doing really—as in the selling of Joseph into Egypt" (*WFB*, 6:711).

Bacon finds it appropriate that Pan is called the god of hunters, "for every natural action, every motion and process of nature, is nothing else than a hunt"; for the sciences and arts "hunt after their works, human counsels hunt after their ends, and all things in nature are either after their food... or after their pleasures." Pan is also appropriately associated with country people because they live according to nature, whereas cities and courts are corrupted by too much man-made artifice (culture). Bacon finds the allegorical reference to Pan being, next to Mercury, the messenger of the gods to be plain and self-evident: "next to the Word of God, the image itself of the world is the great proclaimer of the divine wisdom and goodness. So sings the Psalmist: *The heavens declare the glory of God, and the firmament sheweth his handiwork*" (*WFB,* 6:712). The nymphs that accompany Pan are metaphors for the souls of all living things that are the delight of the world and leap and dance about "with infinite variety." Nature also creates in each living thing fear or caution, which serves to preserve life. But human beings are capable of creating unnatural fears and terrors (panic) through the fantasies of the mind, and these come to prominence during periods of hardship and adversity.

Bacon next offers an interpretation of Pan's various escapades. The fight between Pan and Cupid refers to the fact that "matter is not without a certain inclination and appetite to dissolve the world and fall back into the ancient chaos; but that the oversawying concord of things (which is represented by Cupid or Love) restrains its will and effort in that direction and reduces it to order. And therefore it is well for man and for the world that in that contest Pan was foiled" (*WFB,* 6:712–13). On the other hand, it is fortunate that Pan was capable of catching Typhon in a net, because Typhon represents "that vast and strange swellings" occasionally occurring in nature—"whether of the sea, or the clouds, or the earth"—that must be held in check in order to prevent distraction and chaos. The tale of the discovery of Ceres provides further evidence that discovery of useful things depends upon "sagacious experience and the universal knowledge of nature, which will often by a kind of accident, and as it were while engaged in hunting, stumble upon such discoveries" (*WFB,* 6:713). The incident of the music contest with Apollo is a warning that human judgment (Midas) is more attuned to human capacities than to the capacity for divine harmonies.

In the final paragraph Bacon comments on Pan's marriage to Echo.

Nature is full and complete and, therefore, desires nothing to fulfill it. The only way nature could be enhanced would be through an accurate articulation or discourse. Therefore, the only suitable marriage that can be made with nature is with its own echo, which is true, accurate, natural philosophy. "For that is in fact the true philosophy which echoes most faithfully the voice of the world itself, and is written as it were from the world's own dictation; being indeed nothing else than the image and reflection of it, which it only repeats and echoes, but adds nothing of its own" (*WFB*, 6:714). Because nature is full and complete, when it reproduces or generates, it does so within its separate parts—the whole thing does not generate outside itself. Therefore, when the fable suggests that Pan and Echo produced a daughter, Syringa, it is a comment on "those vain babbling doctrines about the nature of things, which wander abroad in all times and fill the world—doctrines barren in fact, counterfeit in breed" (*WFB*, 6:714).

This description of nature and the study of nature is commensurate with that found in Bacon's other writings. The original natural order is a creation of God that manifests his power and his glory. Fallen nature is the result of human hubris or pride. The rehabilitation of nature depends on true philosophy, which echoes correctly the structure of the celestial and the terrestrial realms. This recovery depends on hunting in the natural world, and this hunting will sometimes produce correct results by good fortune (which always means Providence). Bacon's analysis of this fable also has the familiar criticisms and cautions against human vanity and the impotence of speculative philosophy, and this impotence is contrasted to the productive results deriving from a true marriage between nature and the human intellect. Finally, we find another instance in which Bacon's interpretation of the Greek materials is guided by his understanding of the scriptures.[16]

## *The Advancement of Learning*

*The Advancement of Learning* is divided into two parts. The first book seeks to restore the dignity of learning to its proper place, and the second assesses the current state of learning and prescribes needed reforms. Scholars usually concentrate on the second part, which offers Bacon's critique of Platonic and Aristotelian speculative philosophy and presents his own empirical, epistemological reform.[17] Less attention has been given to book 1 and to the dedications to James I at the beginning of each of the two books or to the frequent allusions to the Jacobean rule as an age of Providence.[18] The analysis offered here will not follow this usual course. Instead it will move through the text from the opening sections to the end, allowing Bacon's argument to unfold as he himself presented it.

The first thing to note is the full title of the text, *The Two Books of Francis Bacon of the Proficiencie and Advancement of Learning Divine and Human.* It is important to take the full title into account because the abbreviated title, *The Advancement of Learning,* and the analysis usually given by scholars, focuses primarily on a reform of philosophy and ignores Bacon's reference to divine learning. Careful reading of the text, however, makes it clear that Bacon regards both as crucial elements of the instauration of learning. The next feature to note is that both parts of the text are dedicated to James I, who was inaugurated in 1603, two years before it was published. As we have seen in other discussions, the court pageantry surrounding James I associated him with Solomon and England with the New Jerusalem. The court iconography associated the rule of James I with the Solomonic virtues—justice, peace, charity—and with Solomonic wisdom. Bacon draws upon these themes and gives them his own special focus in relation to his project for the advancement of learning.[19]

### The First Book

The entire book is addressed to the king, but the first paragraph contains Bacon's dedication. Bacon begins by establishing a correspondence between the oblations of a faithful servant of God to those of a faithful subject of a king, both of which include oblations of debt and of affection.[20] A loyal subject must, first of all, make an offering in recognition of benefits gained. The second oblation is not an extension of his duty; it grows out of the love and affection that a subject has for his lord. Bacon then says that he hopes to discharge the first duty through his direct service through official appointment. The second part of his tribute arises from his high regard for the person of the king, especially for his excellence in learning[21]:

leaving aside the other parts of your virtue and fortune, I have been touched, yea and possessed with an extreme wonder at those your virtues and faculties which the philosophers call intellectual; the largeness of your capacity, the faithfulness of your memory, the swiftness of your apprehension, the penetration of your judgment, and the facility and order of your elocution: and I have often thought that of all the persons living that I have known, your Majesty were the best instance to make a man of Plato's opinion, that all knowledge is but remembrance, and that the mind of man by nature knoweth all things, and hath but her own native and original notions... again revived and restored: such a light of nature I have observed in your Majesty, and such a readiness to take flame and blaze from the least occasion presented, or the least spark of another's knowledge delivered. (*WFB*, 3:261–62)

This opening is in many ways conventional and formulaic. Parallels were regularly drawn between God's rule of the universe and the king's rule of his terrestrial realm. It was also conventional to associate James I with wisdom, and a book about the state of knowledge would appropriately focus on that reputation; but this tribute is more subtle and nuanced than this. First, it asserts that true knowledge is remembrance. Plato develops this concept to explain the difference between the confused state of opinion held by most people and the philosopher's truth. According to Plato, the soul, before being born into the terrestrial realm, participates directly in divine knowledge and has a perfect understanding of reality. This understanding is compromised and fragmented by being immersed into the physical world and distorted by the senses.[22] Through the use of disciplined reason, the senses can be brought under control, and recollection (anamnesis) of the true state of existence can be recalled. Bacon then uses this allusion in order to praise James I as one who has been able to overcome the limitations that plagued most people and to have been able to recover true knowledge. This manner of praising James introduces the primary motif of Bacon's text. The advancement of learning depends on being able to move away from the prevailing ignorance and error. Moreover, this advance is at the same time a recovery and restoration.[23]

This reference to Plato's concept of recollection (anamnesis) is followed immediately by a scriptural reference to Solomon, the wisest king, which in turn is followed by a reference from Tacitus regarding the virtues of Caesar. Bacon then turns from the personal virtues of the king to his civil or political virtues, which he links to the portentous circumstances of the time:

> as in your civil estate there appeareth to be an emulation and contention of your Majesty's virtue with your fortune; a virtuous disposition with a fortunate regiment; a virtuous expectation (when time was) of your greater fortune, with a prosperous possession thereof in the due time; a virtuous observation of the laws of marriage; a virtuous and most Christian desire of peace, with a fortunate inclination in your neighbor princes thereunto; so likewise in these intellectual matters, there seemeth to be no less contention between the excellency of your Majesty's gifts of nature and the universality and perfection of your learning. (*WFB*, 3:262–63)

Since Bacon regards fortune and Providence to be the same, the implication of this passage is that James's virtues are augmented by providential grace, which has created a time of peace and prosperity. Bacon then returns to his praise of the king's knowledge and asserts that "there hath not been since Christ's time any king or temporal monarch which hath been so learned in all literature and erudition, divine and human" (*WFB*, 3:263). After delineating the aspects of James's extraordinary learning, Bacon avers that the king's remarkable achievements have to be considered "almost a miracle." This association of James's wisdom with the age of Christ and claim that this is almost a miracle is another way in which Bacon links the reign of James I with Providence. Continuing his praise of James's erudition in both divine and human spheres of learning, Bacon claims: "there is met in your Majesty a rare conjunction as well of divine and sacred literature as of profane and human; so as your Majesty standeth invested of that triplicity which in great veneration was ascribed to the ancient Hermes; the power and fortune of a King, the knowledge and illumination of a Priest, and the learning and universality of a Philosopher" (*WFB*, 3:263). The reference to Hermes Trismegistus augments Bacon's emphasis on the recovery and advance of both human and divine learning, but it also identifies the characteristics of the learning to be recovered. Hermes Trismegistus had a complete understanding of the workings of nature that allowed him to draw benefits, which he gave to his subjects. His kingdom, therefore, lived in peace, harmony, and prosperity.[24] This reference to a theoretical understanding of the foundations of nature that produces useful knowledge, of course, anticipates Bacon's critique of traditional speculative philosophy and his advocacy of a recovery of the understanding of nature that provides useful results.

We find, then, in the opening paragraphs a compact presentation of several key themes. First of all, Bacon's references to Platonic anamnesis links Bacon's advancement of learning with the recovery of true knowledge. This emphasis on the two aspects of instauration—recovery and advance—is augmented through the reference to both Solomon and Hermes Trismegistus. So the theme of escaping from the present state of ignorance is prominent in the opening paragraphs. A second prominent theme is the allusion to the beginning of James's reign as an epochal turning point or the beginning of a providential age.[25] Bacon catalogs the characteristics of this providential age: first, the reign is marked by human excellence and divine favor; second, there is both internal stability and international peace; and third, there is a cessation of religious strife both within the country and abroad.

Having offered his extensive praise of James's virtue and wisdom, Bacon returns to his starting point: the gift that he wishes to make. "Therefore I did conclude with myself, that I could not make unto your Majesty a better oblation than of some treatise tending to that end [a lasting memorial to the virtues and wisdom of James]; whereof the sum will consist of these two parts: the former concerning the excellency of learning and knowledge, and the excellency of the merit and true glory in the augmentation and propagation thereof" (*WFB*, 3:263). Bacon then indicates that the first task of a treatise on learning is to establish the proper scope and boundary of knowledge. While this would be an appropriate beginning for any text of the kind, it is especially appropriate now because the purpose and the scope of knowledge has been misunderstood for so long. The first step, then, is to "clear the way" so that the "true testimonies concerning the dignity of learning" can be heard without the interruption of tacit objections. This point in the text marks a transition from Bacon's direct address to his king to the beginning of his philosophical critique.

The first objection to be cleared away is the erroneous claim that "the aspiring to over-much knowledge was the original temptation and sin,

# Themes and Images in Bacon's Early Writings

whereupon ensued the fall of man; that knowledge hath in it somewhat of the serpent, and therefore where it entereth into a man it makes him swell" (*WFB*, 3:264). Bacon then cites biblical figures, including Solomon and Saint Paul, who have been used to support the view that a preoccupation with knowledge leads to anxiety and to alienation from God. But Bacon maintains that the nature of Original Sin has been misinterpreted and that the cautions of Solomon and Paul against a preoccupation with knowledge have been misused. The fall from grace was not precipitated by the pursuit of "the pure knowledge of nature and universality, a knowledge by the light whereof man did give names unto other creatures in Paradise, as they were brought before him" (*WFB*, 3:264). The source of man's Fall was the pursuit of "the proud knowledge of good and evil, with an intent in man to give laws unto himself and to depend no more upon God's commandments" (*WFB*, 3:265). This prideful attempt to become autonomous causes man to swell up with pride and to fall from grace. Bacon then returns to claim that God intends humanity to have a full and complete understanding of nature: "God hath framed the mind of man as a mirror or glass capable of the image of the universal world.... If then such be the capacity and receipt of the mind of man, it is manifest that there is no danger at all in the proportion or quantity of knowledge, how large soever, lest it should make it swell or out-compass itself" (*WFB*, 3:265–66). Bacon then affirms that charity—compassion for others—is the corrective against pride. He quotes Saint Paul that "knowledge blows up, but charity builds up" and then quotes another passage from Paul: "if I spoke with the tongues of man and angels, and had not charity, it were but as a tinkling symbol." According to Bacon, the error is not in speaking with the tongues of man and angels; the error is in pursuing knowledge without charity. Having made this clarification he then explains that the cautions of Saint Paul and Solomon are not against pursuing knowledge but against pursuing the wrong kind. At the conclusion of this paragraph, Bacon adds the following statement:

> let no man, upon a weak conceit of sobriety or an ill-applied moderation, think or maintain that a man can search too far or be too well studied in the book of God's word or in the book of God's works; divinity or philosophy; but rather let men endeavor an endless progress or proficience in both; only let men beware that they

apply both to charity, and not to swelling; to use and not to ostentation. (*WFB*, 3:268)

These statements reflect a now familiar theme. Humanity has a God-given or God-imposed obligation to know him and to know the natural world as his Creation. The source of sin is not too much knowledge; it is the rebellion against God and the effort to become a creator rather than a creature, that is, to become autonomous. The guard against prideful rebellion is to allow charity to be the motive for the pursuit of knowledge, because the effort to gain knowledge in order to help others prevents a preoccupation with the self.[26]

Bacon then devotes the next several paragraphs to an inventory of the fields of knowledge, what is proper to them, and where and how knowledge has become derailed. He then identifies three primary sources of error or "distemper." The first Bacon calls "fantastical learning"; the second, "contentious learning"; and the third, "vain learning." He takes up the third distemper first, citing as an example the vain learning of the Church, which studies words rather than things. The reference is to Scholastic philosophy and theology, which Bacon contends has lost sight of the truth of scripture and has devoted its efforts to its own elaborate arguments. Proof that Scholastic learning has been preoccupied with "vain imaginations" is found in the recent recovery of ancient scriptural texts and the study of ancient languages of the texts, which make clear the ignorance and errors of the schoolmen.

> Martin Luther, conducted (no doubt) by a higher Providence, but in discourse of reason finding what a province he had undertaken against the Bishop of Rome and the degenerate traditions of the church, and finding his own solitude, being no ways aided by the opinions of his own time, was enforced to awake all antiquity, and to call former times to his succors to make a party against the present time; so that the ancient authors, both in divinity and in humanity, which had long time slept in libraries, began generally to be read and revolved. This by consequence did draw on a necessity of a more exquisite travail in the languages original wherein those authors did write, for the better understanding of those authors and the better advantage of pressing and applying their words. (*WFB*, 3:282–83)[27]

The second distemper is called contentious learning. This learning has some basis in empirical analysis, usually by the original thinker or founder of that system of thought, but most of the subsequent effort of the followers of this school are devoted to further system building. That is, more effort is put into the system of argumentation than into additional empirical investigation.

> This kind of degenerate learning did chiefly reign amongst the schoolmen; who having sharp and strong wits, and abundance of leisure, and small variety of reading; but their wits being shut up in the cells of a few authors (chiefly Aristotle their dictator) as their persons were shut up in the cells of monasteries and colleges; and knowing little history, either of nature or time; did out of no great quantity of matter, and infinite agitation of wit, spin out unto us those laborious webs of learning which are extant in their books. (*WFB*, 3:285)

As noted earlier, Bacon compares such effort to the spider who spins webs out of its own substance. He also describes such effort as sterile and uses the now familiar reference to Scylla as a monster incapable of the production: "so the generalities of the schoolmen are for a while good and proportionable; but then when you descend into their distinctions and decisions, instead of a fruitful womb for the use and benefit of man's life, they end in monstrous altercations and barking questions" (*WFB*, 3:286–87). The third distemper is vain fantasy, which has no truth. Here Bacon refers specifically to documents that purport to be natural histories but are "fraught with much fabulous matter, a great part not only untried but notoriously untrue, to the great derogation of the credit of natural philosophy" (*WFB*, 3:288). Having identified the diseases that are the causes of epistemological disorder, Bacon contends that a return to true philosophy requires a return to first principles, or to *prima philosophia*. The aim of *prima philosophia* is for "the glory of the Creator and the relief of man's estate," and its purpose is to "separate and reject vain speculations and whatsoever is empty and void, and preserve and augment whatsoever is solid and fruitful; that knowledge may not be as a curtesan, for pleasure and vanity only, or as a bond-woman, to acquire and gain to her master's use; but as a spouse, for generation, fruit, and comfort" (*WFB*, 3:294–95).

Having proposed the restoration of the dignity of knowledge, Bacon presents a listing of subjects appropriate to *prima philosophia*. His description of the subjects of human knowledge are arranged in a hierarchy that moves from the supreme being God to the other immortal and unchanging beings—the spirits or archangels—to the forms God used to structure the created world and finally to the created world itself. The first subject, knowledge of God, is acquired in one of two ways: through the scriptures and direct revelation or through the study of the Creation. Next in order of worthiness are spirits or angels, whose appearance in the list Bacon uses as an opportunity to stress the importance of love and charity over power: "the first place or degree is given to the angels of love, which are termed Seraphim; the second to the angels of light, which are termed Cherubim; and the third and so following places to thrones, principalities, and the rest, which are all angels of power and ministry; so as the angels of knowledge and illumination are placed before the angels of office and domination" (*WFB*, 3:296). From the realm of spirits the next stage or category is the intellectual realm, the realm of forms, and then the Creation. Reminding the reader of the primordial state of Creation, Bacon next turns to humanity's prelapsarian pursuit of knowledge. "After the creation was finished, it is set down unto us that man was placed in the garden to work therein; which work so appointed to him could be no other work than contemplation; that is, with the end of the work is but for exercise and experiment, not for necessity" (*WFB*, 3:296). Man's work could be nothing more than contemplation because the Creation was perfect and readily revealed its purpose and its benefits to humanity. Humanity did carry out empirical investigations and analysis, but this was not labor; rather, it was the pleasure of intellectual discovery. After the Fall, however, humanity was alienated from both God and nature and was required to labor in order to discover the benefits of the Creation. As a result, humanity's primary task was no longer pleasurable contemplation but a laborious effort to attain what had been previously readily revealed.[28]

Bacon moves from this account of the primordial state to the history of humanity after the Fall. Of note for our purpose is his special mention of "the first great judgment of God upon the ambition of man[, which] was the confusion of tongues; whereby the open trade and intercourse of learning and knowledge was chiefly imbarred" (*WFB*, 3:297). This special mention is worthy of note because of its connections to the *New Atlantis* and to the earlier discussion of *Wisdom of the Ancients*. Bacon next turns to representative figures who were able to escape human pride and its consequences and restore humanity's relation to God and nature. Bacon describes Moses as the lawgiver and the possessor of "all the learning of the Egyptians," which made him wise in theology, moral philosophy, and philosophy of nature. He then cites the book of Job as another excellent example of wisdom in all three aspects of learning. The next person cited is Solomon, who is described as one who was "enabled not only to write those excellent parables or aphorisms concerning divine and moral philosophy, but also to compile a natural history of all verdure" (*WFB*, 3: 298–99). Bacon describes the age of Christ as one in which knowledge was perfected: "for our Savior himself did first shew his power to subdue ignorance, by his conference with the priests and the doctors of the law, before he shewed his power to subdue nature by his miracles. And the coming of the Holy Spirit was chiefly figured and expressed in the similitude and gift of tongues, which are but . . . [carriers of knowledge]" (*WFB*, 3:299). The gifts of the Spirit continued to be carried by "the ancient bishops and fathers of the Church[, who] were excellently read and studied in all the learning of the heathen" as well as in the scriptures (*WFB*, 3:299). Bacon then arrives at his own age and the restoration of learning that is under way. "And we see before our eyes, that in the age of ourselves and our fathers, when it pleased God to call the church of Rome to account for their degenerate manners and ceremonies, and sundry doctrines obnoxious and framed to uphold the same abuses; at one and the same time it was ordained by the Divine Providence that there should attend withal a renovation and new spring of all other knowledges" (*WFB*, 3:300). Here again the recovery or restoration of knowledge includes a restoration of both divine and human knowledge, a topic developed more fully in *The New Organon*. In that text Bacon alludes to the restoration of scriptural authority and to overseas exploration, which advances knowledge of the natural world. This compact statement in *The Advancement of Learning* is clearly intended to have the same dual emphasis. Having recited these instances in which recovery of the dignity of knowledge and the proper subjects of study have occurred, Bacon again summarizes the two tasks of knowledge. God has laid "before us two books or volumes to study, if we will be secured from error; first the Scriptures, revealing the will of God, and then the creatures expressing his power" (*WFB*, 3:301). Bacon then states that the historical record demonstrates that progress and knowledge occur most often when supported by learned princes. Bacon gives six examples, ending the list with Queen Elizabeth, whom he credits with reestablishing the truth of religion, establishing peace and security, administering justice, and creating a flourishing state of learning (*WFB*, 3:306). Bacon then makes it clear that James I has the opportunity to further advance the pursuit of knowledge and create an immortal reputation for himself:

> by learning man ascendeth to the heavens and their motions, where in the body he cannot come; and the like; let us conclude with the dignity and excellency of knowledge and learning and that whereunto man's nature doth most aspire; which is immortality or continuance; for to this tendeth generation and raising of houses and families.... We see then how far the monuments of wit and learning are more durable than the monuments of power or of the hands. (*WFB*, 3:318)

Having arrived here, Bacon has returned to his starting point. Bacon began by saying that he wishes to offer the king an oblation out of love and devotion. The most enduring gift that he can offer is to provide the means for the advancement of learning, which will become a hallmark of the reign of James I.

This analysis makes it obvious that the first part of *The Advancement of Learning* is not simply an extended flattering dedication to James I. Key themes are introduced that run throughout Bacon's major writings. He offers James I the opportunity to create a legacy of the restoration of the dignity of learning. This restoration entails a recovery and advance in theology as well as in natural philosophy. The spiritual recovery is under way through the study of ancient languages and the rehabilitation of scriptural texts, and the restitution of natural philosophy has been begun by the opening of the terrestrial realm to overseas exploration, which undermines the authority of ancient texts and paves the way for a new beginning. The advance will be accelerated by Bacon's contribution of the new methodology, and this recovery and advance will contribute to the providential restoration of humanity to its proper relationship to God and nature.

## The Second Book

Much of the second part of the book is taken up by a plea for the king to provide resources for the advancement of learning. Here Bacon addresses practical matters of establishing libraries and research laboratories and providing funding for scholars. He then gives a catalog or an inventory of the various dimensions of learning. This latter part receives the most attention. The analysis provided here will not concentrate on this section but will focus on the elements of book 2 that reinforce Bacon's main themes and introduce new or complementary motifs.

Near the end of book 1, Bacon offered high praise for Queen Elizabeth. The opening paragraph of the second book, however, points to a shortcoming of the queen not found in James I. Queen Elizabeth was unmarried and, therefore, could not generate or create a line of descendants. James I, as a respecter of marriage, is capable of generating or procreating. Bacon then notes that the best legacy that the king can create is found not in family lines or in governmental administration but in those things that are permanent and immortal. In this context, Bacon reminds the king that the advancement of learning would be the most permanent legacy he could create. There is not a more worthy act "than the further endowment of the world with sound and fruitful knowledge: for why should a few received authors stand up like Hercules' Columns beyond which there should be no sailing or discovering, since we have so bright and benign a star as your Majesty to conduct and prosper us" (*WFB*, 3:321–22). Bacon is here repeating the reference to the Pillars of Hercules as a false boundary and now depicts James I as a polestar to serve as the reference or guide to the opening of the intellectual globe. This opening is followed by several paragraphs that outline the practical needs entailed in advancing learning. Bacon then begins his description of the components of human learning. The first he discusses is natural history, and Bacon proposes that an inventory be made of texts and inventions that could serve as the beginning point for assessing the further work that needs to be done. He concludes this discussion with reference to the recent voyages that have opened the terrestrial globe and shown the limitations and errors of ancient teachings, and he once again links the opening of the terrestrial realm with the expansion of the intellectual terrain and associates both with Providence.

> And this proficience in navigation and discoveries may plant also an expectation of the further proficience and augmentation of all sciences; because it may seem they are ordained by God to be coevals, that is, to meet in one age. For so the prophet Daniel speaking of the latter times fortelleth . . . [many shall pass to and fro, and knowledge shall be multiplied]. (*WFB*, 3:340)

While this is the first appearance in print of the quotation from Daniel, we know that it is repeated several times in Bacon's later writings and is one of the key motifs linking overseas expansion with the expansion of knowledge, both of which are the result of human effort and providential design.

Bacon then moves from a description of natural history to ecclesiastical history. On the surface this may appear to be an unusual shift in subject matter and have no connection to the preceding discussion. Bacon explains that ecclesiastical history has three parts: the history of the church, the history of prophecy, and the history of Providence. It is this third component that ties Bacon's discussion of natural history to his ecclesiastical history. According to Bacon, the history of Providence contains the correspondence between God's revealed will and his secret will. In most instances the working of divine Providence remains hidden from the understanding of philosophers and theologians. There are, however, extraordinary times and circumstances in which God reveals his secret design in obvious ways. Bacon's meaning is clear in this context. The preceding reference to the providential advancement of learning through overseas exploration is the primary evidence. Bacon then moves to his second major form of learning, which he calls "poesy" or works of the imagination. Bacon warns that works of this type have a high potential for error because they are not grounded in empirical observation and analysis. On the other hand, works of imagination can be beneficial because they are able to portray ideal conditions, which cannot be found in actual things or events. Works of poesy, therefore, can inspire; and he cites the example of parables, which help to teach morality or provide glimpses into the secrets and mysteries of religion.

Bacon then returns to a discussion of the three aspects of the one universal science or *prima philosophia:* divine philosophy, natural philosophy, and human philosophy. The three contribute to a unified science because their common purpose is to know God through his revealed word and through his Creation. In *prima philosophia* nature links God and humankind. Bacon cautions, however, that natural philosophy cannot broach aspects of the divine that are beyond its scope. Here he has in mind specifically the articles of faith, which transcend the reaches of human reason. Bacon then begins a discussion of the two parts of natural philosophy: physics and metaphysics. We do not need to follow this argument except to note that Bacon includes mention of natural magic as an art that draws together physics and metaphysics. Here he is obviously referring to the original forms of magic and not to the degenerate forms that exist in his own age.

The third topic considered part of universal science is the philosophy of human nature, or anthropology. Bacon examines the physical and the spiritual components of human nature and discusses the individual and his life in society. We will again not engage in an extended analysis of this because it is familiar for the most part; but we will note one or two important elements of this discussion. Bacon identifies the capacity for language as one of the most distinctive attributes of humanity and contends that language is not a human invention but is rather the result of the recollection of knowledge that humans already possess. This statement would be confusing were it not for the discussion in book 1 where Bacon indicated that all knowledge is remembrance rather than invention. There he made the point that true knowledge and authentic language are an articulation of the proper understanding of nature, which is provided to humanity by God. After the Fall, however, this clear understanding was lost and human language was confounded. Bacon repeats this point here. Because of the Fall, "the mind of man is far from the nature of a clear and equal glass, wherein the beams of things should reflect according to their true incidence; nay, it is rather like an enchanted glass, full of superstition and imposture" (*WFB*, 3:394–95).[29] Because of his fallen state, man must be reeducated, and Bacon describes various rhetorical means for training the mind and directing the will toward the pursuit of the highest good. The present state of disorder makes this task difficult but not impossible, because humanity can be reawakened to its proper nature and to the proper source of meaning, purpose, and ultimate satisfaction. In this discussion Bacon maintains that the results of misfortune and of humanity's fallen nature can be overcome through hard work or, to be more precise, "through suffering," a reference that recalls opening sections of book 1 where Bacon describes the consequences of the Fall and identifies hard work as the way for repairing the damage. Bacon then argues that the reorientation and recovery of man's true nature requires constant attention and can be aided through practice. More specifically, humanity can train itself by avoiding evil and practicing good. Here Bacon observes that regard for one's fellow man is a universal trait of good men found in pagan literature as well as in the scriptures:

> only love does exalt the mind, and nevertheless at the same instant doth settle and compose it; so that all other excellencies, though they advance nature, yet they are subject to excess; only charity admitteth no excess: for so we see, aspiring to be like God in power, the angels transgressed and fell ... by aspiring to be like God in knowledge, man transgressed and fell ... but in aspiring to the similitude of God in goodness or love, neither man or angel ever transgressed or shall transgress. For unto that imitation we are called: ... love your enemies, do good to them that hate you, and pray for them which despitefully use you and persecute you; that you may be the children of your Father which is in Heaven. (*WFB*, 3:443)

This section is followed by citations of ancient authorities that discuss human physical and spiritual health and well-being. The great majority of these are taken from the aphorisms of Solomon.

Having promoted the benefits of the restoration of true knowledge, Bacon once again cautions against the sin of pride and the attempt to know divine mysteries beyond the scope of human reason:

> we conclude that sacred Theology ... is grounded only upon the word and oracle of God, and not upon the light of nature. ... This holdeth not only in those points of faith which concern the great mysteries of the Deity, of the Creation, of the Redemption, but likewise those which concern the law moral truly interpreted: *Love your enemies: do good to them that hate you; be like to your heavenly Father, that suffereth his rain to fall upon the just and unjust.* (*WFB*, 3:478)

Further on in this discussion, Bacon again says that the source of knowledge of matters of faith rests "upon the true and sound interpretation of the Scriptures, which are the foundations of the water of life" (*WFB*, 3: 483). Toward the end of this discussion, Bacon contends the restoration of divine knowledge has already begun.

> For I am persuaded, ... that if the choice and best of those observations upon texts of Scriptures which have been made ... in sermons within this your Majesty's island of Britain by the space of these forty years ... had been set down in a continuance, it had been the best work in divinity which had been written since the apostles' times. (*WFB*, 3:487–88)

This spiritual renewal offers the prospects for the advancement of divine learning, and Bacon's proposals for the advancement of natural philosophy serve as its complement; and book 2 of *The Advancement of Learning* ends with this discussion of the recovery of divine truth that serves as a guard against various forms of sin, idolatry, and false religion. It also sets Bacon's work within the context of the providential renewal and restoration of knowledge.

This analysis of the two parts of *The Advancement of Learning* reveals that this early published work contains the fundamental motifs that will occupy Bacon in his later writings, especially the theme of the instauration of divine and human knowledge, the emphasis on divine Providence coupled with human work, and the signs that his own age is a providential age of renewal.

## Conclusion

The themes that we found central to Bacon's major late writings are evident in the early writings examined here. The same allegories and symbols also are present, making it obvious that the preoccupations in the later works were preoccupations from the outset. A significant difference between the earlier and the later works is in the format Bacon uses for presenting his ideas. Nevertheless, it is clear from the mode in which he situates himself that Bacon understands himself to be the possessor of knowledge and wisdom that is very different from contemporary views. He feels an obligation to communicate what he knows to a select few, who are also disenchanted with contemporary philosophy. As he attempts to persuade the select few to join his efforts, Bacon urges them to be persuaded by "signs" or empirical evidence of both the limits of current philosophy and the extraordinary opportunities unfolding in the current age. Bacon's understanding of the developments in his own time is biblically based. He sees God's hand at work, as the references to scripture make clear. He also sees himself as an agent for God, much like the biblical judges or prophets, who were appointed to rescue God's people. This biblical basis is also found in the use of the key term *instauration* and in the description of humanity as the master of nature whose sin of pride has resulted in alienation from both God and nature.

Bacon's appreciation for the ancient wisdom, which precedes Platonic and Aristotelian philosophy, is also evident in the early works. He mentions major pre-Socratic philosophers by name and discusses alchemy and magic. His criticisms against alchemy and magic are of their current condition, which are degenerations from a more noble state. At the same time, Bacon insists that it is more productive to turn the mind toward the investigation of nature than to attempt to rehabilitate an ancient philosophy that exists in a few scattered fragments. Nevertheless, Bacon clearly sees his instauration of philosophy as entirely consistent with the kind of knowledge the ancient magi possessed.

# Conclusion

## Four Key Baconian Themes
Instauration, Providence, Vocation, and Charity

This study has sought to establish the central role religion plays in Bacon's thought by demonstrating the pervasiveness of religious motifs, scriptural references, and biblical doctrines in his writings. Analysis of eight texts spanning from some of his earliest writings through the last reveals that four religious themes permeate his work. The primary theme is that of apocalyptic "instauration." The second religious element, which is also related to his apocalyptic view of history, is Bacon's conviction that his own era is a providential age. The third is Bacon's understanding of his vocation as a prophet and as a priest of nature, and the fourth religious concept is that of Christian charity. These themes and their interconnection now need to be drawn together.

### The Twofold Nature of Instauration

The part of Bacon's instauration that has received most attention is the reform of natural philosophy. In fact, it is often the only part recognized. This reformation involves a direct, empirical study of nature that searches for useful knowledge to bring relief of man's estate. Viewed from this epistemological focus, Bacon's reform clears away the rubble of classical and medieval philosophy and returns to the pre-Socratic foundations of natural philosophy. At the same time, the restoration of natural philosophy is a move forward because recent advances have opened the terrestrial world and new discoveries have accelerated the understanding of nature.

Certainly, the rehabilitation of natural philosophy is a central part of Bacon's instauration and deserves careful attention. Exclusive focus on Bacon's epistemology does not, however, offer an adequate characterization of Bacon's vision of the instauration. In fact, it distorts the nature of the instauration. The broader dimensions of Bacon's project are evident in the frontispiece to the *Instauratio Magna*. The ships sailing toward the horizon represent the expansion of the terrestrial realm, which Bacon celebrates as a concurrent expansion of the intellectual realm. Empirical reports from the New World challenge traditional modes of inquiry and make a new foundation necessary. The epigram from the book of Daniel makes this rebuilding part of an apocalyptic reform initiated by divine Providence. The full scope of this apocalyptic event is reflected in the title itself, the *Instauratio Magna*. Bacon's readers would associate the "great instauration" with an apocalyptic typology found in the Vulgate edition of the Bible. The central event around which this apocalyptic motif develops is the restoration of Zion and of the Temple of Jerusalem. This meaning of the term *instauration* would be familiar to Bacon's readers because of widespread apocalyptic sentiment that identified James I as the new Solomon and identified England as the new Zion or the New Jerusalem. Bacon draws upon this court iconography and augments it through allusions to James's Solomonic learning. This comparison is most fully developed in *The Advancement of Learning*, which was published shortly after the king's coronation. In his dedication, Bacon praises James for establishing peace and stability and for promoting learning, especially the recovery of biblical truth. Bacon then attempts to persuade the king that a complete instauration requires the rebuilding and renewal of natural philosophy as well as religion. "But as both heaven and earth do conspire and contribute to the use and benefit of man, so the end ought to be, from both philosophies to separate and reject vain speculations and whatsoever is empty and void, and to preserve and augment whatsoever is solid and fruitful; that knowledge may not be as a curtesan, for pleasure and vanity only, or as a bondwoman, to acquire and gain to her master's use; but as a spouse, for generation, fruit, and comfort" (*WFB*, 3:294–95).

While this apocalyptic typology clearly focuses on England and England's destiny, Bacon's vision of instauration goes beyond his own country to encompass the restitution of humanity's relation to God and to nature. In fact, Bacon's fundamental conviction is that England has been chosen as God's instrument for the universal rehabilitation of humanity and nature. While Bacon frequently associates instauration with humanity's recovery of its prelapsarian condition, he also depicts it as an apocalyptic installation of the Christian Kingdom of God on earth. True Christianity is characterized by the three Christian virtues—faith, hope, and charity. Faith, of course, refers to the restitution of a proper relationship with God, hope refers to the overcoming of despair due to the futile worship of the idols of the mind, and charity refers to overcoming self-centered pride and loving one's neighbor as oneself. This emphasis on restoration of humanity to its prelapsarian condition and on Christianity's transformation of humanity to a "New Adam" is a key element of Bacon's instauration that is often overlooked. Scholars repeatedly assert that Bacon is one of the primary sources for the modern view of human nature as dominated by materialism, secularism, and ambition. This predominant point of view fails to take account of Bacon's frequent references to overcoming pride and the importance of charitable concern for the welfare of others.

Two additional and interrelated elements of Bacon's religious instauration need to be noted. First, religious and spiritual renewal are the precondition for the instauration of the understanding of nature. Second, Bacon's conviction that religious renewal is already under way gives him confidence that he can help usher in the complementary reform of philosophy. That religious instauration has begun is reflected in *The Advancement of Learning* where Bacon states: "For I am persuaded ... that if the choice and best of those observations upon texts of Scriptures which have been made dispersedly in sermons within this your Majesty's island of Britain by the space of these forty years and more ... had been set down in a continuance, it had been the best work in divinity which had been written since the apostles' times" (*WFB* 3:487–88). Also in *The Advancement of Learning* Bacon says: "we see before our eyes, that in the age of ourselves and our fathers, when it pleased God to call the church of Rome to account for their degenerate manners and ceremonies, and sundry doctrines obnoxious and framed to uphold the same abuses; at one and the same time it was ordained by the Divine Providence that there should attend withal a renovation and new spring of all other knowledges" (*WFB*, 3:300). Bacon is here referring to both a recovery of scriptural truth and a recovery of correct church practices. The key to both aspects is the same—a rehabilitation of God's word. Restoration of scripture will restore church rituals and practices to those practices found in the scriptures and the early church and will eliminate doctrines and practices added by medieval theologians and ecclesiastics.[1]

The restoration of texts is part of the leitmotif of the recovery of God's language. God's words are found in the book of revelation and in the book of nature. The instauration of both religion and natural philosophy involves returning to the same source or foundation, which is the word of God. Part of Bacon's development of this leitmotif is to contrast or juxtapose the word of God to the languages of man. While Bacon uses this theme primarily in his criticism of the philosophy of nature, it is also applicable to the degeneration of biblical Christianity through accretions and distortions of medieval theology. Bacon attributes the errors of interpretation of scripture and errors in church practices to human sin. More specifically, Bacon traces these errors to the human inclination to become fascinated with the inventions of human fantasy and the replacement of truth grounded in God's revelation with idols created by the human mind. This is the same charge that Bacon makes when he discusses the derailment of natural philosophy and offers his famous characterization of the idols of the mind in *The New Organon*. Also in *The Advancement of Learning* Bacon warns that failing to search for the truth of scriptures and to stay close to the text leads to confusion and to error: "as in nature the more you remove yourself from particulars the greater peril of error you do incur, so much more in divinity the more you recede from the Scriptures by inferences and consequences, the more weak and dilute are your positions" (*WFB*, 3:284).

While Bacon repeatedly identified his contribution to the instauration as a restoration of the language of the book of nature, he also carefully studied the scriptures and offered his own interpretations of key biblical passages and doctrines. Bacon's contributions to this biblical exegesis include a reinterpretation of Original Sin. The point of Bacon's reinterpretation is to uncouple "sin" from the quest for the knowledge of nature. Bacon also offers an interpretation of the Tower of Babel as an account of human pride that replaces the language of God with the language of man. This account is the complement to Bacon's account of Original Sin. The two taken together reveal the twofold nature of human sin—direct disobedience against God and the rejection of God's Creation in order to build a second world out of human fantasy. The punishment for both is to remove the language of the book of the world in order to force humanity to recognize the impotence of human language as a tool either to reach God or to draw from nature the benefits God places there for humanity's use. This rupture is not permanent, however. God will provide the means and opportunity for restoration, and Bacon is convinced that his age is the period of apocalyptic instauration.

## Providential Action and Apocalyptic History

Bacon's convictions that this twofold instauration was occurring in his own time were deeply held and due to his belief that there were abundant signs of God's providential action that had precipitated and was leading both the reform of religion and the reform of natural philosophy. Bacon repeatedly cites as evidence technological developments, the opening of the terrestrial world, the restoration of scriptural truth, and the reform of church practice. Bacon especially associates the reign of James I with heightened prospects for England having an apocalyptic or providential destiny. James is the king who would be capable and worthy of being called Solomon because of his intellectual and spiritual commitments and interest. James had already inspired important work in religion and biblical scholarship, and Bacon hopes to persuade him that the reform of natural philosophy is an equally important development and in fact is necessary for England to reach its providential destiny as the New Jerusalem.

An important and distinctive feature of Bacon's concept of Providence is in his understanding of the relationship between divine and human action. We have seen that Bacon maintains that human beings must labor, that is, carry out extensive empirical investigations into nature, in order to discipline the mind and bring it back to a proper investigation of nature. This human labor would be inadequate to accomplish the instauration, however, without Providence actively involved in guiding human effort in the proper direction. Bacon's writings make it clear that he is concerned that the opportunity could be lost because of the failure to recognize providential signs and to understand their meaning. This is a principal reason that Bacon's *New Organon* and *Advancement of Learning* repeatedly point to signs of hope and try to clarify and underscore the evidence of providential action.

Bacon's understanding of providential action is grounded in his apocalyptic understanding of history. What is especially important to note is that the apocalyptic age is one in which humanity's redemption is complete. It is not a transitional phase that is reversible. Apocalyptic or eschatological history is linear and leads to a final result: the end of human sin and error and the restitution of humanity to its original condition. The end of history, therefore, is a return to the beginning of history before the Fall. We have seen from his accounts of the Creation that Bacon identifies the Fall with human pride, which alienates humanity from God and from nature. His discussion makes it clear that instauration requires both spiritual renewal and a restoration of the proper relation to nature. In his portrayal of the apocalyptic nature of his own time, Bacon indicates that the spiritual reform is under way already and that he is providing the means for the recovery of the proper relationship to nature.

Without realizing the apocalyptic thrust of Bacon's view of his providential age, it is not possible to understand his extraordinary optimism that the long history of human ignorance error and suffering is coming to an end and that humanity will live in peace, harmony, and prosperity as Adam lived in Eden.[2] We have seen that Bacon repeatedly portrays humans as weak, prideful, and deluded. Bacon's vision of a remarkable transformation of humanity makes sense only within this broad apocalyptic context. It provides the only way to understand how Bacon's dual instauration will transform and redeem humanity. This context is also the only way to fathom how Bacon can believe that human pride can be overcome and that humanity will devote itself to charitable acts that will improve the human condition.

## Vocation

Bacon's apocalyptic sense of history is tied to his sense of vocation. The stem of this word is "to call," and being called by God for a special purpose is a biblical concept seen repeatedly in the Old and the New Testaments. The Old Testament book of Judges offers repeated instances in which God calls a man or woman to be his agent to remedy a state of crisis, a pivotal moment in the lives of God's people. The Old Testament prophet Amos admits that he lacks the training and the status of a prophet; and yet God has called him to speak to Israel in its time of crisis. This sense of "calling" stresses God's effort to remedy a state of disorder and minimizes the talent of the person. Moses also debates with God about choosing him to speak on behalf of the Hebrews because he has a speech impediment and suggests that his brother Aaron would be better suited to the task.

Bacon understood his calling to be both a prophet and a "priest of nature." As a prophet, he is compelled to speak God's word and lead God's people to the truth. As a "priest of nature," he was God's voice pointing the way toward the true reading of God's divine plan as revealed in his Creation.[3] As a "priest of nature," Bacon understood his role to be comparable to that of the theologians and biblical scholars who were reforming church doctrine by grounding it in the truth found in scripture.

These references to a biblical sense of vocation help to explain Bacon's sense of his special role in ushering in the new age and in restoring humanity's proper relation to God and to nature. In his several references to his contribution to instauration Bacon minimizes his own talents and preparation. God is the agent setting the stage for a renewal and restoration. Bacon says that he has the good fortune to be born in an auspicious time and that he has been chosen to call attention to both the crisis of the age and its cure. His role consists of first attacking the pride and arrogance that have alienated humanity from God and his Creation. The point of this critique is not, however, to create despair. After criticizing human ignorance and error, Bacon points to signs of hope. The principal one is the extraordinary opening of the world to exploration. Another sign is unprecedented and unanticipated technological breakthroughs. Because these developments do not grow out of established learning, they are viewed as isolated and arbitrary or as the happy but arbitrary products of fate. Bacon, on the other hand, recognizes that these are providential breakthroughs aimed at providing "new mercies" and pointing the way to a true understanding of nature and nature's bounty. Reading providential signs and providing the evidence to his fellow man is a part of Bacon's understanding of his calling and the reason he proposed several times to provide a catalog of discoveries and inventions. These catalogs were intended to demonstrate the wealth of benefits God placed in the Creation for man's benefit and were also to confirm that induction was the proper method for keeping nature in focus and keeping the mind disciplined and on track.

Bacon's presentation of himself as an instrument of God's providential action stands in stark contrast to the scholarly characterization of him as the first modern, secular rebel against religion.

## Charity and Piety: The Transforming Effect of True Religion

Scholars who have emphasized Bacon's utopian dreams of transforming humanity and perfecting the world too often overlook Bacon's emphasis on the restoration of religion, which is characterized by religious piety and by charitable works. This study has focused on the central role of piety and charity as the characteristic mark of the instauration. An instauration of piety would clear away the idols of the mind and open it to accepting God's truth, and an instauration of charity would eradicate human selfishness, pride, and materialism. This restoration of humanity to its prelapsarian state is also a realization of a true Christian self, who seeks to obey the divine commandment to love God and one's neighbor as oneself. Bacon's confidence that an instauration can occur is firmly grounded in his conviction that humans are created in the image of God. This means that human beings have the capacity to understand the natural world; it also means that human nature is suffused with love, which is the primary attribute of God. This love in human beings is a love for God, the Creator, but also for other human beings, who are the children of God and therefore the brothers and sisters of all other human beings.

The connection between piety, charity, and right knowledge is repeated throughout the *New Atlantis* and is also a key theme in *The Great Instauration* and *The New Organon*. If these connections are overlooked or ignored, the nature of Bacon's instauration is distorted. Bacon is not proposing a utilitarian exploitation of nature to create a luxurious state, as Howard White and others have suggested. The benefits available in nature can only be brought to light by investigators who are capable of escaping from the idols of the mind and devoting themselves to a pious study of God's Creation.

Given the importance of these religious elements of Bacon's program of instauration, it is difficult to understand how and why so many studies from a variety of disciplines characterize him as anti-religious or irreligious. Bacon was not attempting to purge religion from natural philosophy; he was attempting to (re)establish their proper relationship. This was an enormous undertaking because of the profound disorder in both religion and natural philosophy. But Bacon believed reform in both fields was providentially guided, and he was convinced that he was called to demonstrate how the reform of natural philosophy was an integral component of the reconciliation of humanity, nature, and God. As he attempts to reveal signs of providential instauration, he draws upon and modifies key biblical motifs including the Creation, the Fall, and apocalyptic restoration.

The misunderstanding of the role of religion in Bacon's program of instauration also distorts the understanding of modernity. Scholars who trace elements of modernity to Bacon misconstruct its features by denying or obscuring the strong apocalyptic and millenarian sentiments that Bacon infuses into the modern dream of innerworldly fulfillment through the advancement of science.

# Notes

### Introduction. Bacon's Religion Obscured: The Problem of Reading in the "Future Indicative"

1. Leslie, *Renaissance Utopias.* See esp. 8–11.
2. This is the thrust of Baconianism as it developed in the eighteenth century. See Rossi, "Baconianism," and Pérez-Ramos, *Francis Bacon's Idea of Science and the Maker's Knowledge Tradition,* 7–31.
3. A classic text is Jones, *Ancients and Moderns.*
4. Portraying Bacon as "anti-religious" or "irreligious" has been a predominant feature of scholarship for the last sixty years. F. H. Anderson, for example, credits Bacon with emancipating natural philosophy "from the dominant conceptions of traditional theology" (*The Philosophy of Francis Bacon,* 297), and Moody E. Prior describes Bacon's religious references as "conventional embroidery" that play a "relatively minor role" in Bacon's natural philosophy ("Bacon's Man of Science," 363). Similarly, Harold Fisch characterizes Bacon as "pseudo-religious" (*Jerusalem and Albion: The Hebraic Factor in Seventeenth-Century Literature,* 72–92). On these and other similar works, see Guibbory, "Francis Bacon's View of History," 337n4. Richard Olson also argues that "secular power rather than spiritual well being or pure knowledge was at the heart of Bacon's interests" and contends that "Bacon dissociates spiritual salvation from the notion of man's dominion over nature" (*Science Deified & Science Defied,* 1, 279–80). One of the most highly influential works to treat Bacon's use of religious language as disingenuous is Howard White's *Peace among the Willows,* which is discussed at length in chap. 1.
5. Of course, not all who have read Bacon in the "future indicative" have praised him. Critics have characterized him as an advocate of imperialism, colonialism, misogyny, and ecological rape. Notable examples are Charles C. Whitney, "Merchants of Light: Science as Colonization in the *New Atlantis,*" and Carolyn Merchant, *The Death of Nature: Women, Ecology, and the Scientific Revolution,* and more recently David J. Hawkin, "The Disenchantment of Nature and Christianity's 'Burden of Guilt.'" Nevertheless, these negative assessments, like the laudatory, are developed from the perspective of "the future indicative."

6. These numbers refer to works that include a substantial treatment of Bacon; works that make only a limited or incidental reference to Bacon are not counted.

7. These works include Faulkner, *Francis Bacon and the Project of Progress;* Albanese, *New Science, New World;* Barry, *Measures of Science: Theological and Technological Impulses in Early Modern Thought;* Boesky, *Founding Fictions: Utopias in Early Modern England;* Leary, *Francis Bacon and the Politics of Science;* and Solomon, *Objectivity in the Making: Francis Bacon and the Politics of Inquiry.* The following are representative views of Bacon's religion: Richard Kennington asserts that "Bacon's version of charity is much too worldly to be considered peculiarly biblical or Christian." In fact, he "knowingly altered the meaning of biblical charity to provide a biblical sanction for the humanitarian character of modern science" ("Bacon's Reform of Nature," 45). Thomas M. Lessl maintains that Bacon's use of biblical language is a rhetorical device that allows Bacon to confuse "the identities of religion and philosophy in a selective way that preserves the autonomy of science while also veiling it in religious authority" ("Naturalizing Science: Two Episodes in the Evolution of a Rhetoric of Scientism," 385); and Laurence Lampert, referring to Bacon's utopia, the *New Atlantis,* said "Christianity was introduced [to Bensalem] by a wise scientist as an instrument to lead the sheep" (*Nietzsche and Modern Times: A Study of Bacon, Descartes and Nietzsche,* 31).

8. For an overview of the reassessment under way, see Lindberg and Numbers, eds., *God and Nature: Historical Essays on the Encounter between Christianity and Science.* For an excellent example of the work being done on early modern science and religion, see James J. Bono, *The Word of God and the Languages of Man,* vol. 1, *Ficino to Descartes.*

9. See Zagorin, *Francis Bacon,* and Briggs, "Bacon's Science and Religion." Some earlier studies give attention to Bacon's religion. Benjamin Farrington, for example, stresses the importance of Bacon's use of biblical references and themes (*The Philosophy of Francis Bacon,* 21–26). This approach, however, did not substantially alter the prevailing modes of interpretation. Charles Whitney's more recent study, *Francis Bacon and Modernity,* makes an important contribution to the understanding of Bacon's central concept of instauration as an apocalyptic concept based upon a typology found in the Vulgate edition of the Bible. Whitney, however, is among those who are skeptical of the sincerity of Bacon's religion, and he portrays Bacon as manipulating this typology to fit his re-edification project. Whitney's work will be discussed further in chaps. 1 and 2.

10. Francis Bacon, *The Oxford Francis Bacon.* This new critical edition is edited by Graham Rees and Lisa Jardine. Five volumes have been published to date.

11. Bacon referred to his reform of natural philosophy as *instauration,* and the term is found in the title of one of his best-known works, *Instauratio Magna* (*The Great Instauration*).

12. The pioneering work that has shaped subsequent work on science and Protestantism is Merton, "Science, Technology and Society in Seventeenth Century En-

gland." Two other highly influential works are Hill, *Intellectual Origins of the English Revolution,* and Webster, *The Great Instauration: Science, Medicine and Reform, 1626–1660.* Scholars who examine Bacon's religious views tend to situate them within one of the forms of Protestantism or within the apocalyptic and millenarian currents of his age. Recent examples of this approach include Renaker, "A Miracle of Engineering: The Conversion of Bensalem in Francis Bacon's *New Atlantis,*" and Milner, "Francis Bacon: The Theological Foundations of *Valerius Terminus.*"

13. Titles of works published originally in Latin will be first cited by the Latin titles and then subsequently referred to by their translated English titles as found in the *Works of Francis Bacon* (*WFB*) or *The Philosophy of Francis Bacon* (*PFB*). The only exception to this practice will be when the reference is specifically to the Latin edition of a work.

14. See Whitney, *Francis Bacon and Modernity,* and also "Francis Bacon's Instauratio: Dominion of and over Humanity."

15. Rossi, *Francis Bacon: From Magic to Science,* and White, *Peace among the Willows,* explain that the modernist school was not interested in Bacon's "non-philosophical," literary works. More recently, scholars have recognized the relation between Bacon's philosophical and literary work and argue that Bacon frequently uses myth, parables, and allegory as part of his philosophical exposition.

## Chapter 1. The *New Atlantis*

1. See Weinberger, "Science and Rule in Bacon's Utopia: An Introduction to the Reading of the *New Atlantis.*" Weinberger has also edited a widely used edition of Bacon's *New Atlantis* and *The Great Instauration* and published a book-length study of Bacon's *The Advancement of Learning,* which also treats Bacon's religious language as manipulative and disingenuous. See Weinberger, *Science, Faith, and Politics: Francis Bacon and the Utopian Roots of the Modern Age.* This text will be examined in the discussion of *The Advancement of Learning* in chap. 4.

2. See, for example, Whitney, "Merchants of Light," and Boesky, *Founding Fictions.* Boesky's introduction offers a useful discussion of the cultural and political purposes of English utopias as "founding fictions."

3. The cross is an obvious Christian symbol, and cherubim's wings are a key symbol from the Old Testament, representing God's presence among his chosen people. As we shall see, Bacon makes use of this symbol several times in the *New Atlantis,* especially with reference to Solomon's House. Also see the excellent discussion in McCutcheon, "Bacon and the Cherubim: An Iconographical Reading of the *New Atlantis.*"

4. The name Bensalem also establishes a parallel with England as the New Jerusalem, a common apocalyptic motif during the reign of James I, who was portrayed as the new Solomon who would install the New Jerusalem. This motif is discussed later in this chapter and in detail in chaps. 2 and 3.

5. Accounts are found in Plato's dialogues, the *Timaeus* and *Critias*. These accounts are analyzed and compared to Bacon's treatment later in this chapter.

6. See White, *Peace among the Willows,* for an excellent discussion of the complex symbolization of fertility (177–79) and his argument that the feast has to be interpreted on at least three levels (78–81).

7. This ceremony is another episode of the *New Atlantis* that is frequently misunderstood and cited as evidence of absolute materialism. Within the Renaissance Christian context the emphasis is quite different. There is, first of all, a common practice of identifying the family as the building block of social and political order. This emphasis is clear in this episode. The father of the family is honored—not simply for biological reproduction, but for providing order and stability. Moreover, Renaissance monarchs were frequently likened to the head of a family. Just as children should love their fathers (as commanded in the Bible), citizens should love and honor the monarch. Moreover, this political model mirrors the Renaissance understanding of the natural order. The Christian God is the Father of all his children and, ultimately, instructs the children on the behavior that is required in order to maintain the integrity of the family and the order and harmony of society. In this way a relation is established between social and political order and natural and divine law. In this context it is worth noting that James I made use of the correspondences between God and king and father and king. See, for example, James I, "Speech to Parliament, 1609."

8. The analysis here is restricted to the most literal meaning of the text. We shall see later that Bacon repeatedly uses the marriage image in reference to the productive union of the mind with nature. This image is contrasted to the sterile state when men become obsessed with their intellectual creations. This contrast between productivity and sterility is a key theme discussed in chaps. 3 and 4.

9. White makes the association with the biblical Joab but chooses to focus on Joab as a "man of great cruelty" (*Peace among the Willows*, 245).

10. Here is another instance where Bacon associates knowledge of nature with piety and charity, which he contrasts to the sins of pride and selfishness. Elliot Simon has observed that the thirty-six scientists of Solomon's House may be considered analogous to the thirty-six just men in Jewish Talmudic legend. Both groups are motivated by their sense of charity, have their calling imposed on them by God, and are religious benefactors to humanity. See Simon, "Bacon's *New Atlantis:* The Kingdom of God and Man," 60n31. Also see Fisch, *Jerusalem and Albion,* 257–59. Nevertheless, Richard Olson and others persist in the claim that "the aims of Solomon's House are conspicuous in their lack of religious references" (*Science Deified & Science Defied,* 286).

11. The effort to obtain royal sponsorship was continued with King Charles I, and those who sought to establish such an institute often made direct attribution to Bacon. Recent scholars have also considered it the most important part of Bacon's scientific utopia. Benjamin Farrington, for example, in *Francis Bacon: Philosopher of Industrial Science,* reprints only this portion of the *New Atlantis.*

12. Whitney, *Francis Bacon and Modernity.*

13. Restoration of gospel Christianity was a principal concern, and Bacon wrote several times about the necessity of returning to the pure religion of the early church. Three of his earliest published works express Bacon's conviction that an instauration of gospel Christianity is already under way. In *The Advancement of Learning*, for instance, he says, "For I am persuaded... that if the choice and best of those observations upon texts of Scriptures which have been made dispersedly in sermons within your Majesty's island of Britain by the space of these forty years and more... had been set down in a continuance, it had been the best work in divinity which had been written since the apostles' times" (*WFB*, 4:487–88). See also *Advertisement Touching the Controversies of the Church of England* (*WFB*, 7:75) and *Certain Considerations Touching the Better Pacification and Edification of the Church of England* (*WFB*, 10:122). This important theme will be developed in the analysis of *The Great Instauration* and *The New Organon* in chaps. 2 and 3.

14. The foregoing synopsis summarizes Plato, *Timaeus, Critias, Cleitophon, Menexenus*, 16–31. The association of Solon's account with Hesiod and Homer will be significant in our subsequent discussion of Bacon's statement in the preface to *Wisdom of the Ancients*, where he argues that the fables of Hesiod and Homer are not products of their own age but "sacred relics... caught from the traditions of the most ancient nations" (*WFB*, 6:697–98).

15. Plato, *Timaeus, Critias, Cleitophon, Menexenus*, 35. Subsequent passages are cited in the text by brief title, *Timaeus*, and page numbers. References to the *Critias* will also be cited in text.

16. This description is one source for the legend of the Pillars of Hercules as a boundary of the human realm. It will be returned to later in the discussion of the *Great Instauration* in chap. 2.

17. The text of the *Critias* breaks off just as Zeus is about to address the assembled deities.

18. This work was neglected by scholars for several decades because it was deemed incompatible with the view of Bacon as a patriarch of modernity. This situation has recently changed, however. Rossi, for example, insists that this project is not ancillary to Bacon's efforts to promote the advancement of learning: "the explication of the true meaning of the fables is an integral part of [Bacon's] task of creating a new encyclopedia of learning" (*Francis Bacon: From Magic to Science*, 118). Similarly, White also describes *Wisdom of the Ancients* as being second only to the *New Atlantis* as a key text for understanding Bacon's political philosophy (*Peace among the Willows, 108–9.*)

19. The Latin text is found in *WFB*, 6:648. Where the English reads "restitution and renovation," the Latin is "restitutio et instauratio."

20. The emphasis on the restitution of health and the prolongation of life runs throughout the *New Atlantis*. The European sailors who are sick are given a fruit, prepared by the members of Solomon's House, that has remarkable restorative properties. This causes the sick among the travelers to think that they had been "cast into some Divine Pool of healing." Indeed, no function of Solomon's House appears to be

more important than the preservation and prolongation of life. This emphasis links Solomon's House to the ancient wisdom, or *prisca theologia* tradition. It is also important to note that the original edition of the *New Atlantis* was followed by a list of *Magnalia Naturae*. Several of these deal with the prolongation of life, the restitution of youth, the retardation of age, and the curing of diseases counted as incurable, and other topics deal indirectly with longevity. Others deal with the increase in the intellect, which is another form of restitution or instauration. White and others have seen this emphasis on "prolonging life" and drawing other benefits from nature as evidence of Bacon's materialism and secularism. It is more accurate to see these results as evidence that the reverent study of nature by Solomon's House allows the Brethren to overcome the alienation from God and nature that is the consequence of Original Sin. The Brethren understand nature and are able to enjoy the benefits God intended humanity to possess. This return to Eden is a result of the spiritual quest that has purged the members of Solomon's House of pride (the cause of the Fall), and pious devotion to God prompted them to "love the neighbor as the self." The reference to the "Waters of Paradise" makes associations with Eden and humanity's prelapsarian state explicit.

21. Already in the eleventh century, Michael Psellus contended that scriptural references to the wisdom of Adam, Noah, Moses, and Solomon included esoteric knowledge of God's Creation. He also claimed that the writings of Hermes Trismegistus and Orpheus predated Christianity but were compatible with it. The idea of a *prisca theologia* gained widespread acceptance in the fifteenth century through the work of Ficino and the Neoplatonists, and is found, for example, in Pico della Mirandola's *Oration on Human Dignity*, which is discussed in chap. 2. In the *New Atlantis* this connection is reinforced by Joabin's reference to Moses and the Cabala.

22. Whitney, *Francis Bacon and Modernity*, esp. 23–54.

23. *The Great Instauration*, *The New Organon*, and other texts provide extended critiques of European natural philosophy and set out Bacon's inductive method, which is exemplified in the work of Solomon's House. See chaps. 2 and 3.

24. White, *Peace among the Willows*, 144.

## Chapter 2. *The Great Instauration*

1. This statement refers to *The New Organon*, which was published with *The Great Instauration*.

2. Francis Bacon, *New Atlantis and The Great Instauration*, ed. Weinberger, vii. Weinberger explains further in his introduction that he has coupled *The Great Instauration* with the *New Atlantis* because *The Great Instauration* offers a compact statement of Bacon's critique of traditional epistemology and introduces his epistemological revolution, while the *New Atlantis* provides a description of the social and political transformation, as well as the transformation of the human condition, that will result from the implementation of Bacon's program.

3. See Tomasi, "Image, Symbol, and Word on the Title Pages and Frontispieces of Scientific Books from the Sixteenth and Seventeenth Centuries," and Corbett and Lightbown, *The Comely Frontispiece: The Emblematic Title Page in England, 1550–1660*.

4. Burnett indicates that there is some evidence that Bacon might have been directly involved in the design of the image ("The Engraved Title-Page of Bacon's *Instauratio Magna*," 18–19).

5. Boesky somehow manages to claim that this famous image appears as the frontispiece of the *Advancement of Learning*, which she states was published in 1620. See *Founding Fictions*, 62.

6. Accounts are found in the two Platonic dialogues, the *Timaeus* and *Critias*. The use of these dialogues as a point of reference will be discussed later in this analysis.

7. For a discussion of the Pillars of Hercules and the motto "plus ultra" see Bacon, *The Oxford Francis Bacon*, 4:249–50.

8. Denise Albanese suggests that the focal point of the illustration is the ship, which marks "a moment of transition; poised between the old and the new and informed by both" ("The *New Atlantis* and the Uses of Utopia," 506).

9. The quotation was highly important to Bacon, and versions of it appear in *The Advancement of Learning* (*WFB*, 3:340), *De augmentis scientiarum* (Latin, *WFB*, 1:514; Eng. *WFB*, 4:311–12), and *The New Organon* (*WFB*, 4:92). Its apocalyptic and providential meaning will be examined in chaps. 3 and 4.

10. See Whitney's excellent analysis of Bacon's conception of instauration in "Francis Bacon's *Instauratio:* Dominion of and over Humanity," and in his *Francis Bacon and Modernity*.

11. The *Sylva Sylvarum* was compiled to suggest the range of natural histories. Bacon proposed such a compilation as the third part of his six-part *Instauratio Magna*.

12. The *New Atlantis* was published with the 1627 edition of the *Sylva Sylvarum*, and Elizabeth McCutheon observes that "the title page ... is at least as relevant for *New Atlantis* as the *Sylva*" ("Bacon and the Cherubim," 337n14).

13. In chap. 4 we will see how Bacon develops comparisons between the reigns of Solomon and James I in *The Advancement of Learning*. For additional discussion of Bacon's equation of James and Solomon, see Bacon, *The Oxford Francis Bacon*, 4:35–36; for a related discussion of "Bacon and the British Solomon," see 4:xxxviii–lvi. For treatments of the theme of restoration or regeneration in the iconography of James I court pageantry, see Dollimore, *Radical Tragedy: Religion, Ideology, and Power in the Drama of Shakespeare and His Contemporaries;* Goldberg, *James I and the Politics of Literature*, esp. chap. 2; and Orgel, *The Illusion of Power*.

14. Scylla and Charybdis attempt to prevent the return of Odysseus to his home. This reference is, therefore, a parallel to the image of the Pillars of Hercules, which block the way and prevent an advance.

15. Bacon states that his purpose is to join the empirical with the rational faculty in order to create "a true and lawful marriage and overcome the divorce which has thrown the human family into confusion" (*WFB*, 4:15).

16. In this same section Bacon also characterizes philosophy as static and lifeless, "like statues, worshipped and celebrated, but not moved or advanced." This brief reference to the worship of statues anticipates the famous section on the Idols of the Mind in *The New Organon*.

17. This claim is similar to the myth of Atlantis. The known history is truncated and offers a deformed and deforming vision of human excellence. Also, as we have seen, the loss of true philosophy is a theme in *Wisdom of the Ancients*.

18. Gen. 3:5.

19. The meaning of this term has been the subject of debate in recent literature. Feminist and ecological critics have made Bacon the source of "masculine misogynistic" and "exploitive" destruction of nature. See Merchant, *The Death of Nature*. For a counterview, see Landau, "Feminist Criticisms of Metaphors in Bacon's Philosophy of Science," and Soble, "In Defense of Bacon."

20. The works of D. P. Walker and Frances Yates did much to document the availability of Hermetic and Neoplatonic sources and their transmission into Renaissance writings, including those of Ficino, Pico, Agrippa, and Bruno. Two recent works that trace the connections of the Hermetic and Neoplatonic traditions on the development of natural philosophy are Bono, *The Word of God and the Languages of Man*, vol. 1, *Ficino to Descartes*, and Olson, *Science Deified & Science Defied*. Olson provides an excellent summary of Renaissance Neoplatonism and Hermeticism and its influence on science. In his discussion, he develops direct connections to Bacon, who, he says, borrowed heavily from Hermeticism but modified and transformed some elements. But the primary traits Olson links are the prelapsarian knowledge and the dominion over nature. See chap. 8, "Magic, Astronomy, and the Governance of Nature, Church, and State About 1460 to 1633," and chap. 9, "From Renaissance to Modern Scientism in the Works of Johann Andreae and Francis Bacon," 230–90.

21. See Stephen A. McKnight, "Ficino and the *Prisca Theologia* Tradition."

22. Brian Vickers, in "Francis Bacon and the Progress of Knowledge," 505–7, has chastised Brian Copenhaver for associating Bacon's concept of forms with Neoplatonic magic. I do not intend to trace conceptual derivatives. My intent is to establish parallels with the Judaeo-Christian notions of Original Sin and the restoration to a prelapsarian condition.

23. Pico della Mirandola, *Oration on the Dignity of Man*, 5. Subsequent citations are given in the text with the abbreviated title *Oration* and the page number.

24. Pico's account of Adam's prelapsarian state has close affinities with the Creation account found in the *Corpus Hermeticum*. In book 1, for example, Pimander provides an account of Creation to Hermes Trismegistus. This account explains that Primal Man was the son of God and God instructed all of the celestial beings, who control the terrestrial world, to teach man all the secrets of nature so that man might become a co-creator in the terrestrial world. Here, as in Pico and in Bacon, God grants knowledge; knowledge is not associated with pride or with Original Sin.

25. In this reference to the rebuilding of the Temple and to the transmission of the Cabala, Pico uses the term *instaurato:* "verum postquam Hebraei a Babylonica captivitate restituti per Cyrum et sub Zorobabel instaurato templo." See Pico della Mirandola, *De dignitate hominis,* 80. See also Pico, *Oration,* 62.

26. This reference to the commensurability of the mysteries of the Christian faith with the mysteries of the Cabala is interesting to note in relation to Bacon's description of Joabin in the *New Atlantis.* Joabin is not like other Jews but belongs to a tradition that is compatible with Christianity. It is also Joabin who tells the Europeans that Bensalem follows the laws of Moses and mentions Moses and the Cabala.

27. The Platonic and Hermetic materials may also help explain Bacon's references to marriage and to generation. Bacon complains that the sciences are unproductive and sterile. By contrast, he proposes a marriage between the human mind and the natural world that will produce fruit. Both Pico and Ficino described their epistemological programs of recovery to a wedding of the mind and nature that will bear fruit. There are also the broader or more general images of marriage that are part of the alchemical tradition. These marriage metaphors might also shed light on the discussion of marriage in the *New Atlantis.* Perhaps it can also be read as a parable for his program of edification. At the beginning of his discussion, Joabin contrasts the situation in Bensalem to that in Europe. In Europe men did not take marriage seriously. They allowed their passions to dominate their lives; virgins are ruined and marriages are destroyed. Europe is, therefore, disordered and unproductive. By contrast, the Bensalemites take marriage seriously and have stable families that are a great asset to the nation. It is also worth noting that this episode occurs immediately before the entrance of the Father, who describes the generative work of Solomon's House.

## Chapter 3. *The New Organon*

1. See, for example, Zagorin, *Francis Bacon,* 82–86.

2. This interpretation would also be consistent with both the Vulgate and Septuagint's use of *eidola/idola* to mean "false gods."

3. Spedding identifies the *Timaeus* as the source of this quote (*WFB,* 4:276n39). This passage was discussed in the analysis of Bacon's use of the *Timaeus* in chap. 1.

4. This discussion makes it clear that White, *Peace among the Willows,* has essentially misunderstood Bacon's basis of hope. Bacon is not a modern secularist who replaces God with man. Bacon is convinced that Providence is at work in his own time, and he is an agent chosen by God to initiate the great instauration.

5. The reference to his contribution being "a happy accident" occurs in aphorism 78 and elsewhere.

6. For a fuller discussion, see Stephen Daniel, "Myth and the Grammar of Discovery in Francis Bacon."

7. See the discussion in chap. 2.

8. *WFB*, 4:297n64.

9. The miracle of the wedding at Cana is found in John 2:1–12.

10. For an excellent discussion of Bacon's epistemology in contrast to Aristotle's, see Pérez-Ramos, *Francis Bacon's Idea of Science and the Maker's Knowledge Tradition*, especially the discussion of Bacon's *scientia operativa*, 136–45.

## Chapter 4. Themes and Images in Bacon's Early Writings

1. For a discussion of this circle, see Matthews, "Apocalypse and Experiment," chap. 3, "Bacon's Literary Circle."

2. In addition to the treatises discussed here, Bacon's early philosophical writings include: *De Interpretatione Naturae Proemium* (1603), *Valerius Terminus* (1603), *Cogitationes de Natura Rerum* (1604), and *Cogitationes da Scientia Humana* (1604).

3. In the *De augmentis scientiarum* Bacon refers to this as the "initiative method," which opens the mysteries of science to a select few "sons of science." Bacon also distinguishes between the exoteric and acroamatic. The exoteric is intended for the intellectual elite. For a discussion of these rhetorical methods, see White, *Peace among the Willows*, 111–13.

4. Numbering of the meditations is done by Farrington and appears in his translation. There are no corresponding numbers in the Latin original as it appears in Spedding. See *WFB*, 3:591–620.

5. As we have seen, Bacon repeats this metaphor of water and wine in *The New Organon*.

6. These three inventions are also cited in *The New Organon* and are briefly discussed in chap. 3 of this book.

7. As already noted, however, the ways in which the two works are presented are quite different. *Thoughts and Conclusions* is set out as a series of meditations and is similar to *The New Organon*. *The Masculine Birth of Time* is presented as the pronouncements of a mature wise man to an initiate.

8. Farrington has created an introduction, but this structure does not appear in the Latin original. The Latin text of *The Refutation of Philosophies* (*Redargutio Philosophiarum*) is found in *WFB*, 3:557–85.

9. This reference is obviously to Plato's *Timaeus*, which Bacon also uses in the *New Atlantis*.

10. The reaction of the Europeans when they discover Bensalem is very similar.

11. There are some parallels with the comportment of the stranger and the Father of Solomon's House. Bacon stresses their dignity and compassion. The Europeans in the *New Atlantis* can also be viewed as an audience of initiates who listen in rapt attention to the Father, but they are not an intellectual elite who possess rare abilities.

12. For a useful overview of the Renaissance mythographic tradition, see Purdon, "The Mould and Cast of Renaissance Mythography." Garner also provides a brief overview before a detailed comparison and contrast of the approach of Comes and

Bacon; see "Francis Bacon, Natalis Comes, and the Mythological Tradition." Bacon's book was also widely circulated in the seventeenth century, going through nine Latin editions, five English, two French, and one German. Interest in Bacon's allegorical interpretations of the ancient fables waned in the eighteenth and nineteenth centuries, however, as the Baconians campaigned to make him "the father of the scientific method" and one of the pioneers of modernity. It was not until the middle of the twentieth century that an interest in *Wisdom of the Ancients* as a major philosophical text was rekindled. Bacon's interest in ancient wisdom and his own use of parables and allegory to convey his philosophy are now, for the most part, accepted by current scholars.

13. As these quotations indicate, Bacon refers to both divine Providence and human providence. Divine Providence is God's direct action to benefit humanity. Human providence is humanity's ingenuity properly aligned with divine purpose and directed toward the study of nature and the relief of the human condition.

14. Reid Barbour sees a tension between divine Providence and human providence. A careful reading of this fable, however, shows that the two work in concert. Moreover, in other texts Bacon makes the same point about the interaction between divine and human providence. A more balanced interpretation is provided by Sidney Warhaft. See Barbour, "Remarkable Ingratitude: Bacon, Prometheus, Democritus," and Warhaft, "The Providential Order in Bacon's New Philosophy."

15. This notion of Creation comes much closer to Pico's creation myth than it does to the Genesis account. See the discussion in chap. 2.

16. For a useful discussion of Bacon's biblical hermeneutic in the *Wisdom of the Ancients,* see Manzo, "Holy Writ, Mythology, and the Foundations of Francis Bacon's Principle of the Constancy of Matter."

17. Two book-length commentaries on *The Advancement of Learning* are found in Bacon, *The Oxford Francis Bacon,* vol. 4, and Weinberger, *Science, Faith, and Politics.* Weinberger, a political philosopher influenced by White's analysis of the *New Atlantis,* argues that *The Advancement of Learning* is one of the most important texts in modern political theory, which "tells us more about the causes and problems of the modern age than any other work" (*Science, Faith, and Politics,* 19). Weinberger's interest in the impact of Bacon on the modern age minimizes or totally disregards the intellectual and cultural climate of Bacon's own age. In fact, Weinberger asserts that "Bacon need not be studied in terms of some narrow historical context"; the truth or importance of his teaching cannot be understood or appreciated as "the reflection of some historical moment" (*Science, Faith, and Politics,* 19). Bacon, *The Oxford Francis Bacon,* vol. 4, on the other hand, situates Bacon's *The Advancement of Learning* within the intellectual, cultural, and political context of the age. Perhaps it is because Weinberger dismisses the context of Bacon's writings that he is prone to misread or misinterpret. For a listing of recent monographic treatments, which contain extended discussions of *The Advancement of Learning,* see *The Oxford Francis Bacon,* 4:xxx n148.

18. An important exception is Wong, "Some Baconian Metaphors and the Problems of Pure Prose," which offers a useful analysis.

19. For works that discuss court iconography, see chap. 2 n14.

20. Bacon is basing this on laws found in Num. 28:3 and Lev. 22:18.

21. Bacon, *The Oxford Francis Bacon*, vol. 4, contains a useful account of James's intellectual interests, his own scholarly writings, and his support for learning. Bacon had good reason to expect James's support for his projects. See xxxvii, n203, and the text on xxxix.

22. The myth is found in *Phaedo* 75e.

23. Weinberger, *Science, Faith, and Politics,* ignores the twofold aspect of the advancement of learning, perhaps because of a confused understanding of Bacon's references to ancient learning or ancient wisdom.

24. Bacon, *The Oxford Francis Bacon*, 4:206–7, maintains that the "triplicity" phrasing used in this passage reflects the influence of Ficino.

25. In *Science, Faith, and Politics,* Weinberger juxtaposes human effort to divine Providence, an interpretation that is not tenable in light of this passage or similar passages in Bacon's other texts.

26. Weinberger maintains that Bacon transmutes the biblical concept of charity into a source of political disorder and "dangerous politics" (*Science, Faith, and Politics,* 147). Such an interpretation is not commensurable with Bacon's references to Christian charity in this text or in other writings.

27. Weinberger misreads this passage and makes Luther a source of "vice" rather than an instrument of divine Providence (*Science, Faith, and Politics,* 149).

28. Weinberger misunderstands the redemptive possibilities in the requirement that man "till the soil." He interprets the necessity of the human arts as a result of "divine revenge" and concludes that Christianity teaches humanity that it is in the hands of "a malicious God" (*Science, Faith, and Politics,* 191).

29. This image of a mirror was also used in the opening paragraphs of book 1, where Bacon likened the human mind before the Fall to a mirror.

## Conclusion. Four Key Baconian Themes: Instauration, Providence, Apocalypse, and Vocation

1. According to Mouton, "the ideal that the Church of England should seek, is that of the ancient Church of the earliest Christians. This *primitivist* theme occurs rather frequently in these early writings of Bacon. In 1589 he writes: '... if we would leave the over-weening and turbulent humours of these times and revive the blessed proceedings of the Apostles and Fathers of the primitive church' (*Advertisement, Works,* VIII, 75). And again in 1603 he asks that the Church may indeed be 'restored to the ancient vigour and splendour' (*Pacification, Works,* X, 122). The main reason for this belief, is probably to be found in the fact that Bacon saw in the primitive Church, a liturgy which was 'in all parts agreeable to the word of God.' It was a

church of 'one faith, one baptism, and not, one hierarchy, one disciple' (*Idem*, 108). One faith and one baptism, based on a true exegesis of the Word of God, was the necessary condition for any Church, but it was also a sufficient condition for uniformity. Controversies over discipline and ceremonies were unnecessarily threatening the uniformity of the Church, especially, as we have seen, when it concerned matters that were not fundamental to the principles of faith" ("Reformation and Restoration in Francis Bacon's Early Philosophy," 105).

2. This key idea is amply expressed in the *New Atlantis*. The Elders of Solomon's House possess a prelapsarian religious purity and understanding of nature and are therefore able to extract its benefits.

3. See *WFB*, 4:26, where Bacon describes himself as a "true priest" of the senses (nature).

# Bibliography

Achinstein, Sharon. "How to be a Progressive without Looking Like One: History and Knowledge in Bacon's *New Atlantis*." *Clio* 17 (1988): 249–64.
———. "John Foxe and the Jews." *Renaissance Quarterly* 54 (2001): 86–120.
Adams, Robert P. "The Social Responsibilities of Science in *Utopia, New Atlantis*, and After." *Journal of the History of Ideas* 10 (1949): 374–98.
Agassi, Joseph. "Knowledge Personal or Social." *Philosophy of the Social Sciences* 28 (1998): 522–51.
Albanese, Denise. "The *New Atlantis* and the Uses of Utopia." *English Literary History* 57 (1990): 503–28.
———. *New Science, New World*. Durham, NC: Duke University Press, 1996.
Anderson, F. H. *The Philosophy of Francis Bacon*. Chicago: University of Chicago Press, 1948.
Applebaum, Robert. *Literature and Utopian Politics in Seventeenth-Century England*. Cambridge: Cambridge University Press, 2002.
Archer, John. *Sovereignty and Intelligence: Spying and Court Culture in the English Renaissance*. Stanford, CA: Stanford University Press, 1993.
Ashton, Robert, ed. *James I by His Contemporaries*. London: Hutchison, 1969.
Aughterson, Kate. "The 'Waking Vision': Reference in the *New Atlantis*." *Renaissance Quarterly* 45 (1992): 119–39.
Bacon, Francis. *New Atlantis and The Great Instauration*. Edited by Jerry Weinberger. Arlington Heights, IL: Harlan Davidson, 1989.
———. *The Oxford Francis Bacon*. Edited by Graham Rees and Lisa Jardine. Vol. 4, *The Advancement of Learning*, edited by Michael Kiernan. Oxford: Oxford University Press, 2000.
———. *The Philosophy of Francis Bacon: An Essay on Its Development from 1603 to 1609 with New Translations of Fundamental Texts*. Edited and translated by Benjamin Farrington. Chicago: University of Chicago Press, 1964.
———. *The Works of Francis Bacon*. Edited by James Spedding, Robert L. Ellis, and Douglas D. Heath. 14 vols. London: Longman, 1857–74.
Barbour, Reid. "Remarkable Ingratitude: Bacon, Prometheus, Democritus." *Studies in English Literature, 1500–1900* 32 (1992): 79–90.

Barnaby, Andrew. "Things Themselves: Francis Bacon's Epistemological Reform and the Maintenance of the State." *Renaissance and Reformation* 21 (1997): 57–80.

Barry, James, Jr. *Measures of Science: Theological and Technological Impulses in Early Modern Thought.* Evanston, IL: Northwestern University Press, 1996.

Berns, Laurence. "Francis Bacon and the Conquest of Nature." *Interpretation* 7 (1978): 1–26.

Berti, Silvia. "At the Roots of Unbelief." *Journal of the History of Ideas* 56 (1995): 555–75.

Bierman, Judah. "Science and Society in the *New Atlantis* and Other Renaissance Utopias." *Publication of the Modern Language Association* 78 (1963): 492–500.

Blodgett, Eleanor D. "Bacon's *New Atlantis* and Campanella's *Civitas Solis*: A Study in Relationships." *Publications of the Modern Language Association of America* 46 (1931): 763–80.

Boesky, Amy. "Bacon's *New Atlantis* and the Laboratory of Prose." In *The Project of Prose in Early Modern Europe and the New Worlds,* edited by Elizabeth Fowler and Roland Greene, 138–53. Cambridge: Cambridge University Press, 1997.

———. *Founding Fictions: Utopias in Early Modern England.* Athens: University of Georgia Press, 1996.

Bono, James J. *The Word of God and the Languages of Man: Interpreting Nature in Early Modern Science and Medicine.* Vol. 1, *Ficino to Descartes.* Madison: University of Wisconsin Press, 1995.

Bowers, R. H. "Bacon's Spider Simile." *Journal of the History of Ideas* 17 (1956): 133–35.

Box, Ian. "Medicine and Medical Imagery in Bacon's 'Great Instauration.'" *Historical Reflections/Réflexions Historiques* 16 (1989): 351–65.

———. *The Social Thought of Francis Bacon.* New York: Edwin Mellen Press, 1989.

Brann, Eva. "'An Exquisite Platform': Utopia." *Interpretation* 3 (1972): 1–26.

Brentano, Franz. "The Four Phases of Philosophy and Its Present Condition." Translated by Stephen Satris. *Philosophy Today* 43 (1999): 14–28.

Briggs, John C. "Bacon's Science and Religion." In *Cambridge Companion to Bacon,* edited by Markku Peltonen, 172–99. Cambridge: Cambridge University Press, 1996.

———. *Francis Bacon and the Rhetoric of Nature.* Cambridge, MA: Harvard University Press, 1989.

Burnett, A. D. "The Engraved Title-Page of Bacon's *Instauratio Magna.*" In

*The Durham Thomas Harriot Seminar: Occasional Paper No. 27.* Durham, UK: Thomas Harriot Seminar, 1998.

Burns, William E. "'A Proverb of Versatile Mutability': Proteus and Natural Knowledge in Early Modern Britain." *Sixteenth Century Journal* 32 (2001): 969–80.

Byrne, M. St. Clare. "The Mother of Francis Bacon." *Blackwood's Magazine* 236 (1934): 758–71.

Ciocci, Argante. "Il mito di Prometeo nell'interpretazione di Francesco Bacone." *Intersezioni: Rivista di Storia Delle Idee* 16 (1996): 453–65.

Clericuzio, Antonio. "Alchimia e teorie della materia nel Seicento." In *Storia e Fondamenti della Chimica,* edited by Franco Calascibetti, 109–16. Rome: Academia Nazionale della Scieze, 1997.

Cochrane, Rexmond C. "Francis Bacon and the Architect of Fortune." *Studies in the Renaissance* 5 (1958): 176–95.

Colie, Rosalie. "Cornelis Drebbel and Salomon de Caus: Two Jacobean Models for Salomon's House." *Huntington Library Quarterly* 18 (1954–55): 245–60.

Collins, Stephen. *From Divine Cosmos to Sovereign State: An Intellectual History of Consciousness and the Idea of Order in Renaissance England.* Oxford: Oxford University Press, 1989.

Cooper, Andrew M. "The Collapse of the Religious Hieroglyph: Typology and Natural Language in Herbert and Bacon." *Renaissance Quarterly* 45 (1992): 96–118.

Corbett, M., and R. W. Lightbown. *The Comely Frontispiece: The Emblematic Title Page in England, 1550–1660.* London: Routledge and Kegan Paul, 1979.

Daniel, Stephen H. "Myth and the Grammar of Discovery in Francis Bacon." *Philosophy and Rhetoric* 15 (1982): 219–37.

Davis, Walter R. "The Imagery of Bacon's Late Work." *Modern Language Quarterly* 27 (1966): 162–73.

De Maistre, Joseph. *An Examination of the Philosophy of Bacon: Wherein Different Questions of Rational Philosophy Are Treated.* Translated and edited by Richard Lebrun. Montreal: McGill-Queen's University Press, 1998.

Demers, Patricia. "Bacon's Allegory of Science: The Theatre of the *New Atlantis.*" *Journal of the Rocky Mountain Medieval and Renaissance Association* 4 (1983): 135–48.

Dollimore, Jonathan. *Radical Tragedy: Religion, Ideology, and Power in the Drama of Shakespeare and His Contemporaries.* Chicago: University of Chicago Press, 1984.

Durel-Leon, H. "*The Advancement of Learning* (1605): From Bacon's Study to the Press." *Transactions of the Cambridge Bibliographical Society* 11 (1997): 127–69.

Dzelzainis, Martin. "Milton and Sir Francis Bacon's *A Wise and Moderate Discourse Concerning Church-Affaires (1641).*" *Notes and Queries* n.s. 44 (1997): 182–85.

Elliot-Binns, L. E. *Divine Providence and Human Destiny.* London: Society for Promoting Christian Knowledge, 1943.

Elsky, Martin. "Bacon's Hieroglyphs and the Separation of Word and Thing." *Philological Quarterly* 63 (1984): 449–60.

Farrington, Benjamin F. *Francis Bacon: Philosopher of Industrial Science.* London: Lawrence and Wishart, 1951.

———. *The Philosophy of Francis Bacon: An Essay on Its Development from 1603 to 1609 with New Translations of Fundamental Texts.* Chicago: University of Chicago Press, 1964.

Fattori, Marta. *Francis Bacon: Terminologia E. Fortuna: NEL XVII Secolo.* Rome: Edizioni dell'Ateneo, 1984.

———. "*Spiritus* dans *L'Historia Vitae Et Mortis* de Francis Bacon." *Spiritus: IV Colloquio Internazionale,* edited by M. Fattori and M. Bianchi, 283–323. Rome: Edizioni dell'Ateneo, 1984.

Faulkner, Robert K. *Francis Bacon and the Project of Progress.* Lanham, MD: Rowman & Littlefield, 1993.

Findlen, Paula. "Francis Bacon and the Reform of Natural History in the Seventeenth Century." In *History and the Disciplines: The Reclassification of Knowledge in Early Modern Europe,* edited by Donald R. Kelley, 239–59. Rochester, NY: University of Rochester Press, 1997.

Fisch, Harold. *Jerusalem and Albion: The Hebraic Factor in Seventeenth-Century Literature.* New York: Schocken Books, 1964.

Fletcher, Anthony, and Peter Roberts. *Religion, Culture, and Society in Early Modern Britain.* Cambridge: Cambridge University Press, 1994.

Gadol, Joan. "The Unity of the Renaissance: Humanism, Natural Science, and Art." In *From the Renaissance to the Counter-Reformation,* edited by Charles H. Carter, 29–55. New York: Random House, 1965.

Garcia, Jose Maria Rodriguez. "Solitude and Procreation in Francis Bacon's Scientific Writings: The Spanish Connection." *Comparative Literature Studies* 35 (1998): 278–300.

Garner, Barbara Carman. "Francis Bacon, Natalis Comes, and the Mythological Tradition." *Journal of the Warburg and Courtauld Institutes* 33 (1970): 264–303.

Gaukroger, Stephen. *Francis Bacon and the Transformation of Early Modern Philosophy.* Cambridge: Cambridge University Press, 2001.

Gilbert, Ruth. "The Masculine Matrix: Male Births and the Scientific Imagination in Early Modern England." In *The Arts of 17th-Century Science: Representations of the Natural World in European and North American Culture,* edited by Claire Jowitt and Diane Watt, 160–77. Burlington, VT: Ashgate, 2002.

Goldberg, Jonathan. *James I and the Politics of Literature: Jonson, Shakespeare, Donne, and Their Contemporaries.* Baltimore: Johns Hopkins University Press, 1983.

Green, Mary Elizabeth. "The Poet in Solomon's House: Abraham Cowley as Baconian Apostle." *Restoration: Studies in English Literary Culture, 1660–1700* 10 (1986): 68–75.

Gregerson, Linda. "Narcissus Interrupted: Specularity and the Subject of the Tudor State." *Criticism* 35 (1993): 1–24.

Guibbory, Achsah. "Francis Bacon's View of History: The Cycles of Error and the Progress of Truth." *Journal of English and Germanic Philology* 74 (1975): 336–50.

Hall, Joan Wyle. "Solomon Saith: Bacon's Use of Solomon in the 1625 Essays." *University of Dayton Review* 15 (1982): 83–88.

Hattaway, Michael. "Bacon and 'Knowledge Broken': Limits for Scientific Method." *Journal of the History of Ideas* 39 (1978): 183–97.

Hawkin, David J. "The Disenchantment of Nature and Christianity's 'Burden of Guilt.'" *Leval Theologique et Philosophique* 55 (1999): 65–71.

Healey, Robert M. "The Jew in Seventeenth-Century Protestant Thought." *Church History* 46 (1977): 63–79.

Hill, Christopher. *Intellectual Origins of the English Revolution.* Oxford: Oxford University Press, 1965.

Hodgin, Margaret. "The Ark of Noah and the Problem of Cultural Diversity." Chap. 6 in *Early Anthropology in the Sixteenth and Seventeenth Centuries.* Philadelphia: University of Pennsylvania, 1964.

Horton, Mary. "Bacon and 'Knowledge Broken': An Answer to Michael Hattaway." *Journal of the History of Ideas* 43 (1982): 487–504.

Hutchison, John C. "The Design Argument in Scientific Discourse: Historical-Theological Perspective from the Seventeenth Century." *Journal of the Evangelical Theological Society* 41 (1998): 85–105.

Iliffe, Rob. "The Masculine Birth of Time: Temporal Frameworks of Early Modern Natural Philosophy." *British Journal for the History of Science* 33 (2000): 427–53.

Innes, David C. "Bacon's New Atlantis: The Christian Hope and the Modern Hope." *Interpretation* 22 (1994): 3–37.

Jacob, James R. "'By an Orphean Charm': Science and the Two Cultures in Seventeenth-Century England." In *Politics and Culture in Early Modern Europe: Essays in Honour of H. G. Koenigsberger,* edited by Phyllis Mack and Margaret C. Jacob, 231–49. Cambridge: Cambridge University Press, 1987.

James I. "Speech to Parliament, 1609." In *The Political Works of James I,* edited by Charles Howard McIlwain, 43–44. Cambridge, MA: Harvard University Press, 1918.

Janacek, Bruce. "Thomas Tymme and Natural Philosophy: Prophecy, Alchemical Theology, and the Book of Nature." *Sixteenth Century Journal* 30 (1999): 987–1007.

Jardine, Lisa, and Alan Stewart. *Hostage to Fortune: The Troubled Life of Francis Bacon.* New York: Hill and Wang, 1999.

Jones, Inigo. *Festival Designs: An Exhibition of Drawings for Scenery and Costumes for the Court Masques of James I and Charles I.* Introduction by Roy Strong. N.p.: Meriden Gravure, 1967.

Jones, R. J. *Ancients and Moderns.* Gloucester, MA: Peter Smith, 1961.

Kennington, Richard. "Bacon's Reform of Nature." In *Modern Enlightenment and the Rule of Reason,* edited by John C. McCarthy, 40–54. Washington, DC: Catholic University of America Press, 1998.

Klein, Ursula. "Experiment, Spiritus, und Okkulte Qualitäten in der Philosophie Francis Bacons." *Philosophie Naturalis* 33 (1996): 289–315.

Kocher, Paul H. *Science and Religion in Elizabethan England.* San Marino, CA: Huntington Library, 1953.

Lampert, Laurence. *Nietzsche and Modern Times: A Study of Bacon, Descartes, and Nietzsche.* New Haven, CT: Yale University Press, 1993.

Landau, Iddo. "Feminist Criticisms of Metaphors in Bacon's Philosophy of Science." *Philosophy* 73 (1998): 47–61.

Larsen, Robert E. "The Aristotelianism of Bacon's *Novum Organum*." *Journal of the History of Ideas* 23 (1962): 435–50.

Leary, John E., Jr. *Francis Bacon and the Politics of Science.* Ames, IA: Blackwell, 1994.

Lee, Maurice. *Great Britain's Solomon: James VI and I in His Three Kingdoms.* Champaign: University of Illinois Press, 1990.

Lemmi, Charles W. *The Classic Deities in Bacon: A Study in Mythological Symbolism.* New York: Octagon Books, 1971.

Leslie, Marina. *Renaissance Utopias and the Problem of History.* Ithaca, NY: Cornell University Press, 1998.
Lessl, Thomas M. "Naturalizing Science: Two Episodes in the Evolution of a Rhetoric of Scientism." *Western Journal of Communication* 60 (1996): 379–96.
Levao, Ronald. "Francis Bacon and the Mobility of Science." *Representations* 40 (1992): 1–32.
Lindberg, David C., and Ronald L. Numbers, eds. *God and Nature: Historical Essays on the Encounter between Christianity and Science.* Berkeley: University of California Press, 1986.
Linden, Stanton J. *Darke Hieroglyphicks: Alchemy in English Literature from Chaucer to the Restoration.* Lexington: University Press of Kentucky, 1996.
———. "Francis Bacon and Alchemy: The Reformation of Vulcan." *Journal of the History of Ideas* 35 (1974): 547–60.
Longo, Bernadette. "From Secrets to Science: Technical Writing, Utility, and the Hermetic Tradition in Agricola's *De Re Metallica*." *Journal of Technical Writing* 27 (1997): 353–59.
Longworthy, S. S. "The Separation of the Divine from the Natural: A Perspective on the Thought of Francis Bacon, 1584–1609." Master's thesis, University of North Carolina–Chapel Hill, 1976.
MacGregor, Arthur. "A Magazine of All Manner of Inventions: Museums in the Quest for Solomon's House in Seventeenth-Century England." *Journal of the History of Collections* 1 (1989): 207–12.
Manzo, Silvia Alejandra. "Holy Writ, Mythology, and the Foundations of Francis Bacon's Principle of the Constancy of Matter." *Early Science and Medicine* 16 (1999): 181–92.
Martin, Julian. *Francis Bacon, the State, and the Reform of Natural Philosophy.* Cambridge: Cambridge University Press, 1992.
Massi, Sonia. "A Partial Census of Francis Bacon's *Sylva Sylvarum* (Incl. *New Atlantis*)." *Nouvelles de la Republique des lettres* 2 (1997): 119–24.
Matar, N. I. "The Sources of Joabin's Speech in Francis Bacon's *New Atlantis*." *Notes and Queries* 41 (1994): 75–78.
Mathews, Nieves. *Francis Bacon: The History of a Character Assassination.* New Haven, CT: Yale University Press, 1996.
Matthews, Steven. "Apocalypse and Experiment: The Theological Assumption and Religious Motivations of Francis Bacon's Instauration." Ph.D. diss., University of Florida, 2004.

McCutcheon, Elizabeth. "Bacon and the Cherubim: An Iconographical Reading of the *New Atlantis.*" *English Literary Renaissance* 2 (1972): 334–55.

McKnight, Stephen A. "Ficino and the *Prisca Theologia* Tradition." In *The Modern Age and the Ancient Wisdom,* 42–59. Columbia: University of Missouri Press, 1991.

Merchant, Carolyn. *The Death of Nature: Women, Ecology, and the Scientific Revolution.* San Francisco: Harper and Row, 1980.

Merton, Robert K. "Science, Technology, and Society in Seventeenth Century England." *Osiris* 4 (1938): 360–632.

Miller, John J. "'Pruning by Study': Self-Cultivation in Bacon's 'Essays.'" *Papers on Language & Literature* 31 (1995): 339–61.

Milner, Benjamin. "Francis Bacon: The Theological Foundations of *Valerius Terminus.*" *Journal of the History of Ideas* 58 (1997): 245–64.

Morrison, James C. "Philosophy and History in Bacon." *Journal of the History of Ideas* 38 (1977): 585–606.

Mouton, J. "The Masculine Birth of Time: Interpreting Francis Bacon's Discourse on Scientific Progress." *South African Journal of Philosophy* 6 (1987): 43–50.

———. "Reformation and Restoration in Francis Bacon's Early Philosophy." *Modern Schoolman* 60 (1983): 101–12.

Olson, Richard. *Science Deified & Science Defied: The Historical Significance of Science in Western Culture, Two Vols.* Berkeley: University of California Press, 1982–1990.

Orgel, Stephen. *The Illusion of Power: Political Theatre in the English Renaissance.* Berkeley: University of California Press, 1975.

O'Rourke, Sean Patrick, et al. "The Most Significant Passage on Rhetoric in the Works of Francis Bacon." *Rhetoric Society Quarterly* 26 (1996): 31–55.

Paterson, Timothy. "Bacon's Myth of Orpheus." *Interpretation* 16 (1989): 427–44.

———. "On the Role of Christianity in the Political Philosophy of Francis Bacon." *Polity* 19 (1987): 419–42.

Peck, Linda Levy, ed. *The Mental World of the Jacobean Court.* Cambridge: Cambridge University Press, 1991.

Peltonen, Markku, ed. *The Cambridge Companion to Bacon.* Cambridge: Cambridge University Press, 1996.

Pérez-Ramos, Antonio. "Bacon's Legacy." In *The Cambridge Companion to Bacon,* edited by Markku Peltonen, 311–34. Cambridge: Cambridge University Press: 1996.

———. *Francis Bacon's Idea of Science and the Maker's Knowledge Tradition.* Oxford: Oxford University Press, 1988.
Pesic, Peter. "The Clue to the Labyrinth: Francis Bacon and the Decryption of Nature." *Cryptologia* 24 (2000): 193–212.
———. "Desire, Science, and Polity: Francis Bacon's Account of Eros." *Interpretation* 26 (1999): 333–52.
———. "Wrestling with Proteus: Francis Bacon and the 'Torture' of Nature." *ISIS* 90 (1999): 81–94.
Pico della Mirandola, Giovanni. *De Dignitate Hominis: Lateinish und Deutsch. Eingeleitet von Eugenio Garin.* Bad Homburg v.d. H.: Verlag Gehlen, 1968.
———. *Oration on the Dignity of Man.* Translated by A. Robert Caponigri. South Bend, IN: Regnery/Gateway, 1956.
Plato. *Timaeus, Critias, Cleitophon, Menexenus, Epistles with an English Translation.* Edited by R. G. Bury. Loeb Classical Library 9. 1929. Reprint, Cambridge, MA: Harvard University Press, 1999.
Price, Bronwen, ed. *Francis Bacon's New Atlantis: New Interdisciplinary Essays.* Manchester, UK: Manchester University Press, 2002.
Prior, Moody E. "Bacon's Man of Science." *Journal of the History of Ideas* 15 (1954): 348–70.
Purdon, Noel. "The Mould and Cast of Renaissance Mythography." In *The Words of Mercury: Shakespeare and English Mythography of the Renaissance,* 7–30. Salzburg: Institut fuer Englische Sprache und Literatur, Universität Salzburg, 1974.
Quinton, Anthony. *Francis Bacon.* Oxford: Oxford University Press, 1980.
Real, H. J. "Tradition and Progress in Bacon's *Advancement of Learning.*" In *State, Science, and Modernization in England from the Renaissance to the Modern Times,* edited by J. Klein, 55–86. Hildesheim: George Olms Verlag, 1994.
Rees, Graham. "Atomism and 'Subtlety' in Francis Bacon's Philosophy." *Annals of Science* 37 (1980): 549–71.
———. "The Fate of Bacon's Cosmology in the Seventeenth Century." *Ambix* 24 (1977): 27–38.
———. "Francis Bacon and *Spiritus Vitalis.*" In *Spiritus: IV Colloquio Internazionale,* edited by M. Fattori and M. Bianchi, 265–81. Rome: Edizioni dell'Ateneo, 1984.
———. "Francis Bacon's Semi-Paracelsian Cosmology." *Ambix* 22 (1975): 81–101.
———. "Francis Bacon's Semi-Paracelsian Cosmology and the *Great Instauration.*" *Ambix* 22 (1975): 161–73.

———. "*Instauratio Instauratoris:* Towards a New Edition of the Works of Francis Bacon." *Nouvelles de la République des Lettres* 1 (1987): 37–48.

———. "Matter Theory: A Unifying Factor in Bacon's Natural Philosophy?" *Ambix* 24 (1977): 110–25.

———. "An Unpublished Manuscript by Francis Bacon: *Sylva Sylvarum* Drafts and Other Working Notes." *Annals of Science* 38 (1981): 377–412.

Rees, Graham, and Lisa Jardine, eds. *The Oxford Francis Bacon.* Oxford: Oxford University Press, 1998–.

Renaker, David. "A Miracle of Engineering: The Conversion of Bensalem in Francis Bacon's *New Atlantis.*" *Studies in Philology* 87 (1990): 181–93.

Rice, Eugene. *The Renaissance Idea of Wisdom.* Cambridge, MA: Harvard University Press, 1958.

Rossi, Paolo. "Baconianism." In *Dictionary of the History of Ideas,* Vol. 1. New York: Scribners, 1973.

———. *Francis Bacon: From Magic to Science.* Chicago: University of Chicago Press, 1978. Reprint of English edition originally published by Routledge and Kegan Paul, 1968.

Rustici, Craig M. "A Source for the 'Aethiop' in Francis Bacon's *New Atlantis* (Notes.)" *Notes and Queries* 42 (1995): 366–67.

Schuler, Robert. *Francis Bacon and Scientific Poetry.* Philadelphia: American Philosophical Society, 1992.

Scott-Luckens, Carola. "Providence, Earth's 'Treasury,' and the Common Weal: Baconianism and Metaphysics in Millenarian Utopian Texts 1641–55." In *The Arts of 17th-Century Science: Representations of the Natural World in European and North American Culture,* edited by Claire Jowitt and Diane Watt, 109–23. Burlington, VT: Ashgate, 2002.

Sessions, William A. *Francis Bacon's Legacy of Texts: "The Art of Discovery Grows with Discovery."* New York: AMS Press, 1990.

Simon, Elliott M. "Bacon's *New Atlantis:* The Kingdom of God and Man." *Christianity & Literature* 38 (1988): 43–61.

Singer, Thomas C. "Hieroglyphs, Real Characters, and the Idea of Natural Language in English Seventeenth-Century Thought." *Journal of the History of Ideas* 50 (1989): 49–70.

Snyder, Laura J. "Renovating the *Novum Organum:* Bacon, Whewell, and Induction." *Studies in the History of the Philosophy of Science* 30 (1999): 531–57.

Soble, Alan. "In Defense of Bacon." *Philosophy of the Social Sciences* 25 (1995): 192–215.

Solomon, Julie Robin. *Objectivity in the Making: Francis Bacon and the Politics of Inquiry.* Baltimore: Johns Hopkins University Press, 1998.

———. " 'To Know, to Fly, to Conjure': Situating Baconian Science at the Juncture of Early Modern Modes of Reading." *Renaissance Quarterly* 44 (1991): 513–58.

Sprat, Thomas. *The History of the Royal Society of London (1667).* Reprint. St. Louis, MO: Washington University Press, 1958.

Spurgeon, Caroline. *Shakespeare's Imagery and What It Tells Us.* Cambridge: Cambridge University Press, 1952.

Studer, Heidi D. "Francis Bacon on the Political Dangers of Scientific Progress." *Canadian Journal of Political Science* 31 (1998): 219–34.

———. "Francis Bacon: Philosopher or Ideologue?" *Review of Politics* 59 (1997): 915–26.

Sullivan, Mary Agnes. *Court Masques of James I.* New York: G.P. Putnam and Sons, 1913.

Tate, William. "King James I and the Queen of Sheba." *English Literary Renaissance* 26 (1996): 561–85.

———. *Solomonic Iconography in Early Stuart England: Solomon's Wisdom, Solomon's Folly.* Lewiston, NY: Edwin Mellen Press, 2001.

Thomas, Keith. "The Utopian Impulse in Seventeenth-Century England." In *Between Dream and Nature: Essays on Utopia and Dystopia,* edited by D. Baker-Smith and C. C. Barfoot, 20–46. Amsterdam: Rodopi, 1987.

Tomasi, L. Tongiorgi. "Image, Symbol, and Word on the Title Pages and Frontispieces of Scientific Books from the Sixteenth and Seventeenth Centuries." *Word and Image* 4 (1988): 372–82.

Tovey, George V. "Toward a New Understanding of Francis Bacon's Reform of Philosophy." *Philosophical Review* 61 (1952): 568–74.

Urbach, Peter. *Francis Bacon's Philosophy of Science: An Account and a Reappraisal.* LaSalle, IL: Open Court, 1987.

Vickers, Brian. "The Authenticity of Bacon's Earliest Writings." *Renaissance Quarterly* 47 (1994): 248–96.

———. *Francis Bacon.* Oxford: Oxford University Press, 1996.

———. *Francis Bacon and Renaissance Prose.* Cambridge: Cambridge University Press, 1968.

———. "Francis Bacon and the Progress of Knowledge." *Journal of the History of Ideas* 53 (1992): 495–518.

———. "Francis Yates and the Writing of History." *Journal of Modern History* 51 (1979): 287–316.

———. "The Myth of Francis Bacon's 'Anti-Humanism.'" In *Humanism and Early Modern Philosophy*, edited by Jill Kraye and M. W. F. Stone, 135–58. London: Routledge, 2000.

Walker, D. P. "Medical Spirits and God and the Soul." In *Spiritus: IV Colloquio Internazionale*, edited by M. Fattori and M. Bianchi, 223–44. Rome: Edizioni dell'Ateneo, 1984.

Wallace, Karl R. *Francis Bacon on the Nature of Man: The Faculties of Man's Soul: Understanding, Reason, Imagination, Memory, Will, and Appetite.* Urbana: University of Illinois Press, 1967.

Walsham, Alexandra. *Providence in Early Modern England.* Oxford: Oxford University Press, 1999.

Warhaft, Sidney. "Bacon and the Renaissance Ideal of Self-Knowledge." *The Personalist* 44 (1963): 454–71.

———. "The Providential Order in Bacon's New Philosophy." In *Francis Bacon's Legacy of Texts*, edited by William A. Sessions, 151–67. New York: AMS Press, 1990.

Webster, Charles. *The Great Instauration: Science, Medicine, and Reform, 1626–1660.* New York: Holmes & Meier, 1975.

Weinberger, Jerry. *Science, Faith, and Politics: Francis Bacon and the Utopian Roots of the Modern Age: A Commentary on Bacon's Advancement of Learning.* Ithaca, NY: Cornell University Press, 1985.

———. "Science and Rule in Bacon's Utopia: An Introduction to the Reading of the *New Atlantis*." *American Political Science Review* 70 (1976): 865–85.

Weiser, David K. "Bacon's Borrowed Imagery." *Review of English Studies* n.s. 38 (1987): 315–24.

Wheeler, Harvey. "Francis Bacon's *New Atlantis:* The 'Mould' of a Lawfinding Commonwealth." In *Francis Bacon's Legacy of Texts*, edited by William A. Sessions, 291–309. New York: AMS Press, 1990.

White, Howard B. *Antiquity Forgot: Essays on Shakespeare, Bacon, and Rembrandt.* The Hague: Martinus Nijhoff, 1978.

———. "Bacon's *Wisdom of the Ancients.*" *Interpretation* 1 (1970): 107–29.

———. "The English Solomon: Francis Bacon on Henry VII." *Social Research* 24 (1957): 457–81.

———. "Francis Bacon." In *History of Political Philosophy*, edited by Leo Strauss and Joseph Cropsey, 366–85. Chicago: Rand McNally, 1963.

———. *Peace among the Willows: The Political Philosophy of Francis Bacon.* The Hague: Martinus Nijhoff, 1968.

Whitney, Charles C. "Bacon's Antithetical Prophecy." *Journal for the Comparative Study of Literature and Ideas* 15 (1982): 63–77.

———. "Cupid Hatched by Night: The Mysteries of Faith and Bacon's Art of Discovery." In *Ineffability: Naming the Unnameable from Dante to Beckett,* edited by Peter S. Hawkins and Anne H. Shotter, 51–64. New York: AMS Press, 1984.

———. "Francis Bacon's Instauratio: Dominion of and over Humanity." *Journal of the History of Ideas* 50 (1989): 371–90.

———. *Francis Bacon and Modernity.* New Haven, CT: Yale University Press, 1986.

———. "Merchants of Light: Science as Colonization in the *New Atlantis.*" In *Francis Bacon's Legacy of Texts,* edited by William A. Sessions, 255–68. New York: AMS Press, 1990.

Wiener, Harvey S. "Bacon and Poetry: A View of the *New Atlantis.*" *Anglia: Zeitschrift für Englische Philologie* 94 (1976): 69–85.

Williams, Gerhild S., and Charles D. Gunnoe Jr., eds. *Paracelsian Moments: Science, Medicine, & Astrology in Early Modern Europe.* Vol. 64, *Sixteenth Century Essays & Studies.* Kirksville, MO: Truman State University Press, 2002.

Wolff, Emil. *Francis Bacon und seine Quellen.* Berlin: Emil Felber, 1910.

Wong, Samuel G. "Some Baconian Metaphors and the Problems of Pure Prose." *Texas Studies in Literature and Language* 36 (1984): 233–58.

Wormald, B. H. G. *Francis Bacon: History, Politics, and Science, 1561–1626.* Cambridge: Cambridge University Press, 1993.

Young, R. F. *Comenius in England.* Oxford: Oxford University Press, 1932.

Zagorin, Perez. *Francis Bacon.* Princeton, NJ: Princeton University Press, 1998.

———. "Francis Bacon's Concept of Objectivity and the Idols of the Mind." *British Journal for the History of Science* 34 (2001): 379–93.

Zetterberg, J. Peter. "Echoes of Nature in Salomon's House." *Journal of the History of Ideas* 43 (1982): 179–93.

# Index

Adam: Christ's rescue of, 16, 21; creation and fall, 65, 100, 102, 132, 156; and esoteric knowledge, 39, 70, 166*n21*; and naming of creatures, 60, 90; in Pico's *Oration*, 168*n24*

*Advancement of Learning, The*, 12, 62, 103, 156, 163*n1*, 165*n12*, 167*n9*; charity in, 139–40, 142; concept of Original Sin, 139–40; dedication to James I, 135–38, 144, 145, 152; derailments of learning, 140–41; first book, 135–44; inventory of knowledge, 140–42; James I and Solomon, 136, 138, 139, 167*n8*; *prima philosophia*, 141–42, 146–48; Providence in, 137–38, 140, 143, 146, 149, 150; restoration of knowledge, 143–44, 148–49; second book, 145–49; spiritual renewal, 148–49, 153–54; structure of, 134–35

Albanese, Denise, 11, 35, 44, 162*n7*, 167*n8*

Ancient wisdom, 171*n12*, 172*n23*; and Bacon's new philosophy, 104, 126, 150; and instauration, 70, 121; recovery of, 65; and secrets of nature, 69. *See also Prisca theologia*

Aphorisms, 6, 72–96, 98, 100–101, 143, 148

Apocalypse (apocalyptic), 6, 35, 159, 162*n12*, 163*n4*; Bacon's views of, 2–4, 28, 30, 43–44, 47, 49–50, 55–56, 59–60, 61–62, 64–65, 69–71, 85–87, 88, 92, 95–96, 102, 114, 120, 137, 146, 151, 155–56; in Daniel, 49–50, 56, 71, 85–86, 102, 120, 146, 152, 167*n9*; and instauration, 8–9, 28, 30, 69–71, 151–53, 162*n9*

Aristotle, 150; and Bacon's epistemology, 72–73, 98, 135; and the degeneration of philosophy, 31, 70, 82–83, 104, 107, 112, 121, 126, 141; organon of, 62, 73; Renaissance reverence for, 36–37, 57, 116–17, 129; and the sin of pride, 121

Ark, 4, 15–17, 23–24, 29, 39, 43–44

Atlantis, 12, 18, 20, 30–37, 39, 41, 50, 94, 112, 168*n17*

Bacon, Francis: and ancient wisdom, 12, 37–38, 104, 111–12, 121–22, 125–26, 150; apocalyptic views of, 2–4, 28, 30, 43–44, 47, 49–50, 55–56, 59–60, 61–62, 64–65, 69–71, 85–87, 88, 92, 95–96, 102, 114, 120, 137, 146, 151, 155–56; use of biblical motifs, 3–4, 5, 7, 28, 38–39, 42–44, 46–47, 51–52, 98, 105–6, 143–45, 150; comparison with Columbus, 84–86; criticism of Platonic and Aristotelian philosophy, 7, 62–63, 70, 82–83, 107–8, 111–12, 117–18, 134–35; criticisms of Scholastic philosophy, 6, 140, 151; impediments to knowledge, 56–58; interpretation of Creation and Fall, 26, 60–61, 64–65, 69, 79–80, 89–91, 99–100, 138–40, 147–48; and James I, 7, 12, 39, 56, 135–38, 144–45, 149, 152, 153, 155; method of induction, 5–7, 46, 62–63, 70, 72–73, 86, 89–90, 94–99, 112–13, 144, 152; and modernity, 1–2, 7–11, 46–47, 70, 102, 153, 159; and the myth of a primordial golden

age, 3, 12, 31–37, 50, 94–95, 142–43; and Pico della Mirandola, 65–69; reasons for publishing *The Great Instauration,* 45–46, 53–55; recent scholarship on, 1, 2, 7, 8, 10–11, 12, 28, 40, 42, 46, 158–59; relation of charity and knowledge, 43, 55, 62, 71, 135, 139–40, 158; relation of piety and knowledge, 19–20; religious views and program of instauration, 2–4, 11, 12–13, 26, 28–31, 39–42, 47, 49–50, 51, 53, 70, 92–98, 103–4, 109, 149, 152–55; sense of vocation, 4, 6, 8, 56, 70, 85–86, 92–93, 95–96, 100, 102, 104, 114, 151, 156–58; use of aphorisms, 6, 62, 72–100 *passim;* use of fables, 7, 37–39, 121–34; use of Platonic myth, 12, 31–37. *See also* Providence
Bartholomew, 15–16, 21
Bensalem, 11–12, 20–22, 28, 35, 37–38, 40–42, 44, 71, 169*n26;* conversion of, 14–18, 21, 44; discovery of, 13–14; early history, 18–21, 30–31; and Europe (England), 41–42; as ideal Christian society, 14–15, 41; and Jerusalem, 23–24
Bible (Scriptures), 7, 89, 121, 142–43, 149–50, 151, 154, 157, 159; New Testament, 3, 95, 105, 139–40, 148; Old Testament, 3–4, 20, 23, 27–30, 39–40, 67, 93, 100, 102, 105, 139–40, 152; Solomon, 26–30, 39–40, 43
Boesky, Amy, 11, 25, 28, 35, 167*n5*

Charity, 27, 67–68, 97, 127, 142, 151, 153; of Bensalemites, 13–14, 24, 27, 42, 44; and knowledge of nature, 43, 55, 62, 71, 135, 139–40, 158, 164*n10*
Church, 103, 140, 143, 153–54, 157, 172*n1;* fathers, 67, 143
Columbus, 84–86
Comes, Natalis, 121
Creation (nature), 10, 130–34; alphabet of, 63, 78, 90, 93, 108; and benefits contained in, 17, 30, 36, 40, 61, 70, 91, 125, 142, 152, 155, 158; detailed study of, 57–62, 73, 77–80, 82–83, 102, 156; dominion over, 4–6, 13, 21, 41, 74, 76, 79–80, 97, 99–100, 105–6, 113–14, 150; fallen state, 132, 134; and the human intellect, 53–55, 75, 77–81, 96, 99, 101, 106–8, 114, 115, 129, 142, 153, 154, 155, 157, 158; the marriage of the mind to nature, 105; Pico's account of, 66–69, 168*n24;* pious study of, 36, 40, 70, 92–98, 99, 134, 158–59; Platonic account of, 34; restoration of, 3, 5, 71, 134, 153; as revelation, 157; studied by Solomon's House, 17, 19–21, 26–28, 38–41, 47, 93; true knowledge of, 73–74, 86, 88, 92–98, 105–6, 138, 147
Critias. *See* Plato

Daniel, Book of, 49–50, 56, 71, 85–86, 102, 120, 146, 152, 167*n9*
David, King, 23
Deliverance, 12–14, 26, 40, 44, 47, 71, 95, 129

Edification, 5, 29, 54, 80, 93, 98, 169*n27*
Elizabeth I, 145
England, 35–36, 42, 116, 135, 152–53, 155, 163*n4*
Esoteric knowledge, 38–39, 51, 70, 106, 109, 121, 126, 166*n21*
European sailors, 16, 41–42, 44, 165; discovery of Bensalem, 12–14, 42; and a Father of Solomon's House, 17, 25, 38; and the Governor of the Strangers' House, 14, 18–21, 30–31, 36; and Joabin, 21–24. *See also Prisca theologia*

Fables, 37–38, 82, 117, 121–34
Fall, the. *See* Original Sin
Feast of the Family, 21–22, 104, 164*n6*
Ficino, Marsilio, 65, 166*n21,* 169*n27,* 172*n24*
Fortune (Fate), 57, 85–87, 101, 128, 134, 137, 157
Frontispieces, 26, 47; *Instauratio Magna,* 47–53, 56–57, 59, 71, 83, 85–86, 152; *Sylva Sylvarum,* 51–53, 94

# Index

God, 11, 13, 15, 17, 27, 85–86, 95, 105, 108, 119, 126, 129, 132–33, 135–36, 143, 146, 150, 153–54, 157–58; alienation from, 102, 156; chosen people of, 3, 16–17, 21, 23–24, 43–44, 150, 153; and Creation (nature), 11, 19–21, 26–27, 30, 36, 38, 40, 47, 60–61, 64–65, 77, 79, 86, 92–93, 98, 102, 104–5, 114, 117, 125, 134, 143, 147, 155, 157, 159; and Humanity, 4–7, 10, 13, 16, 40–41, 47, 50, 60–61, 64–65, 70, 89, 92–93, 96, 99–100, 102, 104, 114, 120, 125, 127, 129, 139–40, 142–43, 147–48, 153, 155–57, 158–59, 171*n13;* Kingdom of, 14, 24, 43–44, 153; law of, 16, 43; mercy of, 29, 89. *See also* Providence

Governor, Strangers' House, 12, 14, 18–21, 26–28, 30–31, 36, 42–43

*Great Instauration* (*Instauratio Magna*), 3, 6, 12, 103, 104; Adam in, 60, 65, 75; apocalyptic themes in, 49–50, 62, 64, 69–70, 71; Bacon's epistemology and Neoplatonism, 65–69, 70; Bacon's reasons for publishing, 45–46; charity in, 62, 67–68, 71; concept of instauration in, 50, 56, 64, 71–72; dedication of, 55–56; frontispiece of, 47–53, 59, 84–87, 152; hope in, 57, 62, 70–71; original plan of, 5, 45, 62–64; Original Sin in, 60–62, 64–65; the preface of, 56–62; pride in, 79; proemium, 53–55; Providence in, 59, 64, 65, 70–71; restoration of humanity in, 41, 64, 70, 106; restoration of knowledge in, 47, 51–55, 56, 61–62, 64–69, 74

Hermeticism (Hermes Trismegistus), 3, 65, 67, 69–70, 79, 106, 109, 137–38, 166*n21,* 168*n20,* 169*n27*

Hope, 11–12, 57, 62, 68, 70–71, 115–16, 118, 124, 153; reasons for, 6, 74–75, 84–92, 96–97, 100, 110, 114, 120, 156, 157

Humanity (human nature): Bacon's concept of, 26; fallen, 8, 26, 62, 64–66, 69–70, 89, 139, 142, 147–48; in *Critias* and *Timaeus,* 33–34; human condition, 1, 4, 6, 12, 25, 30, 56–58, 61, 63, 66, 75–77, 79, 83–84, 87, 89, 91, 99, 100–101, 108–9, 114, 123–30, 156; prelapsarian, 4, 8–9, 16, 21, 34, 47, 53, 64, 66, 70–71, 78, 80, 86, 106, 129, 142, 153, 156, 158; relation to God, 4–5, 10, 13, 40, 46, 50, 60–61, 85–86, 90–93, 104, 139–40, 146–47, 153, 154–55, 157–59; relation to nature, 4–6, 9, 10, 12–13, 19–20, 30, 40, 46, 50, 53–55, 60–61, 69, 75–80, 86, 91, 93, 96–97, 99, 100–101, 103–6, 108–9, 112–14, 140, 147, 150, 153, 157–59; vocation of, 74–77, 129. *See also* Charity; Idols of the Mind; Pride

Idols of the Mind, 75, 77–81, 96, 99, 101, 106–8, 114, 115, 129, 153, 154, 158, 168*n16*

Instauration: and ancient wisdom, 37–39, 122; as apocalyptic concept, 44, 47–53, 56, 71, 101, 152–53; and Bacon's religion, 2–3, 21, 26, 28–31, 39–42, 46–47, 72, 76, 92, 101–2, 103, 114, 158–59; of humanity's relation to God, 5, 7, 13, 40–41, 46–47, 50, 106, 153, 157; of knowledge, 29–31, 37–39, 47, 51, 53, 56, 61–62, 64–70, 79–80, 82–83, 102, 105, 121, 135, 138, 149–50, 152, 154; and *New Atlantis,* 39–42; and Platonic myth, 36; as re-edification, 5, 29, 54, 80, 93, 98; of religion, 13, 103, 110, 152, 153–54, 156, 159, 165*n13;* two dimensions, 5, 7, 13, 29–30, 39, 41, 64, 151–55, 156

James I, 7, 135–38, 144–45, 164*n7;* as Solomon, 7, 12, 35–36, 39, 135–36, 152, 155, 163*n4,* 167*n13*
Jerusalem (Zion), 4, 16, 23–24, 35, 49, 152
Joab, 23, 164*n9*
Joabin, 12, 21–23, 43, 169*n27*
Josiah, King, 28–29, 43

Leslie, Marina, 1, 11
Love, 28, 66–67, 69–70, 93, 127, 133, 135, 142, 144, 148, 158, 166*n20*

Marriage, 22, 137, 145; of mind and nature, 57, 105, 119–20, 133–34, 164*n8*, 167*n15*, 169*n27*
*Masculine Birth of Time, The* (*Temporis Partus Masculus*), 6, 8, 103–11, 114, 116, 170*n7*
Millenarian(ism), 2, 3, 4, 43, 97, 159
Moses, 4, 16, 23–24, 39, 66, 68, 102, 143, 157, 166*n21*, 169*n26*

Natural philosophy (science): and ancient wisdom (*prisca theologia*), 37–39, 67–69, 121–34; decline of, 7, 37–38, 58, 84, 110–12, 117, 141, 150, 154; and *prima philosophia*, 146–47; recovery and reform of, 3, 12, 30, 36–37, 39, 46, 59, 62–63, 65–66, 69, 84–92, 112–14, 120, 142–44, 148–49, 151–52, 155, 159, 162*n11*; and religion, 3, 17, 35, 40–41, 55, 59–60, 65, 84, 92–103, 154, 158–59; sterile, 57, 74–75, 79, 82, 111–12. *See also* Solomon's House: activities of
Nature. *See* Creation
Neoplatonism, 3, 65, 69–70, 79, 166*n21*, 168*n20*
*New Atlantis*, 3–4, 6, 47, 50, 51, 55, 69, 71, 72, 81, 82, 86, 98, 101, 104, 106, 158, 173*n2*; Adam in, 16, 21, 39; and ancient wisdom, 37–39, 126, 142–43; and Bacon's instauration, 28–31, 37–42; Feast of the Family, 21–23; Governor of the Strangers' House, 12, 14, 18–21, 26–28, 30–31, 36, 42–43; Joabin, 12, 23–24, 43; prehistory of civilization, 18–21, 31–37, 94; and recent scholarship, 10–12, 17, 18, 42, 44, 46. *See also* Bensalem; Solomon's House
New Jerusalem (New Zion), 7, 35, 49; and Bensalem, 16, 23–24; and England, 135, 152, 155, 163*n4*
*New Organon, The* (*Novum Organum*), 3, 5, 6, 8, 12, 59, 103, 104, 106, 110–11, 114, 143, 158, 166*n23*; Adam in, 90–91, 100, 102; alphabet of nature, 78, 90–91, 93; aphoristic style, 62, 72–73; apocalyptic themes, 71, 86, 88; Bacon's new method, 72–73, 81–84, 86, 89–90, 94–99; book 1, 74–98; book 2, 98–100; charity in, 97; derailment of philosophy by Aristotle and Plato, 73, 82–83, 84; and the Fall, 41, 98–100, 102; flaws of the syllogism, 77–80; humanity's vocation, 75–77; Idols of the Mind, 80–81, 154; interpretation of nature, 72–73; natural philosophy and religion, 92–98; pride in, 79, 87, 92, 93, 97–98, 100–2; Providence in, 74, 85–86, 87, 95, 101; reasons for despair, 84–88; reasons for hope, 88–92, 156; title page and preface, 73–74
New Testament. *See* Bible

Old Testament. *See* Bible
Original Sin (the Fall), 3, 16, 21, 168*n24*; Bacon's interpretation of, 5, 26, 41, 60–62, 64–65, 69, 78, 80, 89, 102, 129, 130, 138–39, 142, 147–48, 154–55, 159; and decline of knowledge, 39, 87, 147–48, 154–55
Orpheus, 37–38, 122, 126

Pan, 121, 130–34
Pentheus, 121, 130
Philosophy, 2; and ancient wisdom, 37–39, 65–69, 70, 116, 121, 122; criticisms of Platonic and Aristotelian philosophy, 6, 7, 31, 36–37, 37–39, 57–58, 70, 82–83, 84, 107, 116–18, 121, 134–35, 141, 151; *prima philosophia*, 141–42, 146–48; criticisms of Scholastic philosophy, 6, 140, 151. *See also* Natural philosophy; Pre-Socratic philosophy
Pico della Mirandola, 65–69, 166*n21*, 168*n24*, 169*n25*, 169*n27*, 171*n15*
Piety, 13, 17, 19, 20, 24, 27–28, 36, 40, 41, 43–44, 71, 125, 127, 158–59, 166*n20*
Pillars of Hercules, 49–53, 57, 82, 94, 145, 165*n16*, 167*n14*

# Index

Plato, 115–16; concept of recollection (anamnesis), 136, 138; concept of the soul, 136; *Critias,* 12, 31, 33–34, 36; derailment of philosophy, 7, 57, 70, 82–83, 104, 107, 121, 126, 134–35; and myth of Atlantis, 18, 30–37; *Republic,* 101; *Timeaus,* 12, 32–33, 34, 82, 170*n*9

Pre-Socratic philosophy, 37, 83–84, 111, 121–22, 152

Pride, 8, 40–41, 49, 50, 60–61, 64, 70, 71, 79, 87, 92, 93, 97–98, 100–102, 104, 108, 114, 121, 126, 129, 134, 139–40, 143, 148, 150, 153, 155, 156, 157, 158, 164*n*10, 166*n*20, 168*n*24

*Prima philosophia,* 141–42, 146–48

*Prisca theologia* (ancient wisdom), 3–4, 5, 7, 12, 37–39, 65–69, 70, 104, 121–22, 126, 150, 165*n*20, 166*n*21

Prometheus, 121, 123–30

Providence, 1, 5, 6–7, 8, 12–13, 16, 29, 30–31, 38, 40, 44, 46–47, 50, 55–56, 59, 64–65, 69, 70, 71, 74, 85–86, 87, 95, 101, 103, 104–5, 114, 120, 122, 124–25, 127–28, 129, 132, 134–35, 137–38, 140, 143, 144–46, 149–50, 151, 152, 153, 155–56, 157–58, 159, 171*n*13, 171*n*14, 172*n*25

*Refutation of Philosophies, The* (*Redargutio Philosophiarum*), 6, 8, 103, 115–21

Religion, 1, 2, 8–9; of Bensalem, 15–18, 20–21, 22; and natural philosophy, 92–98, 107; and political order, 36, 101–2; restoration of, 13, 30, 40, 41–42, 65, 69, 144, 149, 154, 155, 158–59

Rossi, Paolo, 7, 161*n*2, 163*n*15, 165*n*18

Salvation, 3, 10, 11, 13–16, 26, 40, 44, 46, 60, 64

Scylla (and Charybdis), 57, 111, 114, 141

Socrates, 31–32, 36, 84, 115

Solamona, King, 19–20, 23, 26, 27, 36, 101; and biblical Solomon, 26–27; and Solomon's House, 26–28, 29, 30

Solomon, King, 3, 4, 7, 12, 16, 24, 27, 28–29, 36, 39, 43, 56, 136, 139, 143, 148; *Natural History,* 20, 23, 28, 37, 38–39, 40, 51, 143; wisdom of, 3–4, 20, 28, 38–39, 40

Solomon's House, 12–13, 17, 23, 25, 26, 39–40, 41; activities of, 4, 12–13, 17, 19–21, 23, 25–26, 28, 30–31, 35, 37, 38–39, 43, 46–47, 51, 71, 93; founding of, 19–21, 26–28, 29–30, 43; members of, 4, 12, 14, 16–17, 19–21, 23–26, 31, 38, 40, 43, 81, 93; and Solomon's Temple, 12, 24, 26, 28, 30, 40, 43, 93, 94

Solomon's Temple, 4, 12–13, 23, 29, 30, 39, 49, 51, 152; and Solomon's House, 12, 24, 26, 28, 30, 40, 43, 93, 94

Solon, 32

Special election, 3–4, 12, 16, 23, 43–44

Temple of Jerusalem. *See* Solomon's Temple

*Thoughts and Conclusions* (*Cogitata et Visa*), 6, 8, 103, 110–15

*Timeaus. See* Plato

Vanity, 61, 79, 87, 92, 134, 141, 152

Vocation: Bacon's sense of, 4, 6, 8, 56, 70, 85–86, 92–93, 95–96, 100, 102, 104, 114, 151, 156–58; humanity's, 74–77, 129

Weinberger, Jerry, 11, 25, 46, 163*n*1, 166*n*2, 171*n*17, 172*n*23, 172*n*25, 172*n*26, 172*n*27, 172*n*28

White, Howard B., 7, 10–11, 17, 18, 25, 34, 35, 42, 44, 158, 161*n*4, 164*n*6, 164*n*9, 165*n*18, 166*n*20, 169*n*4, 170*n*3

Whitney, Charles, 5, 11, 28–30, 40, 162*n*9, 167*n*10

*Wisdom of the Ancients* (*De sapientia veterum*), 3, 6, 7, 8, 69, 103, 143; degeneration of philosophy, 31, 37–39, 51, 122; fable of Orpheus, 37–39, 122; fable of Pan, 130–34; fable of Pentheus, 130; fable of Prometheus, 123–30; the human condition, 123–30; and instauration, 121; and nature, 130–34; Providence in, 124–25, 127–28, 129, 132

GENERAL THEOLOGICAL SEMINARY
NEW YORK

**DATE DUE**